CAMDEN MISCELLANY
VOL. XXVI

CAMDEN MISCELLANY VOL. XXVI

CAMDEN FOURTH SERIES

VOLUME 14

LONDON
OFFICES OF THE ROYAL HISTORICAL SOCIETY
UNIVERSITY COLLEGE LONDON, GOWER STREET,
LONDON, WC1E 6BT
1975

DA
20
. C175
V.14

38,485

Printed in Great Britain by Butler & Tanner Ltd., Frome and London

CONTENTS

I

ORDINANCES FOR THE DUCHY OF LANCASTER

edited by

SIR ROBERT SOMERVILLE
K.C.V.O., M.A., F.S.A., F.R.Hist.S.

CONTENTS

Introduction

The ordinances for the administration of the Duchy of Lancaster, here printed for the first time, come from a small vellum book in the Duchy Office that has been known there for the last 300 years or more as the Little Cowcher. [1] Like the book itself they are undated, but most of the matter in it refers to the fifteenth century. As a result of a modern rebinding it is impossible to distinguish the separate gatherings or quires of the book, but it probably assumed its present size and arrangement in the reign of Elizabeth I.[2] It begins with a long inspeximus by Edward IV of 4 November 1461 confirming the Duchy's 'Great Charter' of 14 October 1399 and re-affirming the Duchy's separation from the Crown lands proper.[3] Apart from a proviso of 1 Hen. VII and an eighteenth-century addition of an oath, the seven next succeeding entries—mainly acts and statutes—are not later than the reign of Edward IV, or appear to be so. Five, however, are in sixteenth-century hands;[4] another is the eighteenth-century addition mentioned, but most

[1] Ff. 67–88ᵛ. On the Little Cowcher see *Eng. Hist. Rev.*, li (1936), p. 614, where I dated it (wrongly) to Henry VIII. The ordinances are reproduced by permission of the Chancellor and Council of the Duchy. I wish to thank Dr. Godfrey Davis for his help and advice on the dating of the hands and the make-up of the Little Cowcher.

[2] On f. 34ᵛ is an addition made in 1579. Early covers of the book, still preserved, belong to the latter part of the sixteenth century. The foliation is in part of that century, in part of the late seventeenth, but there have been earlier folio numbers subsequently erased or altered.

[3] To f. 32ᵛ; W. Hardy, *Charters of the Duchy of Lancaster* (London, 1845), p. 285. P.R.O. DL 10/386 is the original.

[4] They are Hardy, *Charters*, pp. 141, 279, 151, 182 and the chancellor's oath.

significant for our purpose is the enrolment on ff. 45–50 of what the heading describes as a feoffment by Edward IV of certain Duchy lands.[5] It is in a hand of the late fifteenth century, although not the hand of the first thirty-two folios, and in fact it is not the feoffment but its repeal in 1485. Someone in the sixteenth century has indeed altered the heading accordingly. The feoffment of 1475 is, however, entered at f. 108 in the hand of the first or earliest part of the book; thus the two entries have been transposed in an early binding or rebinding.[6] The ordinances follow immediately after these various items in the first part, and the rest of the book has later entries, including some of the seventeenth century. It can be assumed, then, that before rearrangement and binding in the sixteenth century the earliest part of the Little Cowcher, forming a book by itself, consisted of the present first forty-three folios and the Edward IV feoffment of f. 108, all in the same hand, the latest items in date being three statutes of Edward IV's last parliament of 1483. The ordinances are in another hand, also of the latter part of the fifteenth century, and may or may not have formed part of the book.[7]

We might therefore be justified in supposing that that volume is the 'boke of parchement bounden and couvered with red ledder wherin is writen the chartre and confirmacion of the said duchie with other ordonaunces, actes and statutes made for ye wele yereof' which Thomas Metcalfe, Richard III's newly-appointed chancellor of the Duchy, acknowledged on 24 July 1483 to have received from his predecessor along with other Duchy muniments.[8] If so, we have

[5] Hardy, *Charters*, p. 326, 23 February 1475; repealed by Henry VII, 7 November 1485.

[6] A confirmation of this comes from an early note on f. 32^v, about Edward IV's charter of confirmation in Latin, to the effect that the English version is at f. 45 (*i.e.* in the original foliation, now f. 49; 45 was evidently the earliest foliation before the book was rearranged). It was altered here to 46 by Benjamin Ayloffe, deputy keeper of the Duchy records in the late seventeenth century, and 46 was then correct: the difference in numbering being accounted for by the greater length of the repeal of Edward IV's feoffment (6 folios), which has been bound in place of the actual feoffment (4 folios and a blank folio). This note and many other such glosses seem to me to be in a hand of the time of Henry VII or Henry VIII, perhaps of the clerk of the council of the Duchy. Notes in the same hand appear in other Duchy records of the time. For the altering of the foliation see p. 1, n. 2.

[7] Some half-dozen sixteenth- and seventeenth-century copies of the basic part of the Little Cowcher are extant. None has the inserted words correcting the heading to the repeal of the 1475 feoffment, yet all have the other sixteenth-century additions.

[8] DL 25/3631. The book was perhaps the same as the 'Boke of Actes of Parliament, a red-bordid booke', that was lent to Richard Empson as attorney general of the Duchy in 1497, DL 5/3 f. 229^v, but the Little Cowcher was

a *terminus ad quem* for the ordinances, and as the 'chartre and confirmacion' is Edward IV's confirmation of 4 November 1461, we have the earlier limiting date. The original part of the Little Cowcher is clearly later than February 1483, when Edward IV's last Parliament terminated. The ordinances, however, may have been earlier in date, yet incorporated with the charters and statutes.

The matter is not straight-forward, for Metcalfe also received at the same time two skins of parchment tied together and 'writen and sealed under ye seall of ye said duchie, made in King Henry the VI daies, specifieing ye said ordonaunces and statutes'.[9] On a strict interpretation this means our ordinances date from Henry VI's reign. If so, then it seems they might date from the twentieth year of his reign (September 1441 to August 1442), for Sir James Dyer, in reporting a case in the Duchy in which he had himself taken part in 1561–2, ascribed to that year certain ordinances of the Duchy Court one of which required the insertion in Duchy leases of a proviso *si quis plus dare voluerit absque fraude vel malo ingenio*.[10] Now this proviso occurs in the ordinances printed here (para. 15); hence they might be the ordinances Dyer referred to.[11] But a small book prepared for the Elizabethan consideration of that case, which recites in part some of the basic charters and statutes contained in the Little Cowcher and sets out arguments for the Duchy side, also reproduces verbatim two paragraphs from the Little Cowcher ordinances (nos. 14, 15), the second being the crucial *si quis*, and calls them two especial orders from 'The Booke of the duchie of Lancaster', which 'is without date but yet it apperith to be of greate antiquitie'.[12]

We cannot doubt that there were ordinances of 1441–2, one of which prescribed this proviso. On the other hand it is more than doubtful if they were the ordinances in the Little Cowcher. It would

---

known in the early part of the sixteenth century as *liber ordinacionum*, DL 42/11 f. 73.

[9] No such document under seal is now known.

[10] *Les Reports* (London, 1688), f. 232; also in E. Coke, *Institutes, Fourth Part* (London, 1671), p. 209. The cause, between Hickes and Allott, concerned a reversionary lease and was heard several times under Edward VI, Mary and Elizabeth: it became the celebrated 'great case of the Duchy', fully reported by E. Plowden, *The Commentaries or Reports* (London, 1761), pp. 212–23. The pleadings are not extant.

[11] The proviso is first found in demises under the Duchy seal on 16 February 1445, DL 37/59/39. A small point that may have some significance is that all but one of the leases containing the proviso in this roll of leases of Henry VI's reign have *si aliquis* instead of *si quis*.

[12] Bodleian, Rawlinson MS. D 1086. At that date the Little Cowcher could not have been more than eighty years old.

have been unusual at that time for a formal document under the Duchy seal to be in English, and the English of our ordinances seems in any case to be of a later date. Secondly, these ordinances presume the Duchy to exist entire and complete, whereas in 1441-2 a large part was in the hands of feoffees for Henry VI's will, so much so that one chief or high steward and one auditor sufficed for the remainder, yet the ordinances relate to a Duchy with two chief stewards and two, indeed three, auditors.[13] Moreover, in our ordinances the chancellor is the most important officer (as he was in the latter part of the century), whereas in 1441-2 the chamberlain was superior. Finally, the ordinances refer to the king's son (para. 10). There was no such prince in 1441-2, so that if the ordinances date from Henry VI they must fall between 1453 and 1461. But parts of the Duchy were again in feoffment in that period. The reference to the king's son and the practice of retainer seems to refer to the statute of 1472 that released the Prince of Wales from the restriction upon livery and retainer imposed by an earlier statute of 1468.[14]

The ordinances must on these grounds be later than Henry VI. Dyer may have seen the book of extracts and notes already mentioned, which says specifically that the ordinances had no date, yet he gives the date 20 Henry VI. Both may have been right; in other words there were two set of ordinances: one, now lost, of 20 Henry VI, the other in the Little Cowcher, without date but later than Henry VI. It is not unusual to find two sets of regulations, the earlier incorporated or re-affirmed in the later version.[15]

A weakness in this argument is that it tends to discount the evidence of the memorandum of receipt dated 24 July 1483 which ascribes the ordinances to Henry VI's reign, and it requires the assumption that the writer was loose in his reference to the ordinances.

---

[13] The feoffees' interest ended about March 1442, but possession of the lands was not obtained until May 1443, Hardy, *Charters*, p. 219, R. Somerville, *History of the Duchy of Lancaster*, i(London, 1953), p. 206. Note that the earliest Duchy use of the expression 'particular receiver' (*cf*. para. 51) seems to be in 1461, DL 37/30 m. 30.

[14] 12 Edw. IV, c.4; *Statutes of the Realm*, (London, 1810-28) ii, p. 436. Paras. 10 and 78 of the ordinances provide for a dispensing permission from the king, and it should be noted that Edward IV does not seem to have given dispensations, W. H. Dunham, *Lord Hastings' Indentured Retainers* (New Haven, 1955), p. 82.

[15] For example, the ordinances incorporate, with some amendment, regulations in French made in 1417 for Duchy stewards, DL 42/7 f. 174. Similarly most of the provisions of the royal household ordinance of 1445 were incorporated in the later ordinance of 1478, A. R. Myers, *Household of Edward IV* (Manchester, 1959), p. 8; *cf*. incorporation of earlier ordinances for the Privy Council, *Rotuli Parliamentorum*, iv, p. 20, and v, p. 407.

So far it has been possible to suggest limiting dates of 1461 and July 1483 for the Little Cowcher, and they would also apply to the ordinances if these had been part of the original book. Examination of the internal evidence provided by the ordinances may lead to a closer date for them, but in this we must remember that the statement of a rule or regulation may do no more than recognize existing practice without initiating it, and that there are considerable gaps in the financial records of the Duchy for the second half of the fifteenth century.

Although the few dates that can be readily discerned in the ordinances are of little help, there are other indications.[16] For example, the ordinances cannot be later than Henry VII's reign because the last appointment of a chamberlain (para. 43) was in 1485, and of an attorney in the King's Bench (para. 22) in 1484, and both offices had lapsed by 1500.[17] The reference to livery and retainer in paras. 10 and 78 is an echo of the act of 1468, rather than the later acts of Henry VII's reign, and the inclusion of the king's son (para. 10) must derive from the act of 1472 (p. 4).[18] If the ordinances are Edward IV's, then the mention of the king's son means they are later than 1470, or in effect after Edward's return in 1471. Oaths in Little Cowcher form are recited in 1497 and 1501.[19] Rates for the respite of homage quoted in the ordinances occur in 1480, whereas those current fifty years earlier were lower.[20] The concern shown for swans in the Fens (paras. 63–4) is reminiscent of the statute 22 Edw. IV c.6 of 1483, itself entered in the Little Cowcher, but the 'means test' is different and the ordinances may be slightly earlier.[21] The criticism of the approver in the Fens that is

[16] The dates are 1416 (para. 14) and 'days of Henry IV', para. 68. The authority of Parliament in para. 73 is the parliamentary charter of 14 October 1399, and the statute relating to the carrying of arms (para. 78) is 20 Ric. II, c.1, *Statutes of the Realm*, ii, p. 93.

[17] DL 28/6/1A; Somerville, *History of the Duchy*, i, p. 418.

[18] *Statutes of the Realm*, ii. 426 (1468), printed in S. B. Chrimes and A. L. Brown, *Select Documents of English Constitutional History* (London, 1961), p. 329. The first Henry VII statute about livery and retainer is 3 Hen. VII c. 15 of 1487, *Statutes of the Realm*, ii. 522. In 1476 the Duchy Council was issuing orders against livery and retainer and prohibiting the carrying of arms; Somerville, *History of the Duchy*, i, pp. 225–6.

[19] DL 5/3 ff. 152ᵛ & 153: DL 37/62/43.

[20] DL 5/1 f. 42 and DL 42/19 f. 73 for 1480; Somerville, *History of the Duchy*, i, p. 217n for the others. The procedure for homage to the king in person was still in use about 1495, *Prerogativa Regis*, ed. S. E. Thorne, (New Haven, 1949), p. 63.

[21] *Statutes of the Realm*, ii, p. 474. Detailed regulations in the terms of this statute were promulgated in 1501; Somerville, *History of the Duchy*, i, p. 270.

voiced in para. 41 cannot be unconnected with the council's direction of March 1484 that, as there was little profit, the approver of the Fens in Lincolnshire should be spoken with.[22] Another indication of date comes from the directions (paras. 43-4) for a register of tenants by knight's service: such a register exists, with a date not later than 1485 but almost certainly after 1482; and transcripts as prescribed were ordered for the feodaries before January 1483.[23] The control of timber-felling set out in paras. 34-5 has an echo, if not a direct effect, in a general order of 25 June 1486 against felling without a special warrant under the Duchy seal.[24] The provisions of para. 55 for the control of repairs correspond with directions of March 1480 to the stewards and receivers of the principal lordships, taking note of the practice of lower officers in doing expensive repairs without proper orders, and requiring such repairs to be carried out under the supervision of stewards and receivers. The requirement was restated for two of the lordships in March 1484.[25]

It is probable that the rule for periodical 'progresses' through the Duchy estates derived from earlier regulations, or simply codified existing practice.[26] The same may be true of the reference to the clerk of the council and his book of acts in para. 3. The earliest extant book dates from 1474, but in the seventeenth century it was supposed that this was not the first in the series.[27] If so, the others had been lost at an early date. Be that as it may, the detailed instruction for entries are observed only in the early part of the first extant book of acts.

The arrangements for the great audit after Candlemas are codified in paras. 50 and 73. This audit was originally for the receiver general's account, which ran to 2 February, but at least by 1421 one of the chief stewards had been present and by 1442-3 the chancellor and members of the council, as well as the particular receivers, were

[22] DL 5/2 f. 4.

[23] DL 42/130-2; DL 42/130 f. 73ᵛ for a date after 1482. The clerk of the council was paid in 1481-2 for searching records at Kenilworth Castle to find the names of the military tenants, DL 28/5/11. Transcripts, DL 42/19 f. 120ᵛ.

[24] DL 5/3 f. 51ᵛ.

[25] DL 42/19 f. 58 and DL 5/1 f. 24ᵛ; DL 42/20 f. 61.

[26] Para. 11. Progresses were made in 1474, 1476, 1478; Somerville, *History of the Duchy*, i. 250. Cf. A. R. Myers in *Trans. Hist. Soc. Lancs. & Chesh*, cxv (1963), p. 1.

[27] DL 5/1. Bodleian, Rawlinson MS C 714 has B. Ayloffe's remarks on previous books. Another example of restating existing practice is in para. 72, giving the auditors power to make new rentals. This was in fact a continuing process, but the production of new rentals by commissioners had been put in hand in April 1480, DL 5/1 f. 28.

also present.[28] By 1479 this audit was already the 'old usage and custom' and an order of 1480 renewed the 'old ordinance and rules' for the annual appearance at Candlemas and for the full payment by the receivers by that date or fourteen days later.[29] On 22 June 1440 there had been a direction, evidently an innovation, for payment by the receivers in equal portions at Michaelmas and Easter or forty days after. It is certainly not the arrangement in the present ordinances, which prescribe a payment of one-third within six weeks after Easter and the balance within six weeks after Michaelmas.[30] The payments made by receivers to the receiver general, however, tended to follow no fixed pattern, in spite of rules and regulations. Nor does there seem to have been much consistency in applying the rule (para. 71) that the auditors should not receive their fees from local receivers or other officers, but only from the receiver general. We are on firmer ground with para. 57, limiting the receiver general's payments to those by Duchy warrant or by bill under the seal of the Receipt of the Exchequer, for such bills are first cited in his accounts for 1477–8; they are not mentioned in those for 1438–45, the latest previous accounts now extant.[31]

One of the regulations for the County Palatine of Lancaster (para. 80) has some correspondence with an order of March 1483 for the conduct of business at the Lancaster sessions.[32]

The cumulative effect of the internal evidence suggests a date in the 1480s. Even if the Little Cowcher, including the ordinances, was not the book handed over in July 1483, as I think it was, Henry VII may be ruled out. The earliest date for the ordinances, if of his reign, would be after 19 September 1486, the birth of Arthur. Although Henry took a close personal interest in the administration of his revenues, his work upon their reform and development hardly began in the earliest years of his reign, but it is to these early years that the ordinances would have belonged.[33] Richard III's brief reign

[28] DL 28/4/11, DL 28/5/2 f. 68. The particular receivers' year of account ended at Michaelmas; the receiver general's year was altered to Michaelmas between 1490 (John Rylands Library, Cha. 754) and 1498 (DL 28/6/1A). The 'conciliar audit of land revenue' is named as a Yorkist practice by B. P. Wolffe, *The Royal Demesne in English History* (London, 1971), p. 204.

[29] DL 42/19 ff. 50, 79, cf. para. 19. Further restatements of the old usage came in 1503 (DL 37/62 m. 54) and August 1508 (ibid., m. 71).

[30] Para 51; DL 37/8/52. The proportions given in that paragraph were reaffirmed in 1519 as those 'of old time used', DL 42/95 f. 62.

[31] DL 28/5/2 and 11.

[32] Cf. A. R. Myers in *Trans. Hist. Soc. Lancs & Chesh.*, cxv (1963), p. 27n. A falling-off in revenue from the sessions was noted in 1498, DL 37/62 m. 31d.

[33] B. P. Wolffe, *The Crown Lands 1461–1536* (London, 1970) ,p. 73, and *The*

showed as great a concern for financial and administrative reform; his plan of about October 1484 for 'hasty levy of the king's revenues' and improved management is well known, and its provisions, if not similar in content to the Duchy ordinances, share the same basic ideas.[34] Moreover, Richard issued written statements of duties to some of his officers.[35] The Duchy ordinances might therefore date from his reign, and thus before April 1484, the date of his son's death. But, once more, if the Little Cowcher was in existence by July 1483, there was little time—a few days in fact—to draw up the ordinances following Richard's assumption of the crown.

Upon the whole it seems sounder to assign a date slightly earlier, *viz.* to the closing years of Edward IV's reign, and to select the year 1482 as the most probable date of these ordinances. The years after Edward's return in 1471 had witnessed increasing attention to administrative efficiency and reform and a sustained effort to improve the royal revenue; this activity was manifest also in the Duchy, and it embraced the express definition of duties such as these ordinances prescribe.[36]

The emphasis in the ordinances is not so much upon increasing the revenue, however, as upon establishing an efficient administration and upon the promotion of law and order, although financial matters do receive much attention. Some of the regulations are of general significance, such as the withdrawal of the Duchy from the normal Exchequer procedures (para. 73); most, however, are framed in considerable detail. Some deal with accounting procedures (50–1, 65–8, 73), some with estate management (15, 17, 34–6), others with feudal tenures and enforcement of feudal dues (43–7). A few have a limited, local interest, like those concerned with swans (63–4) or the fen courts (41) or stewards in Wales (24, 37). Only three paragraphs at the end are devoted to the 'good and politic rule of the County Palatine of Lancaster', and this meagre ration creates a suspicion that the ordinances as entered in the Little Cowcher are incomplete.

The most lasting element of the ordinances has been the oaths

---

Royal Demesne in English History, pp. 200–206. Cf. S. B. Chrimes, *Henry VII* (London, 1972), p. 124.

[34] Printed in Chrimes and Brown, *Select Documents of English Constitutional History*, pp. 358–60 and summarized and discussed by B. P. Wolffe, 'The Management of English Royal Estates under the Yorkist Kings', *Eng. Hist. Rev.*, lxxi (1956), pp. 10, 21

[35] Wolffe, *The Crown Lands* p. 61

[36] Somerville, *History of the Duchy*, i, pp. 243–55, Myers, *Household of Edward IV*, p. 37.

embedded in them. There are oaths for the council (para. 1), for the clerk of the council and Duchy officers generally (7–8), for 'foreign' officers and others (10, in effect an oath of allegiance and loyalty), and finally for accountant officers (para. 20).[37] The council oath echoes the oath for members of the king's council early in Henry VI's reign: the ideas are similar and in the same order, but not in the same words. Many generations of Duchy officers have sworn these oaths. Under the Promissory Oaths Act 1868, however, the oaths have been turned into declarations, and as such they are still made by the members of the Duchy council and by certain senior Duchy officers.

The ordinances are printed with the spelling of the manuscript, but punctuation and capitals have been adjusted.

[37] Oaths for the chancellor and the attorney were added in the sixteenth century and one for the auditors in the eighteenth.

1. FIRST THE KING will that all suche persons as shalbe of his Counsaill of his Duchie of Lancastre as well officers, their deputies and clerks as all other shalbe sworne and make an othe in manere folowing:

> THE OTHE for every person that shalbe sworne to be of the Counsaill of the said Duchie

YE shall swere that ye shall gif gode advise & Counsaill after your konyng & knowlage in all suche thinges as ye shall here openned & commoned in the Kinges Counsaill of his Duchie of Lancastre, and moost for the Kinges availe & profit alsferr as right and conscience wil require, and be indifferent in all matiers to all manner of persons that shall pursue or answere byfore the said Counsaill whensoever it shall happen you to be present ther. Ye shall alsoe kepe secrete all things that shalbe commoned in the said Counsaill and them not to disclose or make overt without thadvise and assent of the said Counsaill, but oonly to the Kinges owne person or to suche other of the same Counsaill as your wisdome shall think expedient to be doon. Thise and all other things that may serve for the Kinges well and profit and for the gode rule and governance of the said Duchie ye shall well and truly doo and fulfille to your kunyng & power. So helpe you God and his saintes & by this boke.

(67^v) 2 ALSO that at suche tyme as any matier shalbe commoned in the said Counsaill, that then al peple shalbe voided for the tyme sauf oonly such has have beene or shalbe sworne in maner aforsaid, or suche as the said Counsaill shall calle unto them to declare & yeve informacion of such matiers as they shalbe called fore.

3 ALSO when any matier shalbe commoned, concluded or answered in the said Counsaill, the clerke of the said Counsaill shall make an acte or a remembrance thereof in his boke of actis, wherein he shall remembre the place, the day and yer and in whose presence it is commoned, concluded or answered as abovesaid.

4 ALSO att the begynnyng of every terme the said Counsaill shall mete togiders and doo to be redde byfore yeim by the said clerk all thactes of remembrances of the terme next preceding, to thentent that thay may the better be advertised and have clerely in mynde what matiers were commoned and concluded in the same terme and which rest undetermyned, that they may procede to the deter-

minacion of theym byfore any newe matier presented unto theim, if thay shall seme it convenient and necessarie.

5 ALSO that all billes and supplicacions presented unto the said Counsaill shalbe delivered unto the said clerk to be redde bifor theim, and to remembre theim of the same at tyme convenient that (68^r) thay therupon may common & answere as thay shall seem moost necessarie and byhovefull.

6 ALSO that at every tyme of thassemble of the said Counsaill thay shall appoint or thay depart the next day whan thay shall meete ayein, and so from tyme to tyme as ofte as thay shall assemble, to thentent that the peple that sue by fore theim may have knowlage of their assemble and the rather to be spidde and delivered.

7 The OTHE of the CLERK of the COUNSAILL of the said Duchie and all othir OFFICERS servyng the same

YE shall swere that ye shall well and truly serve our soveraigne lord the Kinge and his heires in that office that ye nowe been admytted unto as Clerk of the Counsaill of the said Duchie, and be obeissant, diligent & attendaunt unto the Chauncellor and Counsaill of the same in all thynges as shal concerne the wele, profyt and gode governaunce of the said Duchie Ye shall also kepe wel and suerly the recordes and evidence of the said Duchie that shall come to your keping and warde, and noon of theim embecille, withdrawe nor suffre to be embecilled nor withdrawen to your power, whereby any hurt or harme may growe to the King by reason of the same. Ye shall also kepe secrete all suche thynges as ye shall here spoken and commoned in the Counsaill of the said Duchie, and the same in nowyse discovere nor make open to any othir (68^v) person then oonly to the Kinges owne persone, or to suche othir of the said Counsaill as ye shall be commaunded to doo. All thise thinges and all othir that apperteigne to your office and charge ye shall well and truely doo & perfourme aftir your kunnyng and power. So helpe you God and halidome and by this boke.

8 AND like OTHE to evry othir officer servaunt of the said Duchie, *Nominando ejus officium et ea que ad suum officium pertinent.*

9 Whoso holdith of the King by knightes service as of his Duchie of Lancastre shal make his homage in maner following:

First he shall stande up right barehede before the Kinges owne person and desire to doo his homage, and if the King be then agreed therto his grace shal sitte downe, and the homagier shal knele upon bothe his knees bifor him and holde his handes jointe togiders betwix the Kinges handes and say thus: I A.B. by comme your man from this day forthwardes, of lyf and lymme and of all worldly honour and worship and trouthe and feithe to beer unto you for those londes (*69ʳ*) and tenementes that I clayme to holde of you by reason of your Duchie of Lancastre, saving the faith that I owe to God. So help me God and all his seintes.

And the King so sitting shall kisse him if he will

10   The OTHE of FOREN OFFICERS and other personnes to be sworn, &c

YE shall swere that ye shalbe trewe & faithfull unto our souverain lord the King and his heires, Kinges of England, and trewe feith & trouth bere unto them, and duly serve the Kinges grace in your personne, and under him in the retenue of N. whan & as ofte as ye shalbe resonably warned & required on the Kinges behalf. And if ye shall fortune any thing to knowe that shalbe prejudiciall or hurtfull to the Kinges grace or my lord prince, ye shall lett it to your power and in all hast with possible diligence ye shall geve theim or their counsel knowlege yerof. Also ye shall wele & truly execute your office &c duryng the tyme that ye shall stond and be officer ther. And ye shall not be reteigned with no maner of personne ne personnes othir than with the king, the quene and my lord prince by lyverey, token, signe, promise, othe or otherwise without the Kinges especial licence duryng the tyme that ye shalbe and stond the Kinges officr there. And in all othir thinges wele & truly behave yourself as to the dutie of your alliegeaunce & the dutie of your said office belongith. So help you God and all Saintes and by this booke.

(*69ᵛ*)   CHAUNCELLER

11 ALSO the King will that the Chaunceller and the High Stiwards of the said Duchie or yair deputies, the Chaumbrelain or his deputie & the general receivour & Attournay shall ride in thair owne persons oones in iiij or v yeris at the leest to every honour and grete lordship of the said Duchie as well in England as in Walis, without thay have resonnable letting soo to doo, to thentent to oversee and understond the state of the same honors and lordships, and to sette suche ordre and rule in the same if nede bee, as may be to the Kinges wele and profit and for the gode rule and governaunce of the said Duchie and of all the tenauntes of the same.

12 ALSO that the said Chaunceller, ayeinst the tyme that any suche progresse shalbe made, doo gife knowlage and resonnable warnyng thereof unto the Recevour and othir particuler officers of that honour or lordship that thay shall goo to, and at the leest the warnyng of xl dayes to thentent that the tenaunts of the same

honour or lordship may be ther then redy to attende uppon their comyng for the lesse cost and charge to the King.

13 ALSO that the said Chaunceller shall take with him the particuler boks of thaccomptes of thofficers and ministres of the same lordship that thay shall goo to, which were yeven up by (70^r) thauditours at Candilmasse byfore that at the general audite, and suche othir bokes also as shalbe thought necessarie for that bihalf, to thentent thereby to understande if the said officers and ministres have truly occupied thair offices & answerd the King according to thair trouthes and duties in the same.

14 ALSO for asmuche as it is ordeigned by statute of the lond that no writinges under any othir seall than under the seal of the said Duchie shall have course or be obeied within the same, therefore the King wil that all officers, ministers and tenaunts of the said Duchie shall duely obey & put in execucion all suche writings as shal come or be delivered unto theim under the seal of the said Duchie.

15 ALSO that the Chaunceller of the said Duchie in using the said seall shall make no leese or graunt of any ferme of the said Duchie but that therbe alway in the said graunte or leese a clause of a proviso: *Si quis plus dare voluerit absque fraude vel malo ingenio*, but if it be by the Kinges warraunt or by thadvise of the Counsaill of the said Duchie or ellis of suche a place or grounde as hath lien wast or unocupied in tyme past and whereof no profit (70^v) hathe growen to the King by meane of the same, and that also the tenaunt that wil take the said place or wast grounde so to ferme can have noon advantage thereof withoute grete costes of reparacion or bilding or othir charge by him to be borne for that byhalve.

16 ALSO for alsmuche as it is oftentymes nedeful for diverse causes concernyng the said Duchie to make owt comissions & othir writinges under the said seall, the King will that whensoever any suche comyssion shalbe made, that then the said Chaunceller shal put therinne oon or two of thofficers of the said place whereto the said comyssion shalbe directed, and oon or two at the leest of othir discreete persons jointly with the same, the which comissions shall holde inne that the said comissioners, aftir they have enquiered, shal doo certifie unto the said Chaunceller and Counsaill under thair seal suche as thay can fynde & understande in that byhalve.

17 ALSO whensoever the Chaunceller of the said Duchie shal have any knowladge or understonding that the fermes therof or any of yeim be not letten unto the Kinges moost availe or profite, that then he doo calle inne before him the fermors of the same to know by what auctorite thay holde the said fermes, and whethir thay have in thair writing the proviso aforsaid or not, (71^r) and if they have not

suche a proviso &c, then the King will that the said Chaunceller shal approwe the said fermes to his moost profit, alway preferring the said fermours to kepe thaim stille by fore any othir, yf thay wil gif alsmuche as other men wil doo, and ellis not.

18 ALSO the King will that the said Chaunceller have auctoritie and power to make from tyme to tyme all suche warrauntes and writinges undir the seal of the said Duchie as shalbe thought by him and the said Counsaill necessarie and bihoveful for the Kinges wele and profits, and for the ease and wele of all his officers and tenauntes of the said Duchie for the tyme being, without any othir lettres or warraunt to be sued unto the King for that behalve.

19 ALSO that the said Chaunceller and Counsaill at the grete audite at Candilmesse, and the Auditours of the same Duchie in their progress, shall not entre into any accompte with eny officer of the said Duchie accomptable unto the tyme that the said officer be sworne and make an othe in maner folowing:

(71ᵛ)   THE OTHE of all ACCOMPTAUNTES

20 YE shall swere that ye shal at this tyme wel and truly accompt, rekenne and answere to the King our soveraigne lord of all the profits & revenues of your office that ye now occupie, NAMYNG his Office, of his lordship of A of his Duchie of Lancastre, namely of all that ye have received or ought to receyve and myght have comen to your handes by reason of your said office, that is to wite, sith the fest of Michelmas the   yere of the Kinges reigne unto the fest of Michelmes now last past; and that ye shal not in the said accompt and rekenyng make noon excuse nor delay, ner aske noon allowance of any parcell or parcellx in the same but suche as shalbe gode & true; and also that ye have during the same tyme wel and truely approved the Kinges landes and othir his revenues of your charge within your said office to his moost availe and profitte asferre as your kunnyng, auctorite and power cowde serve you, with all othir things doing wel and truely that apperteyneth to your charge in this behalve. And suche ministres accomptauntes whatsoever thay be within your Receipt that have be committed to warde and delivered owt by you or youre deputies ye take to your charge & charge your silf in your accompt with the money by thaim due. SO help you God and halidome and by this boke.

(72ʳ)   ATTOURNEYS

21 ALSO the King will that the generall Attorney of the said Duchie shall declare bifore the Chaunseller and Counsaill of the same, the

High Stewardes or their deputies if thay be there present, in the begynnyng of every terme all maner of suetes that bilong to his charge to sue, to thentent that all suche sutz as ben necessarie for the King may be thadvise of the said Counsaill procede & be put in execucion, and noon othir, in abbregging of the Kinges costs and charges for that behalve.

22 ALSO that the particuler attourneys for the said Duchie in the Chauncerie, in the Kinges Benche, Comen Place and in the Eskeker shall deliver in the begynnyng of every terme unto the general Attourney of the same Duchie by writing a remembraunce of all maner suetz or processe in the Kinges name by theim sued or bilonging to thair charge touching the said Duchie, to thentent that the processe thereof be not lachessed, conceled ne discontynued in thair defaultes.

23 ALSO that the Attourney in the Kinges Escheker shall yerely deliver unto the Chanceller (72^v) of the said Duchie thextrete of the Grene Wex of every part of the said Duchie within the Realme of England and of Wales, to thentent that thay may be levied and gaderd by thofficers thereof to the Kinges behofe and profit, as it hathe been usid to be doon in tyme past.

STYWARDS

24 ALSO that the Stywardes in the parties of Wales geve no pardons to fellons attaineted before theim in their courtes there of felony but that their fynes for the same pardon be assessed by the said Stiwards, Receivours and Auditor of the same lordship, and not by two or oon of theim but by all three jointly, and if it be long for keping of the persone or the said iij parties mete, then the felons to fynde sufficient suertie by recognusaunce to paie suche fyne for his pardon as upon him by the said Stiward, Receivour and Auditour shalbe assessed at the next Audite.

(73^r) 25 ALSO the King will that the High Stiwardes of the said Duchie as well the Northe as of the Southe parties shall come unto the said Counsaill when they therunto shalbe required, if thay may resounable soo doo, to thentent to gif thair gode advise, assistens and counsaill in all suche things as shalbe shewed unto theim concernyng the said Duchie, and for the Kinges honour and wele & profit; and also thay shall supporte and maynten thofficers and tenaunts thereof in all their resounable desires and requests and in all complaints that shalbe shewed unto theim be indifferent betwix partie and partie as ferre as thair resons will serve theim.

26 ALSO the King will that the said High Stiwardes in thair owne

persons without a resounable excuse shall oones in two or thre yeris at the leest holde the grete courtes, othirwise callid the stiwards tournes, in every honour & lordship that thay have rule of, to thentent to understond how all other particuler stiwardes & thair deputies & all other officers & tenaunts of the same have been demeaned & governed, and wher nede is to reforme, amende & correcte so as may be to the Kinges well & profit, rest and ease of his officers and tenaunts of the same. And if any (73ᵛ) of thofficers or tenaunts of the said lordship and honours have otherwise demeaned theim then shall accorde with thair trouthes and duties to the King oure soverain lord, or to the hurt or damage of any other his tenaunts, then the King will that the said High Stiwardes shall forthwith certifie to the Chaunceller and Counsaill thair defaultes in that byhalve, to thentent that thay may ther fore be corrected and punysshed according to thair demerits and deseruyng.

27   ALSO thay shall make and ordeigne under theim suche deputies as thay will answere fore, the which deputies shalbe attendaunt and come unto the Counsaill as ofte and whan thay shall therunto be called to gif thair advise & counsaill for the Kinges wele & profit concerning the said Duchie.

28   ALSO the High Stiward of the southe parties or his deputie shall yereley at the fest of St Martyn in Wynter holde the grete court of Arkesden of the said Duchie at London in Walbroke according to the custome and usage usid in tyme past.

(74ʳ) 29   ALSO that the said High Stiwardes or their deputies be yereley present at the grete audite at Candilmasse, and ther to contynue and abide unto thende of the same audite, to thentent that thay may have, here & understand all thaccompts that shalbe shewed there byfore the Counsaill of the said Duchie by the particuler receavours and othir officers accomptable of the same Duchie.

30   ALSO that every particular stiward of the said Duchie, as wel in England as in Wales, which is occupied in the Kings service and may not attende to doo his office in propre person, shall ordeyne a deputie undir him or oon sufficient lieutenaunt or deputie to kepe the grete courtes & letes of the honours & lordships that he is Stiward of and a sufficient clerk in kunnyng to kepe the courtes from iij weekes to iij wekes, and namely suche persons as he will answere fore, yeving yerely unto the said deputie or lieutenaunt and clerk for thair occupacion and attendaunce suche fees and wages as thay can deserve and may lif upon, without oppresion doing to thofficers & tenaunts within thair said office or of taking of eny of the Kinges duties; and if thay be not so governed then the King will that the High Stiwardes of those parties of the said

Duchie, by thadvise of the Chaunceller and Counseill thereof, shal depute suche deputies or lieutenaunts & clerkes as thay shal seem moost profitable for the King, assignyng to that lieutenaunt or deputie and clerke resounable fees and wages for their service and attendaunce of the fees and wages of the said (74ᵛ) particuler stiwards that so failleth to make a sufficiaunt deputie or lieutenaunt and clerke in the same.

31 ALSO the said particuler stiwardes or thair deputies shall calle to every lete or grete courtes all the homagiers thereof, and moost specially the gentilmen to appere in thair owne persons, and charge thaim oonly with the presentmentes of the defaultes of the said court, by cause if thay be excused and the homagiers oonly chosen of the pour men, then the said pour men dare not present the said defaultes as thay shuld doo, to the Kinges grete hurt and to the dishonnour of the said court.

32 ALSO the King wil that the said Stiwardes or thair deputies, aftir thay have kept the said grete courtes or letes, shal not depart from thense byfore thay have visited and overseen with the Receivour or his deputie the presentments of the said homagiers and othir perquisites, casuelties, profites, fynes & amerciaments, as well of the said grete courtes & letes as of all othir iij wekes courtes sithen the grete court holden byfore that; and thoes overseen by theim, the said Stiward or his deputie, shall endent with the Receivour or his deputie of the same, or with suche othir officers as owe to be accomptable of the said proffites, and then fourthwith deliver exstretes to the Baillif or Reves of the same lordship to (75ʳ) gadre and levie theim to the Kinges byhove & profit. And that part of thendenture that shal remaigne with the said Stiward or his deputie, the said Stiward or his deputie shal deliver to thauditour at his cumyng thider to his next audite, to thentent that the said Receivour or the othir officers acomptable may be chargid therwith at thair next accompt.

33 ALSO that every particuler Stiward of the said Duchie as wel in England as in Wales shall holde the grete courtes and letes within his office in his owne person two tymes in the yere, if he be not excused thereof by the Kinges licence or commaundement or of any othir cause resounable.

34 ALSO the King will that nethir High Stiward, particuler Stiward, Receivour nor their deputies ne noon other officer of the said Duchie shal take upon thaim to yeve any licence, commaundement or any othir warrauntes by writing or otherwise to any maner of person to felle, carie or lede away any of the Kinges wode, trees or tymbre out of any of his forrestes, parkes or chaces of the said

Duchie, but if it be underwode to be sold to the Kinges moost profit and availe or for resonnable browsing for deris mete, which shal be taken by the oversight of the Receivour or of his deputie there for the tyme being, and to make accompt thereof as it hathe ben used in tyme past.

(75^v) 35   ALSO that nether maister of the game, forster, parker ne noon othir officer havyng any rule or governaunce of any of the Kinges parkes, forestes or chaces within the said Duchie serve or obey any warrauntes for felling or carrieng away any tymbre, wode or trees out therof but oonly warrants under the seal of the said Duchie, upon payne to recompence the King of asmuche as he is hurted by meane of the same and to be punysshed at the Kinges pleasir.

36   ALSO for asmuche as the High Stiwardes, particuler Stiwardes of the said Duchie as well in England as in Walis have usid in tyme past of thair own auctorite without any othir advise to make leeses of fermes within thair office in thair owne names by endentur and othir writinges, sum for terme of xx yeres & sum more & sum lesse, where if the said leeses had be made by deliberacion and advise of the Counsaill of the said Duchie and by indenture in the Kinges name, it wold have ben to the Kinges grett advauntage and profit, therfore the King will that no Stiward nor his deputie from this tyme fourth make any leese nor lette to ferme any of the Kinges demaynes in the lordship wher he is Stiward of, but oonly of those londes and tenementes that been holden by copie of court rolle aftir the custome of the manour, and yit that by thadvise of the Receivour or of (76^r) his deputie ther for the tyme being.

37   ALSO for asmuche as oftentymes ther hathe been grevous complaintes made upon Stiwardes and ther deputies and othir officers in Wales for gadering of comorthaes and for othir divers grete extorcions and oppressions by theim doon unto the Kinges tenaunts & liege men there, therfore the King will that all suche Stiwardes that shall occupie and holde the Kinges courtes of the said Duchie in Wales hereafter shall fynde sufficient seuerty by recognusaunce in the Chauncerie of the said Duchie that thay and thair deputies shalbe of gode abering anenst the King and his people, and that no Stiward shalbe allowed of his fee of his office unto the tyme he have founde the said suertie.

38   ALSO that no particuler Stiward of the said Duchie nor his deputie fromhensforth make no collectours, bedelles, baillifs ne revis accomptables but suche as the Receivours particulers will agree unto for the bettir spede of the levie of the Kinges monney and for the more seurtie of the same.

39 ALSO that noon of the Stewardes of the said Duchie ne their deputies, lieutenaunts ne the clerke of the courte fromhensforth be reteigned to be accomptable to the King of the perquisites, (76^v) casuelties, amerciaments, fines and profits of the same courte that thay have rule of, ne of the fermes of any landes or tenements by thaim latten to ferme by reason of the said courte but that thay be levied, answerd and accompted oonly by the baillifes, reves or othir officers there that use to gadre and levie othir revenuez of the said lordship, and so to content and paie the Receivour of the same as the said reves or other officers shall doo of othir thair charge.

40 ALSO that the said Stiwardes shall see and ordeyne that all maner of forfaitours and eschetes to the King in his Duchie be praised by xij lawfull men by fore him or his deputie and the Receivour or his deputie of the place where suche forfaitur or eschete happeneth to falle, and aftir the praising thereof to be solde to the moost advaile for the King; and that the Stiward, Receivour, Feodarie, Juras nor noon othir officer of that place nor noon of thaim do bye ne have by bargaine to be made by themselfs nor by noon othir in thair names the said forfaitour nor eschete in no wise, by cause of the disceite yat by means there of myght happe to be in praisment of the said forfaitour for thair singuler profit and advaile.

41 ALSO WHERE it hathe been usid in tyme past unto nowe late that the particuler Stiwardes (77^r) have kepte yerely two grete courts in the fennys in Lyncolnshire called the fenne cortes, where owe to be present the Feodour and Baillif of the fraunchise of the said Duchie in the same shire, that is to wite, oon court aftir Pasche and the othir Michellmasse then nexte folowinge, wherby the King was than answerd of grete profits by meane of the same aiswel of wayfes as of strayes as of fynes, amerciaments and such othir casualties, and also thapprowmentes of the said fennys by thapprower thereof, not conceled as it is thought thay nowe be to the Kinges grete losse and hurt; therfor the King will that the said Stiwardes, and attending upon him the said Feodarie and Bailluy of the Fraunchise or thair deputies, shal yerely kepe the said cortes at the festes abovesaid aftir the olde usage and custome, and that thapprower of the said fenys make yerely his accompt of the revenues of his office in that byhalve byfore thauditour at his cummyng thider, and content, and paie the same to the Feodarie or to the Receivour as it hathe been accustomed to be doon in tyme past.

42 ALSO the King will that no particuler Stiward ner under stiward ne clerc of any Stiward holding any cortes in any of his honours or lordships of the said Duchie shalbe his Receivour or

otherwise accomptable to him of the profites & revenues of any of the said honours or lordships, by cause that every Stiward must controlle & charge the said Receivour or other accomptant byfore thauditour at his progresse with all the profites of the said court.

(77ᵛ)   CHAMBRELAIN

43 ALSO that the Chambrelain of the said Duchie have a registre of the names and of all such persons as hilde of the King by knight service by reason of his said Duchie of Lancastre within England and Wales, making mencion of all the knightes fees belonging to the same

44 OUT of the which registre the said Chambrelain shall deliver to everey Feodarie, Countie Bailluy and Bailluy of Fraunchises of the said Duchie a transcript of alsmany names as holde of the King by that service within the office of the said Feodarie, Countie Bailluy and Bailluy of Fraunchises

45 TO thentent that, whan any of thaim that holde by Knyghtes service happen to decesse and dye, that everey Feodarie & Countie Bailluy and Bailluy of Fraunchisez of the said Duchie doo yeve knowlage to the particuler Stiward of the same lordship that he may fourthwith enquer how the said person holde of the King the day of his dethe, and by what service, and how many knightes fees, and who is his next heire and of what age, in whose kepinge, what the value of the landes is, who hathe received the same sith the dethe of the homagier, what tyme he decessed, with othir points convenient to be enquired of in like casu.

(78ʳ) 46 THE which inquisicion had, the said Stiward fourthwith shall certifie the said Chambrelain by the said Feodarie at his next apperaunce in the grete court of Arkesden holden in London in Walbrok yerely at the fest of Seint Martin in Winter, wher the said Chambrelain or his deputie owe to be present. And the said Chambrelain shal certifie the same to the Chaunceller and Counsail of the said Duchie, to thentent to charge the Feodarie, Countie Bailluy and Bailluy of Fraunchise with the custodie aswel of the ward as of the londes, or to doo that that the King will commaunde to be doon in that byhalf; and over that yerely at the generall audite shewe and declare to the said Counsaill in writing the proffites that have growen to the King by meane of the same.

47 ALSO that the said Chambrelain shall oversee that no person that holdith of the same Duchie by knightes service be respited of his homage doing over the terme of an half yere without thassent & aggrement of the Chaunceller & Counsaill of the said Duchie, which

have auctorite & power to gif any lenger respite for more advaile and profit to the King.

48 ALSO that suche fynes as shalbe made for suche respits be paied in maner and fourme folowing, that is to wite, a Duc for every knightes fee that he holdith of the said Duchie xx^s, an (78^v) Erle, xiij^s, a Baron, vj^s viij^d, a Becheler Knight and all othir, iij^s iiij^d.

49 ALSO that the said Chambrelain or his deputie be yerely present at the grete audite at Candilmesse and ther abyde unto thende of the same audite, to thentent to knowe and here all thaccomptauntes that shalbe shewed ther byfore the Counsaill by the particuler Receavour & other officers accomptable of the said Duchie.

(79^r)

RECEIVOURS

50 ALSO the King will that the Receivour Generall and all the particuler Receivours of the said Duchie shall come and appiere byfore the Chaunceller and Counsaill and thauditours therof every yere at the fest of Candilmesse or within xiiij daies aftir the same fest at the ferrest, upon payne to lose thair rewarde of the portage of monney and all othir rewardes accustumed to be allowed unto them, and there the said particuler Receivours shall shewe thair charges & discharges of thair office in writing in fourme of accompte, wherby it may be understond and knowen if thay have contented and satisfied to the said general Receivour the hool revenuez of thair office or not, or alsmuch thereof as they have received or ought to receive by reason of thair said office, to thentent that if they have so doon that the said general Receivour may be chargid with the same aftir the olde custome & maner of the said Duchie; and if thay have not, that then they be committed to prison by thadvise of the said Counsaill and Auditours, there to abide to the tyme they have aggreed with the said general Receivour. And if it can be sufficiently approved at any tyme that any of the said particuler Receivours or any othir accomptant of the said Duchie or any of thair deputies, for fere of themprisonment above said, doo concele or hide in any of their accomptes any some or summez of monney by theim received, or that (79^v) by theim myght have been received, and will not during the said accompt confesse ne knowlage their said receite, that then he or thay yat shall soo be founde in default to abide suche punycion as the King and his Counsaill shall ordeyne for the same.

51 ALSO that all particuler Receivours and othir officers accomptable shall make redie levie of thissues of their receibt by two tymes

in the yere, soo that within vj wekes next aftir the termes usuelx of paiement or sone upon, that is to say, at Pasche and at Michelmesse, they doo make paiement unto the said Receivour General or to such persons as it shalbe assigned unto, that is to wite, aftir Pasche of the thirde part of thair receite for that terme and at Michellmesse or sone upon the remenaunt without lenger delay

52 ALSO that all maner of sales of wardes and mariages, wode, tymber or any othir thing within the Duchie which shall mowe growe to the Kinges profit, that thay be doon & made oonly by the King or by the Chaunceller and Counsaill of the said Duchie by his commaundment and by examinacion of the Stiward, Receavour, Auditour and Feodarie of the place where suche profit shall growe; and that the hoole monney of thoo sales be chargid (*80ʳ*) upon the Receivour, ⟨that⟩ at his next accompt, if the sale thereof be not othirwise made by the King himselfe or by othir persons by his special commyssion.

53 ALSO that at every session, lete, court or tourne the Receavour of the lordship where suche session, lete or tourne shalbe holden be ther present in propre person, onlesse than he have any resonnable cause of excuse to be absent, and at the leest than to have ther for him a sufficiaunt deputie to occupie & answere to all things as he him self shuld doo if he were present.

54 ALSO that noon of the said Receivours nor their deputies do make or doo to be made any new bilding in any of the said lordships byfore thay sufficiantly certifie the same to the Chanceller & Counsaill of the said Duchie & the causes therof, and if by theim it be thoughte expedient to bee doon, then the said Chanceller shall yeve therfore a sufficiaunt warraunt to the said Receivour or his deputie by the which, if he bild of newe, that he mowe have allow-aunce thereof at his next accompte, provided alway that if any soden cas of reparacions happen to falle in any of the said lordships which must hastly be made and may not abyde the cummynge of the (*80ᵛ*) said warraunt, oonlesse then it shulde be to the Kinges grete hurt and more charge unto him therafter, then the King will that the said Receivour, by the oversith of the Stiward there, have auctorite and power to make of newe that that soo nedith to be made or repaired, and alsone as he godely may, sue his warraunt of the same.

55 ALSO that no Stiward nor Receivour suffre nor permite any ministre or bailluy, parker or any other officer of any lordship of the said Duchie or of any parcell thereof, to make any reparacions but by their owne ouersight or by the ouersight of suche persons as shalbe appointed for that byhalve, and that the said reparacions ben doon

& fully made in Somer byfore the fest of Michelmesse then next folowing, of the which reparacions wel and truely doon the said ministre or bailluy, parker or other officer, upon sighte and certificat of the said Stiward, Receivour or of the othir persons so assigned, shall have due allowaunce by the bokes of the said Receivour at his cummyng to the grete audite at Candilmesse.

56 ALSO that no particuler Receivour nor his deputie shall deliver, content nor paie to any person noo monney nor somes of monney cummyng or growing of the revenues of his office, or the paiementes of fees, wages, annuiteis, rewardes ordinarie & reparacions but oonly by warraunt under the (*81ʳ*) seall of the said Duchie, or ellis by bille from the generall Receivour, by which warraunt or bille the said particuler Receivour shall have allowaunce and be dischargid therof at his accomptes from tyme to tyme.

57 ALSO that the generall Receivour make no paiement but oonly by the said warraunt or by bill under the seall of the Receipt of the Kinges Escheker at Westminster, by which warraunt or bill the said generall Receivour shall have allowaunce from tyme to tyme and be dischargid therof at his next accompt to be made of the same.

(*81ᵛ*) FEODARIES & BAILLIFES of FRAUNCHISES

58 ALSO for asmuch as the Feodaries, Countie Baillifes and Baillifes of Fraunchises of the said Duchie have not diligently in tyme past exercised & occupied yeir offices, nether accompted nor annswered the King yerely of the revenues and profites therof, that is to wite, nether of the certain revenues nor of the casuelties, mariages nor reliefes, nor of other eschetes nor forfaitours that have fallen in thair tyme within the precincte of thair said office, therfore the King wil that from hensforth every Feodarie, Countie Bailluy, and Bailluy of Fraunchise shal yerely bring in his accompt of the revenuez of his office byfore thauditour of the said Duchie, and be sworne for the same truely to answere of the revenues of his said office, and thereof to make true contentacion and paiement to the particuler Receavour or his deputie of that lordship or honour where he is officer of.

59 ALSO whensoever any person that holdith of the King by knightes service decesse and dye and his heire within age, that then fourthwith the said Feodarie, Countie Bailluy or Bailluy of Fraunchise doo seasse for the King aswel the said heire as the said livelode so holden by knightes service, and to require the Stiward of that lordship or honour in the Kinges byhalve to enquire of the same, and to certifie the Chaunceller and Chambrelain thereof in

contynent as he hathe made the said seisour, aftir the manour and fourme as is comprised in the first Article made upon (82ʳ) thoffice of Chambrelainship (see para. 43).

60 ALSO the said Feodaries shall yerely serche the Kings recordes of all outlawed men and fellons that dwelle within the precinctes of his office, or ellis make suche othir due inquisicions as can be thought moost expedient for that byhalve, and such as shalbe founde in that cas the said Feodarie shall seasse thair goodis to the Kingis bihove, or to take fynes yerely of thaim for thair said goodis as shalbe thoughte lawful and convenient, and to answere the King of the same as thay shall doo of all othir revenuez of their office, and also to levie all thextretes of the Grene Wex that shalbe sent unto theim out of the Kinges Escheker at Westminster.

61 ALSO that all the Feodaries, Countie Baillifes and Baillifes of Fraunchises of the said Duchie of the Southe parties, or thair deputies, shall apper and be present at the fest of Seint Martyn in Wynter at the grete court of Arkesten holden in the Citie of London in Walbroke, and ther present and shewe to the Stiward or his deputie and Chambrelain or his deputie suche thingis as apperteyneth to thair office, accordinge to thauncien usage & custome of the same court; and that the Feodarie of the said Duchie in the Shire of Kent be there in propre person withoute a resonnable excuse, by cause that unto his office as Bailluy of Franchise apperteyneth to levie & answere of all the perquisites and profits of the said court.

(82ᵛ) 62 ALSO for asmuche as diverse Feodaries, Countie Baillifes and Baillifes of Fraunchises of the said Duchie have no certain fee ne rewarde for their attendaunce in the said office, wherfore thay be more lachesse and lothe for to labour diligently in the same for the Kinges moost advaille and profitt, therfore the King will that aftir the quantitie that thay shal approwe to his profit soo shal the quantite of thair rewardis be, that is to wite, of every xxˢ of approwement by their meanes xxᵈ thereof be allowed at their accomptes made of the same.

63 ALSO where the King had in tyme past grete game of swannys, eyvers and othir in the fennys beside Boston in Lincolnshire, which did serve yerely to thexpence of his moost honourable housholde, and a swanne herde or a Maister of Game aswel for thattendaunce therunto as for all othir mennys games in the said fennys, and the King yerely answered of the profit of the said swannys: now it is so that for default of a gode keper of the said game the Kingis game and othir mennys games for moost partie be destroied and stollen and no profit comyng of theim to the King for his parte, therfore

the King wil that whensoever that office shal be voide herafter that
the particuler Stiward by thadvise of the Feodarie and thapprower
of the said fennys, bycause that thay have the moost knowlage who
shulde be moost mete to be keper of the said game, shal name (*83ʳ*)
to the Chaunceller of the said Duchie iiij or iij persons at the leest,
nygh dwelling to the said fennys, of gode name and fame and that
have understanding in keping of the said game, and then the said
Chaunceller shal shewe the same to the King to take which of them
as shal please him; and that doon and chosen the said keper to have
for his labour and attendaunce suche wages as othir kepers have had
in tyme past, fynding sufficient suertie to the King truly to deale in
the said office and thereof to make accompt byfore thauditour every
yere of ye profits [of] the said game, and to answere the said
Receivour according to this trouthe and dutie in that byhalve.

64   ALSO that the said keper shall suffer no man to have any
marke of swannys within the said fennys without he have office or
lyvelode within the shire of Lincoln to the verray value of xl:s. by
the yere over all charges, &c.

AUDITOURS

65   ALSO that thauditours of the said Duchie aswel for England
as for Walis shal yerely oonys in the yere sitte upon audite, that is to
wite, aftir the Fest of Michelmes and not byfore the said Fest, and
there here all thaccomptaunts within his circuite accustomed to
come to the same, and be indifferent betwix the King and thofficers
in their charge and discharge, and moost to the Kinges availe and
profit according to reason and conscience, and aftir the tenour of
thordrenaunce preceding; and such officers and ministers as thay
shall fynde in arrerage to the King thay shall committe theim and
every of thaim to prison to the next gaole within the said Duchie by
endenture bytwix the said Auditour and the lieutenaunt, constable
or keper of that place where the said officer or ministre is committed
unto, ther to abide unto suche tyme as thay and every of thaim
have contented and paied the said arrerages, or othirwise satisfied
the Kinges Receivour thereof to his pleasure.

66   ALSO that the said Auditours by viij or ix daies or more byfore
thair commyng to thaudite shall doo make warnyng to thofficers
and ministres, where thay shall sitte, that thay may make thair
parcells redy anenst thair said commyng, in suche maner that the
said Auditours ne noon of thair clerkes have cause to be taried the
lenger, wherby the King shalbe put to (*84ʳ*) more cost and charge
by their abiding there.

67 ALSO that the said Auditours shall charge euery Receivour with the hole rent and revenuez of the lordship that he is Receivour of, and with all the monney of every parcell that is chargid upon eny other officer or ministre accomptaunt undir him, and to discharge the said Receivour and allowe him ayein by his othe of the parcelles of the said officer and ministre by thadvise and oversight of the Chaunceller & Counsaill at the grete audite.

68 ALSO WHEREAS diverse officers have graunts of thair offices in thair lettres patentes undir thise termes: *Cum vadijs & feodis debitis & consuetis*, the King will that thauditour shal not take for a president the grettest allowance by serche made of the said officis, but where as suche graunts have ben made under general termes, that the said Auditours shall allowe aftir the lest wagis accustumed by suche presidentes for the Kinges availe, and over that to discharge the fees and wagis of all suche officers as have new offices graunted unto theim that were noon offices in the daies of King Henry the iiijth, ne offices that nede noon actuel exercise nor attendaunce.

69 ALSO that the said Auditours at all suche tymes as thay shal ride in circuite of their (*84ᵛ*) offices shall come and certifie unto the Chaunceller and Counsaill of the said Duchie the first day of their riding forthwardes, to thentent that it may be commoned, advysed and appointed amongest theim to which lordshipes the said Auditours shall first ride, and to which aftir that.

70 ALSO the said Auditours aftir thay have sitten upon thaudite shall doo make billes endented bitwene theim and the particuler Stiwardes or thair deputies of every lordship that thay shall come to, by the oversight of the Receivour or his deputie for the same, making mencion of the first day of his sitting at thaudite there and the day of his departinge and the noumbre of als many daies as he shal abyde upon the same; and the billes endented to be seen by the Chaunceller and Counsaill yerely at the tymes of the general audite of the said Duchie, and theruppon by thadvise and discrecion of the said Counsaill the Auditours to have therfor suche wages or rewardes as shalbe by thaim thought resonnable, and that no wages nor rewardes be in any wise to theim allowed for the said daies without thadvise of the said Counsaill in manier aforesaid.

71 ALSO that noon of the said Auditours take their annuel fees ne wagis of their offices of noo (*85ʳ*) fermour nor particuler Receivour nor Feodaries nor othir officers accomptauntes, but oonly by the hands of the General Receivour, or of suche an othir officer as thay shalbe assigned upon by the said Chaunceller and Counsaill & the said General Receivour; and if so bee that thay doo the contrarie

herof, then that officer that hathe so content theim to be disallowed therof in his accompt at his cummyng to the grete audite.

72 ALSO that the said Auditours have power and auctorite by the moost sure meanes that thay can best devise, by thadvise of the particuler Stiward or Receivour or thair deputies of every lordship, to make newe rentalls in all suche places as shalbe nedefull and as ofte as the case shal so require without ferther auctorite to be pursued for that byhalve, provided alway that the said Auditours have noon auctorite by reason of the premisses neither to distrese ne diminnissh thextent nor value of the lordship where the said rental shalbe renewed nor to chaunge any rent from any parcell of lond to any othir without evidence[or] recorde to be had of the same.

73 ALSO where by auctoritie of parliament the Duchie of Lancastre is severed from the Corone soo (85ᵛ) that noon accomptaunt of the said Duchie shall accompt in the Kinges Escheker ne in noon othir court, but oonly byfore the Chaunceller & Counsaille and Auditours of the same Duchie, the King wil that every yere at the Fest of the Purificacion of oure Lady the said Counsaill shal assemble and sitte in audite and the Auditours of the said Duchie aswel of England as of Walis with hem at a certain place by the said Counsaill limited, byfor whom all the particuler Receivours of the said Duchie or thair deputies and all othir accomptauntes accustumed shall ther appere, and aswel declare & shewe the state & rule of the lordship where he is officer, as also to make thair accomptes of their receipt and charge by their othis to be made of the same, and they thereof to be chargid and dischargid aftir the discrecion of the said Chaunceller and Counsaill; the which doon than the said Chaunceller and Counsaill shal procede to the hering & determinacion of the accompt of the General Receivour of the said Duchie, the which fully ingrossed the said Chaunceller & Counsaill then forthwith, or ellis at the ferthest in the terme of Pasche then next folowing, shal shewe the same and the state of the said Duchie to the Kinges own person or to such othir of his Counsaill as he will assigne for that byhalve; of the which accomptes and of every of theim the said (86ʳ) Auditours shall deliver as well bokes of parchemyn engrossed of all the particuler accomptes of the ministres and officers of the said Duchie unto the said Chaunceller & Counsaill, as of all the said Receavours, to thentent that thay may remayne & be kept emongst oyer recordes and evidences of the said Duchie, and the copie of theim to abide in keping of the said Auditours.

74 ALSO that the said Auditours shall gif noon allowance to any Receivour, ministre or any othir officer accomptaunte for any newe bilding or any reparacions to be made by any of thaim above

the some of xl^s, and yit that allowance to be made according to the tenour of the vjth Article comprised emongst othir Articles made for the Receivours of the said Duchie (*see para. 55*).

GENERAL ARTICLES

(*86^v*) 75   ALSO for asmuche as diverse persons having annuities, fees or wagis assigned to be paid of the said Duchie have taken fermes in thair owne handes, to thentent to stop the Receyvour particuler and othir officers accomptauntes at the terme usuely of the monney of the said fermes, and will take their annuiteis, fees & wagis in thair owne handes and rathir will be paied of their duties then the King shalbe for thexpences of his moost honourable household, the King wil therfore that suche fermours shall take no paiement of thair wagis, fees or annuiteis in that wise, but oonly by the handes of the Receivours or of suche as they shalbe assigned unto or as their patentes specifie, but that thay truly content & paie the monney of their fermes to the particuler Receivour at the times usuely of paiement of the same.

76   ALSO that all Bedelles, Revis and Baillifes which occupie by the Kinges lettres patentes and all othir shall fynde sufficient suertie afore the Chaunceller and Counsaill of the said Duchie or to the Receivour of that lordship tha thay be officers of, truly to answere of all suche thinges as shalbe in thair charge and make a true accompt and paiement to the said Receivour or his deputie therof, (*87^r*) whan by him thay shall therto lawfully be required.

77   AND that every lieutenaunt, constable and keper of any castel or maner, to whose keping and warde thauditours of the said Duchie at the tyme of thair audite comitte to warde any person for debte that he oweth to the King, suerly and saufly doo kepe the same person without any mainprise, suertie or deliveraunce out of his warde unto suche tyme as he have content & paied the said dutie to the King or to his Receavour ther, upon payne that whoso enlargith any suche person so committed to warde to content and paie the same dutie that that person ought to doo him self.

78   ALSO that noon inhabitaunt, resident nor dweller within the said Duchie nor noon officer of the same use to bere any unlieuful wepen defended by the statute nor be retayned with any person by othe nor promesse, nor were nor use any clothing, liverey, signe or token of any person of what estate or degre soever thay be without the Kinges licence, onlesse then he be menyall seruant, bailluy, receavour, stiward, auditour or any other officer of him that yevith him the said lyveray.

79   ALSO the King will that if any officer or ministre (87^v) of the said Duchie that owe to make his accompt byfore thauditour at his commyng to the lordship where he is officer or ministre of come not & make his accompt at the being of the said Auditour there, or that refuseth to make an othe for his said accompt, or that maketh noo redye paiement to the Receivour of the said lordship as he shuld doo, according to the termes usuely of paiement in the same, that then the said officer or ministre shall come and appere byfore the Chaunceller & Counsaill of the said Duchie at the Fest of Candilmesse next then folowing at the grete audite upon his owne cost & charge, and there make his accompt and paiement as aforesaid.

(88^r) Here folow APPOINTMENTES necessarie for the gode and politique Rule of the Countie Palatine of Lancastre

80   FIRST it is appointed and ordeyned that the Sessions at Lancastre at all tymes whan thay shalbe holde be holde xij or x dayes at the leest, and if it nede moo dayes, than to be holde moo, to thentent that all maner suetes, as wel for the King as for the partie, may be better spedde at gode and resonnable laisour and the King the more availed for his seall there.

81   ALSO that the Sherif and Undersherif, Coroners and othir clerkes and elusours also of the said countie for the tyme being be chargid and openly sworne, in plain session bifore the Justices at Lancastre and other of the Kinges counseill ther, to empanell knightes and squieres and the moost sufficiaunt men of lyvelode within the said countie in enquestes bothe for the King and for the parties, not letting neither for lucre nor for affeccion, drede, ne love of any person, and that thay empanell in semble wise byfore the Justicz of the Pees ther.

82   ALSO that the Justices of the Pees there for the tyme being be sworne in the Chauncerie of the said Countie Palatine duely to execute there offices, and that thay kepe Sessions of Pees iiij tymes a yere in due place and oftir if nede be, according to the Statute thereof made.

II

'A BREVIAT OF THE EFFECTES DEVISED FOR WALES', c. 1540–41.

edited by

P. R. ROBERTS, M.A., Ph.D., F.S.A., F.R.Hist. S.

CONTENTS

Introduction

This manuscript is one of a number of draft instruments of legislation dating from the 1530s and 1540s which survive as fragments of proposed or rejected programmes of reform. Some of these, though cast in the diplomatic form of a bill, were not necessarily presented in parliament.[1] There can be little doubt of the official provenance of the present document, since its secondary features either reflect the provisions of the so-called 'act of union' of 1536 or else anticipate those of the final parliamentary settlement of 1543.[2] Its interest and significance lies in that both its principal features and the format suggest an original quite different from the statute enacted in 1543.

The document outlines a new hierarchy of jurisdictions for Wales on the foundation laid in 1536, and defines the relations between the various courts. From the internal evidence of appointments to certain offices it is possible to date it as drafted sometime between September 1540 and June 1541. The system of great sessions, which was to be the most novel and prominent feature of the act of 1543, is seen in embryo in the 'breviat', but it is overshadowed by a remarkable proposal to abolish the Council in the Marches and institute a court of Chancery in its place. By this date the

[1] G. R. Elton, 'Parliamentary Drafts, 1529–1540', *Bulletin of the Institute of Historical Research*, xxv (1952), pp. 117–32.

[2] 27 Henry VIII, c. 26 and 34 and 35 Henry VIII, c. 26: *Statutes of the Realm*, ed. A. Luders *et al.* (London, 1810–28), iii, pp. 563–89, 926–37.

administrative, if not the judicial, changes introduced in 1536 were virtually complete, and the Marcher lordships had been converted into shireground.[3] According to the 'effectes devised for Wales' five itinerant chief justices were to hold their sessions in each shire in turn within three circuits. While a justice of Chester was to continue to have jurisdiction over Flint, two of the remaining four justices were to be entrusted with a circuit of six shires and two with a circuit of five shires. These shires are not named, but a likely division would have been between the shires of North and South Wales. This would have been the more plausible pattern had it been the intention to retain the administrative centres of the former northern and southern principalities at Caernarvon and Carmarthen to serve the new circuits. But the central chancery was evidently intended to replace those local ones which had functioned alongside the regional exchequers. Clearly the pattern was not yet definite, but it is significant that at this stage there was no intention of repeating in the new circuits the arrangement of courts which had obtained in the old principality. But neither was there a tendency to regard the six new shires of the Marches (excluding Monmouth and Flint, which were to be provided for separately) as forming a unit distinct from the rest of Wales.[4] This new dispensation under a central Chancery for Wales would have given the country a greater degree of judicial independence than the scheme that was to be adopted or the system it replaced.

The articles of account contained in a schedule to the 'breviat' reveal the ostensible objection to the continuance of the Council in the Marches to be financial. It is argued that justice and the king's advantage would be better served under the economies of the envisaged new order. However, there may have been more realistic political pressures at work to replace Rowland Lee, the President of the Council in the Marches, and his entourage.

The 'breviat' is not the only extant document which suggests improvement on the act of 1536. There were other petitions and proposals for institutional reform, particularly for an equity juris-diction which would obviate the inconvenience of a journey to London for Welsh suitors and appellants. Many of these recom-mendations from the Marches were not only echoed in the 'breviat' but—with the exception of the Chancery—realized in the act of 1543.[5] Those responsible for defining the Welsh settlement after 1536

---

[3] P. R. Roberts, 'The "Acts of Union" and the Tudor Settlement of Wales' (unpublished Cambridge Ph.D. thesis, 1966), chapter iv, *passim*.

[4] Cf. William Rees, *An Historical Atlas of Wales* (Cardiff, 1951), plate 56.

[5] P. R. Roberts, *op. cit.*, chapter v.

appear to have respected the opinions of local men as expressed in petitions. But there is little doubt that the brief, even if it incorporates some of these proposed reforms, is itself the product of an office of the central government. It may reasonably be taken to be what it purports to be: a memorial or digest of proposals already designed for the government of Wales, rather than a sketch of potential reforms. By the early seventeenth century a legislative procedure had developed in the Commons whereby the clerk, after each reading of a bill, would read the title and a summary of its contents from a breviate filed to it.[6] There is little reason to suppose that procedure in the Lords, where the 'ordinances' of 1543 were first introduced in parliament,[7] would have been different in the reign of Henry VIII. That it is a brief of a larger document fuller in detail is seen by the reference to particulars of officers' fees elaborated 'in the order' (sections 9, 12). We can be sure that the brief reflects an early stage in the business of legislation, though it is not necessarily a document which relates to the parliamentary proceedings.

It is possible to argue that the original intention was to proceed not by act of parliament but rather by ordinance, and that the 'breviat' represents an order in council which required only the king's approval to be made law. As an administrative order, such an elaboration on the settlement planned in 1536 had been legalized by parliament in advance, by a proviso of the act 27 Henry VIII, c. 26. Precaution had then been taken to augment and elaborate the settlement by authorizing the king to erect courts of law and to appoint justices. This special power of legislation was to extend for five years, and at the end of that period, by 1541, the new legal system, consisting of quarter sessions and great sessions, was already in operation in Wales and the Marches. The act of 1543 for the 'ordinances of Wales' was therefore legislating after the event when it purported to introduce these courts, since the king had in effect enforced this aspect of the settlement by an exercise of his prerogative sanctioned prospectively by parliament. The aim in 1543 was not to innovate but to regularize and codify the whole settlement of Wales.

The statute 34 & 35 Henry VIII, c. 26, would therefore emerge as a modified version of a projected or rejected ordinance. It can be shown that, while there survived into the sixteenth century a residuary distinction between statute enacted by the king in

[6] J. E. Neale, *The Elizabethan House of Commons* (London, 1949), p. 394.
[7] See the endorsements on the bill in the Parliament Office, House of Lords.

parliament and ordinance promulgated in council, there is evidence for a deference to statute in the business of legislation which became increasingly more apparent in the second half of the reign of Henry VIII. It appears that council ordinances or administrative orders, dealing as they did with matters bearing on the king's household and government and having therefore a more lasting importance than the emergency authority exercised in proclamation, tended finally to become converted into acts of parliament.

The act of 1543 is one instance of such a tendency. If the 'breviat' does not resemble what has been defined as a 'proper' draft for a bill at this time, neither does the engrossed bill of 1543 conform to the usual Henrician act of parliament. It reads less like an act than a catalogue of legislative orders, and it was not only its great length which determined its division into articles. The diplomatic of the document betrays its original to have been something other than a bill, and it is possible to reconstruct the process whereby the 'effectes devised for Wales' became 'an acte for certaine ordinances in the Kinges Majesties Domynion and Principalitie of Wales'.[8] Plans for an instrument under the great seal may have been discarded on realizing that the enabling provision of the 1536 act was about to lapse in the summer of 1541. Again, once it had been decided to abolish Welsh laws entirely, and once the proposal for a court of Chancery had been jettisoned, the common lawyers in the king's council may have felt that, though not essential, the confirmation of statute was desirable for the establishment of new courts of common law. The memory of a suspicion of prerogative action which had been provoked in parliament by the bill of proclamations in 1539 may have discouraged the government from proceeding by ordinance to the settlement of Wales.

That a deliberate decision was made to change the instrument of enactment is reflected in the enacting clause of the act of 1543:

> [The king] . . . hath devysed and made dyvers soondrye good and necessarye ordinances, which his Ma[jes]te of his moste habundaunte goodnes, at the humble sute and peticion of his said subiectes of Wales, is pleased and contented to be enacted by th'assent [and authority of parliament].

This unequivocally reveals the sequence of decisions: the king had devised ordinances for Wales, and then had been prevailed upon to enact them through parliament, presumably by the Welsh members

---

[8] I intend to rehearse this argument in detail on another occasion. The relationship of some of the clauses in the 'breviat' to those in the final act is set out in the appendix below.

who were attending parliament for the first time as a result of the enfranchising provision of the 1536 act.

Apart from the Chancery for Wales, the most novel provision of the 'breviat' was that for the erection of a new principality for Prince Edward. The settlement as conceived at this stage involved the incorporation of the new shires with the existing 'shireground' of the ancient principality. The whole of Wales would now constitute a principality which, according to historical usage, would form a separate province for the young prince under the king's suzerainty. In this respect the policy for Wales was associated with the central problem of the succession to the throne in the years after the birth of an heir in 1537. That occasion was construed by the authors of the 'effectes devised for Wales' as conferring a special status on the constitution already designed for that country, which was now unified administratively and at the same time brought under uniform, if indirect, royal control. That plans for both a new principality and a Chancery were abandoned in the event shows that the provisions of 1543 were by no means an inevitable development from those outlined in 1536. In the interval between 1541 and 1543 other counsels prevailed and the government resolved upon a settlement which preserved some of the features of the previous order. Had the alternative scheme been adopted, a very different 'union' with England would have been forged. As it was, the definitions finally agreed on did not materially alter or qualify the conception of sovereignty which had been formulated for Henry VIII in the statutes of the 1530s.[9]

As seen in this light, the 'breviat' is not only a seminal document for the reconstruction of the legislative programme for Wales in the years 1536–43. It also provides valuable additional evidence for the study of the relationship between statute and ordinance at the time of the controversial 'act of proclamations' of 1539.

Note on editorial practice

The manuscript is to be found among the Cotton MSS at the British Museum (Vitellius C I, fos. 39–44[v]). It is written in a clerkly hand of the period on both sides of pages of approximate size 7″ by 11″, the spacing between the lines being about ¼″, and is in places corrected in the original hand and ink. Interlineations and

[9] For a discussion of the role of the principality in the 'union', and an analysis of the relevant section of the 'breviat', see P. R. Roberts, 'The Union with England and the Identity of "Anglican" Wales', *Trans. Royal Hist. Soc.*, 5th ser., xx (1972), pp. 49–70.

deletions are indicated in the transcript within parentheses; extended abbreviations are italicized and the punctuation is modernized. The leaves of the manuscript are charred on the outer edges and some of the words consequently lost. However, an attempt has been made to recover the sense by supplying obvious omissions and conjecturing the more obscure ones, and these have been italicized and rendered in modern spelling within square brackets. Where there remains some doubt as to whether a word is obscured at all, this is indicated by a query.

A BREVIAT OF THE EFFECTES
DEVISED FOR WALES

[1] Furst, the Principalitie and Domynyon of W[ales is?] made shire grounde according to the acte mad[e for?] Wales, and ther be xij shires appointed in the s[aid]? Domynyon severed into hundredes according to the s[aid?] acte.

[2] Item, it is ordeyned that there shal be oon Chauncerye [and?] oon Chauncelor to be named by the Kinges Maiesti[e] for all the said Domynyon of Wales, whiche Chau[ncellor] shall have the custodie of the Kinges Highnes se[al] to be devised by his Maiestie for that purpose, [with] the whiche seale, patentes and leases for terme of [life?] or yeres and wrytes, commissions and other proces [of?] comen iustice to be mynystred in Wales shal be [sealed?] as it is used in the Chauncerye in Englond, a[nd] the Kinges Highnes to be aunswered of the profyttes [of the?] seale.

[3] Item, there shal be oon clerk of the crowne of the Ch[ancery] in Wales whiche also shal be clerk examyner of th[e] Chauncerye and shall examyn all witnes that [shall be?] deducyd into the said Chauncerye of Wales bytwe[en party] and partie, whiche clerke of the crowne and cl[erk] examyner shal be named by the Kinges Highnes[and] have the hoole profyttes of all examynacions of w[itnesses?] and for copies of deposicions of the same.

[4] Item, there shal be oon clerk of the hanaper of the s[aid] Chauncerye of Wales to be named by the Kinges M[ajesty] whiche shall receyve all the profyttes of the said seale [and] also the profyttes of three other iudiciall seales tha[t?] shall remayne with the iustices as herafter shal be [?] declared and shall accompt for the same to the Ki[ng's] highnes use.

[39ᵛ]

[5] Item, ther shal be another clerk of the Chauncerye in Wales whiche shal be the clerk comptroller of the hanaper in Wales to be named by the Kinges Maiestie and also twoo other clerkes of the said Chauncerye in Wales, wherof oon to be named by the Kinges Highnes and the other to be named by the Chauncelor of Wales, and everye of them shall attende upon the said Chauncelor. And the clerk of the hanaper and thiese iij other clerkes above named shall have the profyttes for wrytyng of all patentes, leases, writtes, enrolmentes and proces that shall passe under the seale of the Chauncerye of Wales, and be comen attorneis in all causes brought into the said Chauncerye bitwene partie and partie.

[6] Item, it is ordeyned that ther shal be oon sergiaunt at armes and three messengers to be named and appointed by the Kinges Highnes to attende upon the said Chauncelor of Wales. And also oon persone to be named by the said Chauncelor to chaffe the waxe and seale all thinges that shall passe under the seale of the said Chauncerye.

[7] Item, ther shall be fyve principall iustices wherof the iustice of Chester shal be oon, and foure other to be lerned in the lawes of the land, whiche shal be named by the Kinges Majestie, emonges whiche fyve iustices the said xij shires shal be devided and the iustice of Chester shall have allotted to hym the shire of Flynte, oon of the said xii shires, and twoo of the other iiij iustices shall have vj of the said shires and the other twoo v of the same shires.

[40r]

[8] Item, the said iustices shall hold ther session[s within?] the said shires to them severallie allotted twy[ce a year?][1], abydyng at every sessiones by the space of vi [days] and shall have auctorytie to hold al maner of pl[eas of] the crowne and for comen iustice within ther circuytes [as?] the iustices in England maye do.

[9] Item, ther shal be three pronotaries to be devided to [?] attende upon the said iustices within ther circuites, w[hich] office of pronotarye as often as they shal be voide [?] shal be gyven by the Kynges Majestie, and noone of the[m to?] have eny ffee but onlye the profyttes of entrees [of?] plees and writynges (and what fees every pronotarie sh[all have?] it is declared by the said order).[a]

[10] Item, ther shal be three iudiciall seales to be [?] devised by the Kinges Majestie to remayne with th[e] said iustices, with the whiche all iudiciall pro[cess?] to be sued bifore them in ther sessions and cyr[cuits] shal be sealed.

[11] Item, ther shal be three persones to be named by th[e] said iustices to chaffe the waxe and seal a[ll things?] under the same iudiciall seales whiche shall p[roceed] from the said iustices. And thes persones shall re[ceive?] the profyttes of the said seales to the Kinges use a[nd account for?] the same to the clerk of the hanaper of the Chauncerye [of] Wales.

[12] Item, ther shal be marcyalles and cryors to atte[nd] upon the said iustices in the circuites to be named [by?] the said iustices and they to have no ffee of the k]ing?] but the profyttes to suche offices belonging being ex[pressed?] in the order.

---

[a] Added later in the same hand.

---

[1] Cf. 34 and 35 Henry VIII, c. 26, s. 5, and below, item 13.

[40*]

[13] Item, over and besides the sessions to be holden by the iustices twys in the yere in every shire as is aforesaid, ther shall be foure termes holden and kepte byfore the said Chauncelor and iustices, or three of them at the leste, at foure tymes in the yere and every of the said termes shall endure oon moneth at the leste. And twoo of the said termes to be kepte at the towne of Ludlowe and the other twoo there or else where it shal be appointed by the Chauncelor and iustices. And the said Chauncelor and iustices in the said termes shall have power to heir and determyn all maner of causes and use suche proces after the course of the Chauncerye and Sterr Chamber in Englond.

[14] Item, bisides the said termes the Chauncerye shall alwaies be open to all sutors wheresoever the Chauncelor shal be, to award proces and heire and determyn causes as the case shall require.

[15] Item, there shall also be iustices of peax and clerkes of the peax in everye of the said shires whiche shall kepe sessiones and have like auctoritie and fees as iustices of peax and clerkes of the peax have in England, with a certaine declaracion for the ffees of the clerkes of the peace to be taken of the Kinges subiectes. And for this furst tyme the iustices of peax shal be named by the Chauncelor of Englond under the great seale and afterward by the Chauncelor of Wales under the seale of the Chauncerye there, with a proviso that ther shall not be above viij iustices of peace in eny oon shire.

[16] Item, ther shal be oon persone to be the Kinges Attorney and oon other persone to be the Kinges Solycitor within the said Domynion of Wales, and bothe to be named by the Kinges Ma*j*estie and they to attende upon the said Chauncelor and iustices at the said iiij termes alternis vicibus.

[41*]

[17] Item, there shall be shireffes in every of the s[*hires*] to be named yerelye by the Kinges Highnes, [*which*] shireffes shall have like power and auctoritie as sh[*eriffs*] in England, with a declaracion what ffees they take [?] of the Kinges subiectes, and for the yerly no[*mination*] of them the Chauncelor of Wales and twoo of th[*e*] said iustices at the leest shall every yere at the feast of [*All*] Seyntes name three gentilmen in every of the said sh[*ires*] and certyfie the same, and then the Kinges Ma*j*estie [*shall?*] appointe oon suche in every shire as shall stound [*with?*] his most graciouse pleasure, and as his High[*ness*] doth in Englond.

[18] Item, ther shal be excheitors in every of the said shire[*es to be?*] named by the Lord Treasourer of Englond by [*the*] advise of the Master of the Wardes. And tha[*t there*] shal be coroners in everye of the said shires to be [*appointed?*] by wryte de coronatore eligendo,

and also h[*igh*] constables to be appointed in every hundred by th[*e justices*] of peace in like maner as it is used in Englond.

[19] Item, it is declared that the Kinges Highnes shall have [*the profits of the?*] seale of wryttes, patentes and leases according to [*those?*] used in the Chauncerye in Englond. And it is also de[*clared?*] what ffees the clerkes of the crowne, hanaper and oth[*er*] clerkes of the Chauncerye aforesaid shall take for t[*heir*] paynes of wrytynges, enrolmentes and examynacion[*s of?*] witnesses, and what ffees shal be taken for a[*ppearance?*] of the Kinges subiectes.

[20] Item, that statutes and recognisaunces made in Englon[*d*] by Walshemen shal be certified into the Chauncerye in W[*ales*] and therupon execucion shal be ther had by the Kinges M[*ajesty?*] as it is used in Englond.

[21] Item, it is ordeyned that suche as have patentes of offices [*of?*] iustice, chauncelor or steward shall not medle in comen [*justice*] nor with sealyng of eny patentes or process but onlye [*the*] [*41ᵛ*] said Chauncelor and fyve iustices, but that they shall have ther certaine ffees lymyted in ther patentes during ther interest therin, and no casuelties incydent to ther offices, with a proviso that chamberlayns maye make processe against accomptaunces afore them for the Kinges fermes and rentes.

[22] Item, it is ordeyned that the shirefes shall have iailes to kepe prisoners in every shire in the Kinges castelles there by the appointment and order of the said Chauncelor and iustices, and that they shall make bailiffes of the hundreds within ther shirefwyke and kepe ther counties, turnes and hundred courtes as is used in Englond.

[23] Item, the Kinges Majestie shall have all fynes, issues, amercyamentes, forfeytures of recognisaunce, and all maner of forfeytours lost in eny of the said termes, grete sessions, sessions of peace, countees, turnes or hundredd courtes to be levyed by the shireffes by extractes[a] and to be accompted for (and) aunswered by them to the Kinges use byfore the Kynges auditors to be appointed for the same.

[24] Item, it is ordeyned that leases and grauntes of londes, offices, ffees or annuyties in Wales out of the Duchie of Lancaster or apperteignyng to the survey of the Courte of Augmentaciones shall passe under the severall seales of the Augmentacion and Duchie as it is used in Englond.

[25] Item, it is ordeyned that no persone for murdre or felonye shal be put to his fyne, but shall suffer according to the lawe, onles the Kinges Highnes of his petie will pardon hym.

[a] Or estreats: see George Owen, 'The Dialogue of the Government of Wales', in *The Description of Penbrokeshire by George Owen of Henllys*, ed. Henry Owen (London, 1906), part iii, pp. 67, n. 6, 68, n. 4.

[26] Item, that noo wepons bee boren in the termes, grete sessions and sessions of the peace in the presence of the iustices or Chauncelor.
[*42ʳ*]
[27] Item, that the Welshe tenures shall dis[*cend to the?*] oldest soone according to the course of th[*e common law?*] and not to be departible amongist heires m[*ale*], that all morgages there herafter to be made [*shall be?*] after the lawes in Englond and noone otherwis[*e ?*] and that they maye sell ther Welshe (tn)ᵃ tenure[*s as?*] londes been used to be sold in Englond.
[28] Item, all wrytes, billes, plaintes etc. shall be used a[*s*] is in North Wales and (as) shal be devised by the Cha[*ncellor*] and iustices, except that the Kinges Highnes for bi[*lls*] under xl s. shall have ij d. for the seale and [*for?*] billes above xl s., vj d. for the seale like as [*his*]? highnes shall have for originall writes.
[29] Item, suche acciones personalles as be under xl s. a[*nd?*] cannot be tryed byfore the iustices of the grete [*sessions*] for shortnes of tyme shal be remytted to a pet[*ty*] sessiones byfore a depute iustice as is used [*in*] Northe Wales.
[30] Item, if eny murder or felonye be comytted t[*o a*] persone, the partie to whom the offence is comytt[*ed*] shall not agre with the offendor without the Cha[*ncellor*] and iustices there be made privie therunto.
[31] Item, that all londes suppressed or attainted now [*in the?*] Kinges handes shall have none other liberties or [*rights?*] then be conteyned in the Statute of Wales mad[*e anno?*] xxvij° H. viij, except that all proces shal be ser[*ved by*] the Kinges Highnes Bailifes there and by noone [*other*].
[32] Item, everye persone being in peasyble possession [*of land?*] and tenantes by the space of v yeres without clay[*m?*] or chalynge shall not be amoved from the sa[*me?*] but by proces of the lawe.
[33] Item, that if eny indytement of murders or felon[*ies*] comytted or don in eny of the xij shires of W[*ales*] [*42ᵛ*] bee taken in eny of the shires of Salop, Hereford, Wurcester, Glowcester or Mounmouth without licence of the said Chauncelor or of oon of the said iustices, that then the Chauncelor shall remove the same by certiorare or habeas corpus and to examyn the mater and returne it agayne to be tryed by procedendo of [*recte,* if] the cause so require.
[34] Item, in accions personals pursued (bifore) eny of the iustices, if nyne of the iure be sworen in triall therof and the residue make defaute the shireff shall retorne the residue de circumstantibus.
[35] Item, if goodes stolen be sold in open market it shall chaunge noo propertie.

ᵃ Struck through.

[36] Item, every man that maye dispende eny freeholde in ffee symple, fee taile or for terme of liff shall passe in all trials as well in accions realles as personalles as in triall of liff and dethe, except in attainte wherin he mooste dispende xl s. at leeste, and all other chalenges to be used as they be in Englond.

[37] Item, if eny catall be stolen and trake therof founde, yt shal be pursued from lordship to lordshipp after the custome in Wales.

[38] Item, tenantes and resiauntes in Wales shall paie tallages and mysys at the chaunge of the lordes as have byn used in tymes paste (and (all o)*a* do all other service and customes, the redempcion of Sessiones onlye except.)*b*

[39] Item, ther shal be knightes of the shires and burges of parliament chosen in everye of the said xij shires by the Kinges write oute of the Chauncerye in Englond, and (Welshemen) shal be charged and chargeable to subsidies and taxes as the Kinges subgiettes be in Englond.

[40] Item, upon erronyouse iudgement gyven bifore eny of the said iustices in (Englond) accyons reals and myxte, a wryte of error shal be directed out of the [*43ʳ*] Chauncerye of Englond retornable in the [King's Bench]*c* and there to be determyned. And in all [*actions*] personalles the errors shal be redressed bifore [*the*] Chauncelor and iustices of Wales in the terme [?] by write of errour from the Chauncelor of W[*ales*].

[41] Item, proces shal be directed into Wales upon urg[*ent*] causes by the commaundement of the Chauncellor of Englond or eny of the Kinges Counsaill as h[*as*] byn used in tymes paste.

[42] Item, all patentes, leases, writes, commissions and proces [*which?*] shall passe under the seale of the Chauncerye [*of*] Wales as long as the said Domynyon shall [?] remayne in the Kinges handes shall be made in t[*he*] Kinges name and the teste to be teste m[*e ipso*] as it is used in the Chauncerye of Englond [*and?*] the teste of all the iudiciall writes and proces [*shall pass?*] under the name of the iustice from whom s[*uch*] proces shall be awarded.

[43] Item, if it shall please the Kinges Majestie to g[*rant the?*] said Domynyon to his most dere and entier[*ly*] beloved son, Prince Edward, with the hoole prof[*its and?*] the full auctorytie of iustice therof, and the [*gift?*] of all offices ther, all proces shal be made in [*the*] Princes name with teste me ipso expressyng [?] the yere of the Kinges reigne and newe s[*eals?*] to be devysed for that purpose for the Ki[*ng's and?*] princes hono*ur*, as shal be devysed by the K[*ing's*] Maiestie.

a Struck through.   *b* Added later in the same hand.
c Thus in 34 & 35 Henry VIII, c. 26, s. 113.

[44] Item, it is ordeyned that the Kinges Maiestie gyff the said Domynion to the Prince after such[h] facion and forme as shall stound with his graces [?] pleasure, with a proviso that the Prince s[hall] have no auctorytie to pardon eny treasones except [the?] King will so appoint it.

[45] And fynallie the Kinges most Roiall Majestie to reserve his Roia[l?] auctoritie to chaunge, adde and reforme all maner thinges biforesaid [from time]*a* to tyme as to his most excellent wisdome and discrecyon shal b[e thought?] convenient for the comen welthe and good government of his said dominion.

[43ᵛ]   A declaracion what fees and diettes the Kinges Majestie yerely paide for the Commissioners, Iustice of North Wales, and Shireffes in Wales, Furst for the dyettes of the President and Counsaill:

For the diettes of the President and Counsaill by the weke	xiij li. vj s. viij d.
Item, to Sir Edward Croft, knight	x li.
To Sir Rice Mauncell, knight	x li.
To Thomas Holt, esquier, attorney	xiij li. vj s. viij d.
John Vernon, esquier	xiij li. vj s. viij d.
Item, to John Apprice, secretorye	xiij li. vj s. viij d.
Richard Hassall, solicytor	C s.
Foren² expenses by the yere	lxvj li. xiij s. iiij d.
To William Carter, armeror, by the daie	vj d.
Item, a sergiaunt at armes, by the daie, xij d., sum	xviij li. v s.
Pakyngton's ffee for North Wales	xxxiij li. vj s. viij d.
Portes ffee, deceased	xxvj li. xiij s. iiij d.
Fitzherbertes ffee	x li.
Item, iiij messengers yerelye	xij li.
Item, the ffees for shireffes, whiche be discharged by acte of parlement³	(lxxx li.)*b* lxxxx li.
Sum of all the said diettes and ffees M¹ xxiiij li.⁴	

[44ʳ]   Memorandum, if it shall please the Kinges Majestie to fou[nd a?] new order and brek up the Counsaill and

a Thus in 34 & 35 Henry VIII, c. 26, s .119.
b Struck through.

---

² *I.e.*, miscellaneous.
³ *I.e.*, 32 Henry VIII, c. 27, which was read in the Lords on 17, 19 and 22 July, and received the royal assent on 24 July 1540, the last day of the Parliament. *Lords Journals*, i, pp. 158, 160.
⁴ *Recte*, £1,024. 7s. 6d.

Com[*mission*] that is now used, then his graces yerelye charges [*for the?*] mynystracion of iustice in Wales for ffees, wages and diettes shal be as folowethe.

Furst to the Chauncelor for his fee
CC markes and v li. for his roobes   Cxxxviij li. [*vi s. viii d.*]

Item, it is ordeyned that twoo of the
justices and the Kinges attorney or
solycytor shall have mete and drynk
for them and certaine ther servantes
in the tyme of the termes to be holden
and that the clerk of the crown and clerk
examyner and the clerk of the hanaper,
and the other iij clerkes of the Chauncerye,
and the sergiaunt at armes, iij messengers
and the chafer of waxe shall have mete,
drynk and lodging with the Chauncelor
at all tymes of ther attendaunce and
that the Chauncelor shall have yerlye
for ther diettes   CC li.

Item, everye of the iiij justices shall
have yerely oon hundred markes   CCCC [*marks*]

Item, the Kinges attorney shall have
yerely xx li and the Kinges solycytor
yerelye x li   xxx li.

Item, the clerk of the crowne yerelye
x markes and xl s. for his lyverye   viij li. xiij s. [*iv d.*]

Item, the clerk of the hanaper
yerelye xviij li. for his ffee
and xl s. for his lyverye   xx li.

Item, to the clerk comptroller of
the hanaper yerelye   iiij li.

Item, to everye of the other twoo
clerkes of the Chauncerye
liij s. iiij d., sum   x li. vj s. v[*iii d.*]

[*44ᵛ*]

To the sergiaunt at armes xij d. bye
the daie, sum   xviij li. v s.

To every of the iij messengers
yerelye iiij li., sum   xij li.

To the chafer of the waxe, yerelye   iij li. vj s. viii d.

Item, to twoo of the kepers of the
iudiciall seales, to every of them
iij li. vj s. viij d., and to the
thirde xx s.   vij li. xiij s. iiij d.
To every of the xij shireffes
vj li. xiij s. iiij d., sum   lxxx li.
Item, to the excheitor if he fynde
eny office for the king, xl s.   xl s.
    Sum of the charges   DCClxxxxviij li. xij s. viij d.[5]
    ys yerelye
And so the Kinges Maiestie
is lesse charged by the
newe order then he was
by the old   CCxxv li. xiiij s. x d.[6]

[5] *Recte*, £801. 5s. od.
[6] The difference between the two sums given should be £225. 7s. 4d.; the real saving would have been £223. 2s. 6d. (£1,024. 7s. 6d. — £801. 5s. od.).

APPENDIX

CORRESPONDING DIVISIONS OF THE 'BREVIAT' AND THE STATUTE 34 & 35 HENRY VIII, c. 26

(The original of neither document is numbered.
Some points are unavoidably duplicated owing
to the overlapping of approximate matter.)

Sections (Statutes of the Realm)	Statute Articles (after Ivor Bowen, The Statutes of Wales (London, 1908))	Breviat Items
I	1–2	1
II	3	—
III	4	2–6
IV–VI	5–12	7–8, 13
VII	16–20	2
VIII	21–2	21
IX–X	23–5	—
XI	26	—
XII	27	—
XIII	28	—
XIV–XV	29–39	10
XVI	40–3	—
XVII	44	9
XVIII	45–6	12
XIX–XX	47–52	9
XXI	53–60	15
XXII	61–4	17
XXIII	65	—
XXIV–XXVI	66–70	18
XXVII	71–5	22
XXVIII	76–7	23
XXIX–XXXI	78–83	–
XXXII	84	25
XXXIII	85–7	—
XXXIV	88–9	—
XXXV	90	26
XXXVI–XXXVIII	91–3	27
XXXIX	94–5	20

Sections (*Statutes of the Realm*)	*Statute* Articles (after Ivor Bowen, *The Statutes of Wales* (London, 1908))	*Breviat Item*
XL	96	28
XLI	97–8	—
XLII	99	29
XLIII	100	30
XLIV	101	31
XLV	102	32
XLVI	103	34
XLVII	{ 104–5	35
	106	37
XLVIII	107–8	36
XLIX	109	38
L	110	39
LI	111	—
LII	112	23
LIII–LIV	113–14	40
LV	115	41
LVI	116	—
LVII	117	—
LVIII	118	—
LIX	119–20	45
(schedules)		
LX–LXVI	121–30	

III

'THE MUSTER-MASTER'
BY GERVASE MARKHAM

edited by

CHARLES L. HAMILTON, M.A., Ph.D.

CONTENTS

Introduction

The Muster-Master is a small quarto pamphlet ($5\frac{3}{4}'' \times 6\frac{3}{4}''$) of 40 folios (two of which are blank) now in the possession of the Henry E. Huntington Library in San Marino, California.[1] As far as is known, no other copy exists. The manuscript is in two hands: the first wrote the title page, table of contents and chapter four while the second chapters one through three.[2] The text itself is divided into two sections. The first three chapters discuss the position of the muster-master in the county militia while chapter four describes the duties of the muster-master with the army in the field.

According to the title page, *The Muster-Master* was written by *G. M.* These initials coupled with a reference by the author (27[v]) indicating that he wrote *The Souldiers Accidence* confirm that *The Muster-Master* was written by Gervase Markham (1568?–1637). The third son of Robert Markham of Cotham, Nottinghamshire, a respected but ultimately impoverished Elizabethan courtier, Markham produced a vast array of literary and practical works.[3]

[1] The Library acquired the manuscript in April 1964. I wish to thank the Library for kindly allowing me to prepare this edition of *The Muster-Master*; in addition I would like to express my appreciation to Miss Jean F. Preston, Curator of Manuscripts at the Library, for answering several questions concerning the manuscript.

[2] An emendation on fo. 27[v] of *The Muster-Master* suggests that the first scribe read through the work copied by the second. Neither hand appears to be that of Gervase Markham; for an example of Markham's hand see plate IIA in F. N. L. Poynter, *A Bibliography of Gervase Markham, 1568?–1637* (Oxford, 1962).

[3] For a detailed account of Markham's career see the Introduction (pp. 1–31) to Poynter's scholarly study. Some confusion has arisen in the past about

The former have perhaps been too harshly judged by critics, although it is clear that Markham's fame will continue to rest—where it did with his contemporaries—on his enormously popular books relating primarily to horsemanship and husbandry. Few good copies of these remain because, as Dr. Poynter notes, 'they were almost literally read to pieces'.[4]

Well educated and a keen observer of the world around him, Markham was possessed of a compelling drive to write, although declining family fortunes made an economic necessity of a passion. But for all his early patronage by Elizabethan luminaries and the commercial success, at least to printers, of his popular works, Markham was to spend much of his later life in London hard-pressed for money; he died a poor gentleman.

While a young man Markham had been a soldier, serving in both the Netherlands and Ireland, and in 1615 he published his first military manual, a broadsheet entitled *A Schoole for Young Souldiers*. Ten years were to lapse before his second military work, *The Souldiers Accidence*, appeared; this was quickly followed by *The Souldiers Grammar* and *The Second Part of the Souldiers Grammar*. No exact date can be given for *The Muster-Master*, although presumably it post-dates the first edition of *The Souldiers Accidence* (1625). Some references to recent shortcomings within the English militia (21^v–22^r) suggest that the pamphlet was written after the humiliating military ventures of Charles I and the Duke of Buckingham. Perhaps the work was prompted in part by Charles I's efforts to reform the militia. If these inferences are correct, *The Muster-Master* dates from about 1630.

As the only professional soldier among the officers of the trained bands, the muster-master was originally charged with overseeing the selection, training and equipping of the citizen soldiers of Elizabethan England as well as periodically informing the Council of the state of the militia.[5] He played, therefore, a significant role

---

Markham by historians who have attributed to him activities of his distant kinsman and namesake, Gervase Markham of Dunham, Nottinghamshire. In 1597 the latter fought a duel with his cousin, Sir John Holles, and in 1616 he was fined £500 in Star Chamber for challenging Lord Darcy; in 1627, although an invalid living in Dunham, his home was searched for arms and he was falsely accused of aiding a recusant while his failure to pay ship money in 1636 again brought him to public attention; see Poynter, *op. cit.*, p. 16, n. 1, *D.N.B.*, xii, p. 1053, and *Acts of the Privy Council, 1627–28*, pp. 282–3.

[4] Poynter, *Bibliography*, p. 4.

[5] Lindsay Boynton, *The Elizabethan Militia 1558–1638* (London, 1967), pp. 105–7, gives a general description of the duties of the muster-master with the militia. Much of what follows is based on Dr. Boynton's valuable study. For a contemporary comment on the duties of the muster-master with the

in the government's efforts to improve the armed forces in England, an effort which, as Dr. Boynton has convincingly argued, was more successful than previous historians believed.[6]

Improvements prompted by the challenge of Spain, however, soon lapsed during the more pacific reign of James I. Indeed, the position of the muster-master had changed before the Queen's death. Originally the muster-master was paid by the Council and was presumably responsive to the government's demands, but the burden of payment was soon shifted to the county while appointment of the muster-master was given to the lord-lieutenant. These developments had deplorable results. Not only did the government lose much of its leverage in local military affairs, but the new arrangements invited the nomination of muster-masters who were either unqualified or corrupt, or both. Furthermore, friction soon developed between the county and lord-lieutenant over the payment of the muster-master's fee. Opposition to paying the muster-master arose not so much because the office was venal or the appointees inefficient—indeed the local gentry probably preferred an unprofessional muster-master who was more likely to be lax in reporting their military shortcomings to the Council—but because the muster-master was now part of the lord-lieutenant's patronage. As Dr. Boynton states, the county paid but had no voice in the appointment.[7] Disputes over the payment of the muster-master also led to questions concerning the constitutionality of the assessment for his fee,[8] while during the reign of Charles I unwillingness to pay the muster-master reflected growing opposition to the lieutenancy and, ultimately, to Caroline government.[9]

Given Markham's previous interest in producing military manuals, it is not surprising that he wrote one about the muster-master. But his purpose in the first three chapters was more than that of providing a description of the duties and responsibilities of the good muster-master, however important that might be, for he, too, lamented the decline of the office from its Elizabethan apogee. A desire, therefore, to advertise the deleterious effects of the appointment of unqualified and corrupt individuals was clearly one reason why Markham wrote the pamphlet.

---

militia, see a statement by the Earl of Hertford, who served as lord-lieutenant of Wiltshire and Somerset during the reign of James I, in *The Earl of Hertford's Lieutenancy Papers 1603–1612*, ed. by W. P. D. Murphy (Wiltshire Rec. Soc., Devizes, 1969) p. 103.

[6] See the introduction in Boynton, *The Elizabethan Militia*.

[7] *Ibid.*, p. 226.

[8] *The Earl of Hertford's Lieutenancy Papers*, ed. Murphy, pp. 103–4.

[9] Boynton, *The Elizabethan Militia*, p. 291.

The second part of *The Muster-Master* (chapter four) discusses the muster-master with the army in war-time. His duties differed considerably from those of the muster-master with the county militia. The muster-master with the army was an auditor responsible for ensuring that claims for pay, supplies and equipment were justified and, when honoured by the government, were properly distributed, especially to the common soldier. If the muster-master and his subordinates were honest—and Markham argued that even the appearance of dishonesty could not be tolerated—the kingdom and the decent officer and soldier gained. Markham also insisted that the muster-master's returns taken on muster days be accurate. To this end he suggested that the muster-master develop a secret code whereby he would record the distinguishing marks of soldiers and horses so that efforts by captains on muster days to deceive him would not succeed. No doubt the honest muster-master was unpopular, especially with unscrupulous captains.[10]

It should be noted that some of Markham's advice to the muster-master in the field follows very closely the description of the good muster-master made by Thomas Digges who was first muster-master with the English forces in the Netherlands.[11] Although Markham's account is longer than Digges's and there is some difference in emphasis (Digges's principal point was the necessity of paying the muster-master a proper salary in order to remove the need for corruption), some of the passages in chapter four so closely parallel and in a few cases almost directly quote Digges that Markham must have used Digges's tract as the basis for his last chapter.[12]

Why was *The Muster-Master* not published? A writer of proven success in treating practical military questions produced a work aimed at assisting the citizen soldiers of Caroline England to under-

[10] C. G. Cruickshank, *Elizabeth's Army* (2nd ed., Oxford, 1966), p. 136. See also pp. 140–41 for an account of how captains used false musters to defraud the government during Elizabeth's Irish wars.

[11] *A Conference of a Good and Bad Muster-maister, . . .* in *Foure Paradoxes, or politique Discourses. Concerning Militarie Discipline, written long since by Thomas Digges, Esquire. Of the worthiness of warre and warriours, by Dudly Digges, his sonne* (London, 1604).

[12] Concerning payment of the muster-master with the army, Markham writes: 'It is against the honour of this Offycers place to take the valewe of a Pennye from any Captaine or Souldier more then the Fees due unto his place, Neyther may he Receyve that privatlie and Concealed, as thoughe it brought a Benevollence with it; But publiquelie and in open shewe that the world may say, This he deservethe.' (38ʳ.) The comparable passage in Digges is as follows: 'This Officer will not accept penny nor penni-worth of any Captaine, or Souldier, more, than the fee due to his Office, and that not as a benevolence secretly, but as his due openly.' (p. 33.) Markham's use of Digges could account for the stylistic differences between chapter four and the rest of the text.

stand the functions of an officer who was of prime importance in the trained bands as well as in the army. A ready item for a ready market, or so it would seem. There may have been private reasons for *The Muster-Master* remaining unpublished. Perhaps Markham, who had been fleeced before by printers, could not negotiate a fair contract. But another explanation is also possible. As noted above, Markham unfavourably compared contemporary muster-masters with their Elizabethan predecessors. Although it was by now commonplace to contrast Stuart ineptness with the glories of the Tudor past, to do so in print would surely have won for Markham the disfavour of the government. Furthermore, he made critical comments about the lord-lieutenants. While he is properly deferential to the lieutenancy and acknowledges its right to name the muster-masters, none the less it is clear that Markham accuses the lord-lieutenants of being accessories before the fact in creating the venal, corrupt and incompetent muster-masters common to early Stuart England. His opinions, if published, would probably have ensured for Markham the enmity of many powerful men, men perhaps more inclined than the crown to act to defend their honour. Indeed Markham recognized that there was a limit to his ability to suggest reformation when, after comparing many muster-masters to lions who devour their neighbours, he wrote, 'This Starre is out of my firmament, and I am fitter to praye, then to Accuse.' (24^{r}.)

Note on Editorial Practice

In preparing *The Muster-Master* for publication I have generally followed the recommendations in the 'Report on Editing Historical Documents' in the first volume of the *Bulletin of the Institute of Historical Research*. Reconstructions about which there is little doubt have been placed in square brackets and italicized. Deleted words, if they appear to be significant, have been noted; otherwise, minor scribal errors, blotches and decorative pen strokes have been ignored. The punctuation of the manuscript has been altered only where necessary for clarity, although a full stop has been substituted for the virgule. Capitalization has been changed to the extent that each sentence begins with a capital. The spelling of the manuscript has been retained except for u and v and i and j, where modern use has been followed.

The Muster-Master

Contayning the Institution,
Office, Dutie, Place, Use and
Abuse of the Muster-master
in the Lande of Peace
and the Mustermaster
in the Lande of
Warre

By G.M.

(1^v)   blank

(2^r)   The Contents of the
Booke

Off Mustermasters and the dyversities; The first use, and the present Abuse—Chapter 1.

The Office place and dutie of the Muster-master in the Lande of Peace—Chapter 2.

Certain Preceptes & Instructions which the Muster-master in the Lande of Peace ought ever to carrye in hys Memorie—Chapter 3.

The Office, Place and Dutie of the Muster-master in the Lande of Warre—Chapter 4.

(2^v)   blank

(3^r)   Of Muster-maisters and
the diversities: The first
Use, and the present
abuse.
Chapter 1

There is not in any publique Armie, Private Cittie, or well governd Commonwealthe, a place of greater profit to the King, or Generall, nor of more advantage or advauncement for the Souldier (soe Long as Justice, and an upright conscience swayes the Ballance) then this, of which I intend nowe to intreat, and which wee call *Muster-Maisters*, or Commissaries of *Musteres*.

Of *Muster-maisters*, there be twoe kinds, in general, but Diverse in particuler.

The twoe generall kinds of *Muster-maisters* are a *Muster-maister* in the *Land* of *Peace*, & a *Muster*-maister in the *Land* of *Warre*.

(3^v)   A *Muster-maister* in the Land *of Peace* is the same which *Vegetius* (writing to *Valentinia* the Emperor) calleth *Campigeni*, or

Antesignani, because, by them, the exercise of Martiall discipline was mainteind and increased.[1] Others Imagine them (by the Authoritie of the same *Author*) to be those, which he calleth, the under *Tribunes*, Which with us, is a *Colonell* of a *Regiment*. Because (saieth *Vigetius*) they not onely sawe the Inferior Captaines Discharge their duties, in excercising of their souldiers, but did allsoe themselves, in their owne persons (being men of eminent skill) exercise their owne *Bands*, and *Troopes*.

But howesoever names have alterd with the times, the Office, Nature, and Dutie of the place, is all one, and we call them Muster-maisters, in the *Land* of *Peace*.

(*4ʳ*) The ordinance, and Institution of this Muster-maister in the Land of Peace, albeit hath bin, and is as auncient, as the *Romans* or *Grecians*, as both *Rome*, and *Lacedemon* can witness, Yet will I heere speake of the excellencie, and use thereof but in theis moderne times, since the Raigne of the thrice blessed Ladie of ever happie remembrance, & Mistress of the most famous and fortunatest Souldiers, never Conquered *Elizabeth*.

This Queene, taught by experience that the *Excercise* of Arms in peace, made States Invincible, when they came to Mannage true warre; and a little awakened, by home *Rebellion* (as in the Northe, and others) as allsoe, with the pride of Spaine, which then she sawe gapinge to devoure, & Gorge up all the Whole Soveraigntie of Europe; foorthwith the S[t]ate elected soe many old and experienced *An[n]o 1577* Captaines, and approved officers (*4ᵛ*) in the Warres, as might furnishe everye Countie in the Kingdom, with one able, and sufficient Commaunder, whoe was not onely to instruct, and teach all the Cautionarie & Trained Bands, together with their supplies, in all manner of Martiall discipline, but allsoe, to take vewe of the persons, Armor, and all manner of Munition, belonging to the same, and where Default was found, to certifie the Commissioners of *Musters* that speedie redresse might be had for all inconveniences.

Nowe because the Laborer is woorthie of his hire, it was intreated at the hands of the Commissioners of every severall Countie, that they Would, according to the Abillities of the Counties, and the Industrie & paines of the partyes imploied, as allsoe, the profitt received,

---

[1] Vegetius's *Four books of martial policy* was a principal source of medieval and renaissance opinion on Roman military practices. Markham clearly derived much of his information on the Romans from Vegetius, although he was not an unqualified admirer of Greek and Roman practices. Dr. D. M. Loades notes that Sir Thomas Wyatt the Younger used both Polybius and Vegetius in his treatise on the militia, but that he, too, was free from excessive dependence on ancient writers; *The Papers of George Wyatt Esquire*, ed. D. M. Loades, Camden 4th Series, v (London, 1968), p. 163.

by such carefull instruction, think upon some convenient paye or Stipend, on which (5^r) this Muster-Maister (for soe they were all Intituled in their Comissions) might Live, without the offence of base Necessitie.

This woorke was no more prudentlie, and happilie begun, then it was faithfully, and skillfullie perfourmed, Not by inferior, or petty officers, which knewe no more, but the bare *A B C* of warre; but by such, as had ron throughe everie *Grammer rule* thereof; such as had borne the office of Captaines from Desert, and not from private Letters, gaudye cloathes, or Lustfull imployments; such as had their Wounds in their faces, chasing the Enimie, not such, as had whole skins, by ronning awaye, Which they now call a *Violent Retyring*. Insomuch that the Cuntries, seeing their Abillities, and Industries, bestowed upon them Woorthye yearlie pensions: as some fortie pounds a yeare, as in *Darbishier*, and others; Some fiftie, (5^v) as in *Nottinghamsheire*, and others; some threescore, as in *Buckingham-sheire* and others; some fourscore, as in *Lincolnsheire*, and others; and some, an hunderd pounds a yeare, as in *Yorkesheire*.[2]

After theis Muster-maisters had thus excercised, and brought the Trained Bands to some perfection, The State, seeing the Glorie, and Benefit of it, thinke it not amisse nowe, to make every severall Countie, a severall Armye. And because the *Cautionarie Bands* consist both of *Horse*, and *Foote*, and that in some reasonable nombers, it was thought meete, to Devide them into Troopes, and Companies, and to place over them *Generalls, Liuetenant Generalls, Colonells, Captaines*, and all other Inferior officers.

Hence came the Election of the *Lords* Liuetennants of Counties, whoe, as *Generalls*, have the Supreame Command and universall Disposure, of all (6^r) Militarie affaires whatsoever, within their severall Counties.

Nowe because many of theis Noble personages had their Imployments, some in the Court, some in forraine Commaunds, as *Embassages, Goverments*, and the like; and some, in other remote places, and were not resident in their Counties, therefore, it was made Lawefull for theis *Lords-Leiuetenants*, to elect, in their severall Counties, of the best reputed, and most ablest knights & gentlemen,

---

[2] Dr. Boynton (*The Elizabethan Militia*, p. 180) suggests that the fees paid to the muster-master during the latter part of Elizabeth's reign were increasing. As an example he cites the salary of the Hampshire muster-master which had risen to £80. In the reign of James I the fee requested for the Somerset muster-master was £115, while the Wiltshire muster-master's salary was about £60; *The Earl of Hertford's Lieutenancy Papers*, ed. Murphy, pp. 11–12. Against this trend towards higher remuneration must be set the fact that the muster-masters' fees were seldom paid.

a certain choice Companie, as three scoure, or more,[3] to whome the *Lords-Leiuetenants* gave *Deputation* for the excersising of all Martiall Affaires in their absence, and called them by the names of *Deputie-Leiuetenants*, Whose office, and place (in the Land *of Peace*) is the same, that the *Leiuetenant-Generall* is, in the Land *of Warre*.

Theis Deputie-Leiuetenants recommended (6ᵛ) to the *Lords* Leiuetenants a Role, of the most ablest knights, & gentlemen for Revenue and person; and the Woorthiest for Wisedome & goverment, and valor, within their severall Counties Out of which, they chose some for *Colonells of Horse*, some for *Colonells of Foote*; and some for Captaines *of Horse*, and some for Captaines of foote.

The other Inferior officers, as Leiuetenants of *horse*, Leiuetenants of foote; *Cornetts of Horse*, and *Ensignes* of foote; *Corporalles of horse*, & Serjants of foote, as allsoe *Trumpetts, Droms, Fifes*, and the like.

Theis were referd to the election of the Captaines *of horse*, and the Captaines of foote themselves.

Nor in this *Election*, Was there any strict necessitie, that either theis *Colonells*, Captaines, *Leiuetenants*, or Inferior officers, should be chosen, approved, or experienced (7ʳ) souldiers. It onely was sufficient, if they were men of honorable woorthie, and vertuous Disposition, such as their Contries Loved to followe both for their bloods & vertues sakes and such, as were able to support, & uphold the honor of their places, and persons, out of their owne meanes, and Revenues, without taxing the Cuntrye, or pilling the private souldier. For it was presupposed, that touching their skill in Martiall Discipline, and the true Manage of Arms, the *Muster-maisters* before spoken of (of which every Countie had one) should not onely perfect them therein (if they pleased to call him to that service) but alsoe train up out of their severall Troppes and Bands, such as might serve them in all Inferior offices, the *Trumpetts Drums* and *Phiphes* onely excepted, which is to be intended, that they must be foretaught, the sounds and Beatings of Comaund; But the (7ᵛ) use, and Manage thereof is onelye in the Captaines Discretion. And the best *Trumpett*, and the best *Dromme*, I have seene, grossely to erre, in the use of Discipline.

But *Hinc illae Lachrimae*,[4] this fairer sunshine Daye is not without stormes, and theis good intentes, often bring foorth evill effects;

---

[3] This appears to be an enormously inflated figure. For example, there were only seven deputy lieutenants for both Somerset and Wiltshire in 1601, a figure which rose to 11 in 1610–11; *Earl of Hertford's Lieutenancy Papers*, p. 9. See also Gladys Scott Thomson, 'The Origin and Growth of the Office of Deputy Lieutenant', *Trans. Royal Hist. Soc.*, 4th series, v, p. 164.

[4] Terence, *Andria*, Act I, sc. 1, line 99.

for nowe the sword of Authoritie, being put into one private mans government, as namelye the *Lords-Leiuetenants* of Counties, whoe take upon them (as by good right they maye) the settling, bothe of the *Muster-maister*, and other superior officers, many things maye stagger, out of the right waye. And althoughe this Lord-Leiuetenant maye be, bothe by supposition, and the Reall excellencie of his owne noble, and proper Nature, soe good a man as vertue herself can wishe, Yet (as before I saide) what throughe their Dependance, on the *(8ʳ)* Court, and person of the king, their abroad imployments & necessarye absence from theis places of command, they cannot chuse but commit most of theis affaires to report, Manye unto trust, and some, to Affection. Nowe if Report erre; If Trust faile; or if Affection over flatters vertue, then must the Whole Labor reele, and the Noble goodnesse of this good man being abused, the Whole Cuntrie must suffer, as thus for example.

A *Muster-maisters* place falls void in a Countie, and one of the *Lord-Leiuetenants* folowers, or some other contracting with him, procure one of Reputation, with the Lord, to report that he is fitt and woorthie for the place. Then trust, which is not accompanied with doubt, and Affection, which ever hangs about a mans owne folowers, becoming *(8ᵛ)* Solicitors, the Suite is obtained, and this man is made a *Muster-maister*, Who neither was souldier, is Souldier, Nor will Indeavor to be a souldier. It was the Fee, and *glorie* which Were the Markes at which he aymed with comming, the Excercise & Industrie was the ground, betweene the Markes, over which he ran, with neglect, and carelessnes.

But heere you Will aske me if this man be soe insufficient, how can he secure, and make safe his place, or give contentment to his Countrye?

To this I answeare, He can doe it, with greater safetie, then the best Deserver. For, like the Asse, that caried the *Godesse Isis* on his backe, having Greatness for his Countenance, to make him feard, gaudie cloathes, to make him admired, and a fewe Crownes, to inchaunt Clearkes and *parrasites*, What Beast *(9ʳ)* in the feyld, but will fall downe, & Doe him Reverance?

Besides, as he is a Newe *Muster-maister*, and of a newe making, soe doth he bring in with him, new Lawes, and newe Statutes. He saies he is not bound by his *Place*, to excercise the Souldiers, to Informe the Captaines, or to save their purses by instructing their officers; He sayes it was a woorke of Supererrogacion, in the former *Muster-maisters*, and that he is not tyed unto their Imitations. He affirmes that the Whole Fabrique of his place consists onelye, in the election of able men, in the veweing of Arms, and in the sorting of Weapons.

The first of which, the *Deputie* Lieuetenants and Captaines can doe much better then himself, and soe he is needelesse; The Second he performs by a Substitute, as some Cuttler (9^v) Smithe, or half Armorer, whose onely proffit, is to find fault, and abuse Arms, and soe, he becomes noysome to the Countrye; And the Last, he finds finisht to his hand, in the Captaines severall Lists, Where every Weapon is punctually ordered, and the Number dilated; and yet for this ease, and nothing Doeing, will he abate the Countrye, a penny of his *Fee*? Naye he is soe farre from such *Charitye*, that thoughe his Conscience tell him he hath no power to deserve any thing, Yet will Covetousnesse, make him soe audatious, that he will not sticke to invent newe exactions, as raising Twelvepence, six pence, or groates a peice, for the sealing, or stamping of every Corslett, or Muskett, with a world of other Injurious *Perquisittes*. The poore Ignorant man still striving, to make himself, a *Muster-maister*, or Controuler (10^r) of musters in the Warres, When in truthe, he is but the Countries Servant, and a *Muster-maister*, in the Land of *Peace*, the several Dutyes of both which, shall be at large sett Downe heerafter.[5]

I would the abuse of this *Election*, & execution, of unskillful *Muster-maisters*, were but my feare, or my suggestion; but it is too frequent, And I am not ignorant, that many Industrious, and well deserving Gentlemen, have fared the Woorse for their Ignorance, some Cuntries finding Wusses[6] & starting holes in the Lawes, by which they detaine, and refuse to paye, any *Muster-maisters* fee, at all;[7] soe that the painefull, and good souldier, is weakened and discouraged, and the glorie of Martiall Discipline, is likely to be ecclipsed, and all through the error of evill *Muster-maisters*, whoe either are soe ignorant, that they cannot instruct; or els soe proude (10^v) and peevish, that they will not instruct; or Lastlie, soe overladen, With more gainefull employmentes, that they cannot attend this *Ploughe*, unlesse twoe letters miscarie.

Againe by this newe Liberty of theis newe *Muster-maisters*, thus wrongfully undertaken & expounded the Captaines of the Trained Bands, being chosen (as before I saied) rather for their vertues and Abillities, then for their skilles, finding themselves deceived in this

---

[5] The last sentence of this paragraph seems out of context, although there is no break in the manuscript.

[6] Meaning unclear.

[7] Presumably Markham is referring to those who argued that the repeal of the statutes of 1558 regarding obligations to provide arms and attend musters destroyed the legal basis of assessments for the militia and the muster-master fee, see Hertford's comment to James I in *The Earl of Hertford's Lieutenancy Papers*, p. 103.

C M—E

hope, Yet loth, that the service should receive Injurie, are inforced from the strength of their owne purses, to hire strange officers to undergoe the Labor. And althoughe for once, twice, or thrice, they may passe over the Burthen or charge, with a myld sufferance, Yet if it come on fast (as that must be proportiond, according to the Necessitie of times) (*11^r*) it will prove such an Intollerable Loade, that it will make his heart greive, and his tongue cannot chose but Murmure.

Againe, in the hiring of theis stranger-officers (which the Captaines are forced to doe, and take from other mens reports) they often times light on unskillfull & Ignorant men, who rather marre, then make the worke they goe about, and this is an error soe frequent, that for mine owne part, I have seene in a Countie, where there hath bin 4, six, or more, severall Bands of foote, and every Band, taught by a severall Commaunder, no 2 Commanders hath agreed together, either in woords of Commaund, or the manner of Discipline, soe that should those Bands have bin brought, into a well excercisd Armye, they had ben as farr to seeke, as those, which had never handled weapon. And it is well (*11^v*) knowen, to all knoweing[8] souldiers, that there is nothing more necessarye then a constant continewance of unalterable woords of commaund, & a setled, and controuleable forme of Discipline.

Lastlie, this great neglect, and Libertie of the *Muster-maister*, and this intollerable charge, thrust upon the Captaines, makes the Captaines neglect, and out of heart, to excercise their *Bands*, soe that if the *Deputie*-Leiuetenants call not upon the Captaines, the Captaines will be sure, never to awaken the *Deputie*-Leiuetenant, or looke for any excercise, in soe much, that both striving, Which shalbe the Last caller, the Worke Lyes undone, and bothe the State deceived, and the Cuntrye unprepared.

For whoe knowes not that to se a Cuntrie excercised, once, in 2 or 3 yeares, is held tollerable, and good. But if once (*12^r*) a yeare, o! excellent! But if twice a yeare, *O quam te memorem!*[9] past example. Whereas might there be constant, and setled times of exercise, as once a monthe, or once in two monthes, and that Done, by an understanding *Muster-maister*, and before such Commissioners of *musters*, as would without affection se every thing amended, that was Woorthie of complaint, there is no nation under the sun, but would stand in awe, of our *Examples*.

It is not the calling together of Bands, one daye in a Yeare, and to spend half that daye, in argueing of greivances, and the other halfe

---

[8] Inserted with a caret over *conning*, which is crossed out.

[9] I have been unable to discover if this is a classical quotation.

in calling mens Names, & noting Downe of Defects, in wishing of reformation, and threatning punishment, and then to let all things sleepe, till that time 12 monthe; at which time, all things (*12ᵛ*) are woorse then before; Which [n]either breedes good souldiers, or faire Arms. Noe, it must be encouragement, gotten by excercise, that must make men; and Commaundment, mixt with severitie, that must force Arms; and both Jointlie togeether will make the kingdome fortunate.

And this maye be done, by Noble, and vertuous Deputie Leiuetenants; forward and Ingenious Captaines, assisted by a painefull & skillful *Muster-maister*; and with the same *Fees*, and Pentions, Which are at this Daye, allowed and given for nothing[10] Doeing without any further exactions, Laied either upon the Cuntrie, or Captaines, more then their owne free Bounties.

(*13ʳ*)

The office, place, and dutye
of the Muster-maister, in
the Land of Peace
Chapter 2

A Muster-maister, in the *Land of Peace*, ought to be a man of faire vertue, good Birthe, temperate, & myld Nature; of great skill, highe valor, and deepe Judgement.

The first that he may give good example; the second to Defend him from Contempt; the third, because he hathe to doe with *Rudeness*; the fourth that he maye expound the misteries of the Warres; the Fift, that he maye not be scard with Greatness; and the Last, that he maye distribute, all Jointlye together, equally, honestlye, and Justlye.

(*13ᵛ*) *This Muster-maister* is chosen (at Least should be chosen) from the List, of the ouldest Captaines, by the Lord-Leiuetenant of the Countye; But where he is not, then by the State itself.

And this ould, and experienced Captaine ought to be, such a one, as hath spent his meanes, his *Blood*, and all his best times in the Warres, such a one, as to preserve his Countrye (or the freinds, and Allies of his Countrye) from Danger, and that they might quietly rest, and repose themselves, everie man, under his owne *Vine*, hath imborquet[11] himself into all Dangers, and made Wounds, wantes, hunger, thirst and Watchings faithful Monuments of his obedience and sufferings.

And indeed, the true ground, & first Foundation of this place, Was

---

[10] A blank space of about half a line follows *nothing*.
[11] Embarked?

to give (*14ʳ*) releife to true Desert, not to add substance, to light shadowes.

The meanest, and wretchedst soldier in all our English Armies (that is prest for his countrye) if he retorne home Disabled, or maymed, can flye to a statute Lawe, and find releefe, from the Nations Bountye, but soe cannot Captaines, they Want the Letter of the Lawe; sure I am, they have the testimonies of everie good conscience, and they will Justifie that such places as this, or the like, were not founded, without Noble, and Divine considerations, but to my purpose.

This Officer, or Muster-maister, is an Assistant, and a Councellor (when at any time he shall be called) unto the *Deputie-Leiuetenants*, in all Martiall affaires.

He ought to be present in person, at (*14ᵛ*) all *musters, shewes,* vewes, or Impressing of men, either for Forraine, or home service. And therefore, his place, and seate in those affaires, or in any assistance of counsaile, or otherwise, is upon a stoole, at the upper corner of the Table, where the deputie-Leiuetennants sitt, and somewhat remote from the Table; yet in the most perspicuous and best place, for taking the vewe, bothe of men, and Armes.

He ought to have a able, and sufficient Clearke, whose place is among the *Deputie-Leiuetenants* Clearkes—and this Clearke, is to take a true note and List, of every mans name, Dwelling & Arms, that is within the traind *Bands*, together with all supplies & others which are to reinforce the Troopes upon anye change, Death, or other (*15ʳ*) casualltie.

Allsoe, he is to keepe a true Role of all manner of Defects, wants, & Insufficiencies, either in Men, or Armes, which shall be set downe by the *Muster-maister*, for this shall keepe the *Muster-maister* blamelesse in all Controversies, and occasions, When at any time, errors shall be examined.

For you must understand, that allthoughe the *Muster-maisters* have power, to find faults, and to Informe of Defects, Yet it is onely in the *Lord*-Leiuetenants, and their *Deputie*-Leiuetenants to force reformation. And for mine owne part, I have knowen Defects, hang seaven yeares without any amendment; naye, soe Long, that the owners of those evill Arms have (as it were) overswaied the *Muster-maister* (*15ᵛ*) and Defended those Arms for Lawfull by his owne approbation, had not his *Booke*, borne witnesse against them. Therefore (as I saied) this Role of Defects, must carefullye be kept. It is the office and Dutie of the *Muster-maister*, When any man is

---

[12] C. G. Cruickshank, *Elizabeth's Army* (2nd ed., Oxford, 1966), pp. 184–8, gives a summary of legislation relating to maimed soldiers.

calld, or presented, before the Leiuetennant, or *Deputie*-Leiuetennants, Whether he be private or publique, to take vewe of his person, and to informe them, for what Arms, or weapon he is fittest, and soe (upon their allowance) to record him.

He is allsoe to take vewe of all manner of armes & Weapons, and to see that they be alloweable and sufficient, according to such orders and instructions as shall be Delivered by the State, or Councell of Warre, as Namelye (if he be a Pikeman) that he have all (*16ʳ*) the severall peices of Armor which belong to that weapon, that they be of highe pikeproofe and Buckled, and Jointed, according to directions, that his Sword have a close, and good *Hilt*, a well temperd Blade, a strong scabberd and a sufficient Belt, to cary it in, That his pike be of true size, and Lengthe, streight, Nimble, and well headed, With a steele head. And soe of all other things, belonging to that Weapon.[13]

If he be a Musquetteere, he shall se that he have all manner of Armes, belonging to that weapon, as Comb—cappe, Sword and Belt, Bandeleires with Bullet—bagg, wherein is Mould, worme, screwe, scourer and *Bullets*; a sufficient *Rest*, with a string, and the Rest soe small, that it maye goe, into (*16ᵛ*) the *Barrell* of the Musquet. He shall see that the Musquett be of true Lengthe, and Bore; and to that end he shall have a gage, made according to the kings true height and Standard, and with that gage, he shall trye every Musquett Downe to the Bottome; He shall see that the Stocke be of sound wood, and true proportion, the neather end shodd with Iron; the *Locke*, [*T*]*ricker*,[14] and *pan*, serviceable, and the scouring sticke, strong, and sufficient. And as theis, soe for any other Arms whatsoever which shall be brought before him, Whither it belong to horseman, or footeman. And to that end, he shall have a gage, and Size, for the dutch Pistoll with firelocke; for the Long Pistoll with the *Snapphaunce*; for the [*D*]*ragoone*,[15] and the *Carbine*.

As theis, soe he shall Looke to the necessaries (*17ʳ*) belonging unto them, as keyes, screwes, pinns, Moulds, wormes, Flaske, Touchboxes, or Cartilages, and the like.

Allsoe, he shall looke to the arming and Apparrell of the *Horse*; as *Brydles*, *Bytts*, *Chaines*, Saddles, Pettrells, Croopers; sackes for cariage, and the like, and where any defect, fault, or want shall be

---

[13] For additional information concerning the arms and armour of the soldiers discussed by Markham in this and subsequent paragraphs, see John Hewitt, *Ancient Armour and Weapons in Europe* (Graz, 1967; reprint of 1860 edition), iii, *passim*.

[14] The scribe has written *Bricker*; tricker is a form of trigger.

[15] The scribe has written *Bragoone*; the dragon was a cavalry pistol used in the early 17th century, Boynton, *The Elizabethan Militia*, p. xvi.

found, there the *Muster-maister* shall first informe the Leiuetenant, or his deputies; then, by theire allowance, he shall record the Defects, and Lastlie, shall shewe every severall Want, to the partye, or parties, that should amend that, and give unto them, the best advice and Instruction, he can, for reformation of the same, Declaring unto them the true & due prizes of every thing, soe that neither the subject maye be cousend nor the service Disapointed. (*17ᵛ*) And if the partie shall intreate the *Muster-maister*, and delyver him his monye, he ought himself, out of his goodnes, to see the defects amended.

Nowe heere ariseth a *Question*, which allthoughe it be easily resolved, Yet hath it bred (of my knowledge) much discontent, & murmuring, in manye places: Whether the Muster-maister, maye, out of his owne power and Authoritie, deface or breake Arms, that are Insufficient, I, or noe.

To this I answeare, that according to a Modest Limitation, & allowance, he may deface, some Insufficient Armes; but not according to his owne will, or passion; as thus: When Insufficient Arms are brought before the *Muster-maister*, he shall shew them to the Leiuetenant, (*18ʳ*) or his *Deputies*, then sitting in Comission, and to the partye that is the owner thereof; and not onely make the Defect plaine, unto them, but allsoe give a sound and sufficient reason, for suche his fault finding, Defending it, either by the priviledge of the Warres, or by some other particular Instructions, sent from the State, the Leiuetenant, or his *Deputies*. Nowe when this is taken into Consideration, the Leiuetenant or his Deputies, shall give the partye (owner of these evill Arms) a peremtory daye, for the amendment of those Defects; & if at the daye appointed, he bring in those Arms againe, as defective as before, either in part, or all, then he shall undergoe reprehension, and peradventure *Fine*, according to the Nature (*18ᵛ*) of the Contempt, and the pleasure of the Leiuetenant, or his Deputyes. But if the third time he appeare with those evill, & defective Arms, then the Leiuetenant, or his *Deputies*, shall commaund the *Muster-maister* to deface them, and he shall doe it, and the party offending shall undergoe both Fine and Imprisonment.

It is the office of the *Muster-maister*, that as he veweth the Men, and Arms, soe he shall take vewe allsoe, of the *Magozine*, or store of Powder, Match, Bullet, and all other Implements of Warre; and if he find anye Defect in them, to informe the Leiuetenant, or his *Deputies*, that Redresse may be had for the same.

And indeed, it is his true place to see the Buyeing of all newe (*19ʳ*) provisions, and to have the change of the ould, and to doe it at soe easie rates, as is possible, bothe for the Cuntryes good, and his owne Reputation.

It is his place, to have the charge, and safe keeping of the same *Magozine*, and to have the Distribution thereof, in the time of neede, and upon the dayes of Excercise, Whereby the Leiuetenant, and his Deputies, may be blamelesse, the Cuntrye Strengthned, all Services performed, and the Captaines encouraged.

It is the office of the Muster-maister, to be present, at all Daies of exercise, whatsoever, or Wheresoever, within his owne Countie. And if the Captaine of the Band to be excercisd, shall intreate him thereunto, he ought (*19ᵛ*) and it is his Dutie, to excercise the Souldiers before him; and to shew in his person, What the Captaine himself, ought to performe, in his owne person: To teach his Inferior officers, the true Woords of Commaund, both for Posture, and motion, and to make the Souldiers performe them with cheerefull[n]esse, come-linesse, and good order.

Nowe, if the Captaine be soe well opinionated, either of himself, or his owne skill, or soe tyed in Affection to another mans knowledge, that he will save the *Muster-maister* this Labor, and either by himself, or some other, Will have his Band excercisd, then it is the office of the *Muster-maister* to stand by as a Beholder, or silent Judge of the (*20ʳ*) Discipline.

And if he shall find, that the Captaine, or his officers, shall bring in any new, or unknowen Discipline, which is contrarie, or repugnant to those orders, and Instructions which are comaunded and published by the Council of Warre, then it is the office of the *Muster-maister*, in a modest, private, and humble manner (without giving suspition of Dislike, or the Least shewe that maye be, Whereon to kindle disgrace) to informe the Captaine of his mistakes, mildlye wishing, a better consideration, yet referring all, to his owne pleasure; Which if the Captaine take (as it is meant) in a Noble manner, and recall his errors, then there is a good worke, well finished.

(*20ᵛ*) But if he be refractorie, and stubborne, the *Muster-maister* shall forbeare any further to presse him, and onely informe the Leiuetenant, or his Deputies, that they maye argue the offence, and see Reformation.

Upon every generall Daye of Excercise, When the whole Contrye, both *Horse*, and *Foote* shall meete in one place, and everie Captaine, shall shewe bothe himself, and his men, in the height of *Gallantrie*, and in the Depthe of Art and Discipline, In this daye, it is the office of the *Muster-maister* (by the allowance of the Leiuetennant, or his *Deputies*) to take upon him the place of a *Sergeant-Major* of the *Feyld* (*21ʳ*) Distributing Souldiers, according to the art Militarie, and giving rules, for the Embattailing, and draweing of Crosses together; all which himself must se performed in his owne person, reconciling all sorts of Doubts, and giving assistance and Incouragement, both from his person & knowledge, to such as are weake and unable.

It is the office of the *Muster-maister* to be present With the Leiuetennant, or his Deputies, at the Impressing of all Souldiers which be sent into the Warres, and to give his service and assistance in the election, to se them Armd, Coated, and accomodated, with things, fit for their Journie.

And if they shall be conducted (*21ᵛ*) to any *Port, Haven, Towne,* or other *Rendevous*, it is the office of the *Muster-maister* to be theire Conductor (unlesse some other be appointed by the State) and for the same, the Contrie ought to allowe him, a Captaines full entertainment, during his Journie.

And the neglect of this hath bred manye mischeefes, and Inconveniences in the kingdome especially, When thes have made Servingmen, Casheired *servants,* and king Harryes souldiers[16] their Conductors; the Baseness, and Lowenesse of their quallitie, & their unskillfullness & Weakenes in the manage of such actions, meeting with the barbarous (*22ʳ*) rudenesse of *Debausht,* and insolent persons (for suche have bin, the most of our Late Presses) what hope or Issue could possiblye be expected, but such, as we have seene too plentifullye brought foorthe; as namelye: Assaults and Batteries, Murders, Rapes, and what not? Wheres, had the Conductors bin men of account, and place, men fearing god, and skillful in their Professions & undertakings, the first, Would have kept their rudenesse in such subjection; The Second have appeard soe terrible against offences; and the Last soe Watcht over them, with the Justice of severe Discipline, that Errors, like evill Chickens, Would have bin kild (*22ᵛ*) in the hatching; and the ease of obedience, would have looked soe Lovelie, that Barbarisme would have become odious, & the Woorst in the company wold have fled from it, as from a Bugbeare.

Lastlie, to conclude this office of the Muster-maister, in the Land of *Peace,* It is his Dutie, whensoever Arms or Munition shall be sent out of the Contrie, upon any urgent Necessitie, or suddaine emploiment, first carefullye to keep a true note of everye peice of particular Armor, weapon and Munition that is soe sent awaye; The Towneshipps and persons to which they belong; the true State of the Arms, and all other Necessaries, as they were at (*23ʳ*) the

---

[16] An old soldier. See also a quotation from *The Art of Archerie* in F. N. L. Poynter, *A Bibliography of Gervase Markham, 1568?–1637* (Oxford, 1962), p. 186.

Deliverance; And the names of the Captaines, Leiuetenants, and other officers, to whome they were Delivered. Then, When the Cuntrye is Discharged of such Arms, or Munitions, it is the Muster-maisters Dutie, to Informe, and call upon the Lord-Leiuetenante, or his *Deputies*, that Levies maye be made in the *Countie*, for the reinforcing and Buyeing of newe Arms, for the supplye of those which are wanting, Least the Cuntrye by neglect, be found un-prepared and soe bring Danger to the state, or otherwise, it be compeld, to buye Arms on the suddaine, and in unreasonable times, when Rates are brought to a double advancement.

(*23ᵛ*) And it is the office of the Muster-maister to have the bestowing of this monye, and the Buyeng of all such Arms, and Munition; and not Armorers, Cutlers; mine, or my friends kinsman, or Dependant; or indeed any man ells, Whose woorke is done, as soone, as his wages is paied. For thus have many Contries (of my knowledge) bin infinitelie abused. As, if I should enter into particulars, it would make a Vertuous mans eares glowe.

Therefore (as I saied) it is the Muster-maisters office, to discharge this Taske, for he must stand by it, at all times, and in all occasions; and if any thing in him, be found woorthy [of] controule, besides the affliction of his owne (*24ʳ*) Conscience, the Leiuetenant, and his Deputies, knowe where to find their amends, and keep their contrye from being a Looser.

Thus in fewe Woords, you have seene the effect of this mans true place and office; and howe farre it Differs from the Libertie of our Moderne, and present use thereof; many *Muster-maisters* using their Counties, as caged-up Lions doe their Neighbors; when they get Loose, they never come amongst them then, but affright, or hurt them. And theis, never desire to se the Souldiers, till they maye fetch Monie from the Contrie. But *Cynthius Aurem Vellet*.[17] This starre is out of my firmament, and I am fitter to praye, then to Accuse.

(*24ᵛ*)

Certain precepts and
Instruction, Which the
Muster-maister in the
Land of Peace, ought
ever to Carrie
in his
Memorye
Chapter 3

Because this officer (which I call a *Muster-maister*, in the Land of *Peace*) hathe, and ought to have, a peculiar respect, to the election

17 Possibly a quotation from Virgil; see *Eclogue* vi, ll. 3–4.

of men & Armes, to the Manage, and use of Weapons, to the Dexterities & persecution of excercise, and sundrie other things all readie declared, I thinke it not amisse (before I proceede further) to give unto him heere some (25^r) briefe precepts, & Instructions, which maye fortefie, and enable his knoweledge, for the performance, of all Duties, whatsoever.

Nowe for the Ground, or Base, whereon I will build these *Precepts*, and instructions though nothing be more worthie then the Imitation of the *Auncients*, Which are our famous *Schoolemaisters*, in this Art *Militarie*; and of which the *Græcians* and *Romans*, are received as most exact, and excelling all others, Yet I will neither relye absolutelie, on the one, nor on the other, but as neare as I can, I will take the perfection of bothe, so far forth as they agree, With the strengthe (25^v) of reason, the Mutabillitie, and revolution of times, and the setled experience of our Moderne Excercise.

And first, as touching the election of men to be trained for the Warres, it was Disputable, among the Auntients (especially the *Romans*) out of what Cuntries, or Provinces, and whether out of the Cittie, or out of the Countrie, Young Souldiers should be chosen.

And herein they tied themselves to a Philosophicall resolution; and held, such as were nere the *Sun*, to want *Blood*, and soe, subject to feare; Those which Were farr off from the *Sun*, to be throughe too much *Blood*, rash and unadvised; and that onelye, the temperate Climate, Did best affoord Souldiers.

Likewise, for the Citty and the Cuntrye, they held the Cittye by (26^r) reason of its Delicacie, nicenesse, and want of grosse and robustious Labor, unfit for Militarye *Excercise*; And the Contrie, because of its much toyle, and continuall use of all manner of hardnesse, to be onlye aptest for the same.

But *Bothe* theis are *Parradoxes*, and no man of Judgement, will constantly relie, on either Resolution.

It is certaine that Valor growes everyewhere; and Cowardise, ariseth more from *Education*, and *Custome*, then from any Inclination of the mynd, or Temperature of Ayer and *Climate*.

And of this, We have experience from the Boorish Countries,[18] which howesoever they have formerlye bin contemned, are now become great *Maisters* in the Warres, (26^v) and the onely example-givers.

Nowe for the difference, betweene the Cittie, and the Contrie, it is ever found, in our general experience, that never *Clowne* yet was able to outfast, outwatch, out-travell, or out face the *Sun*, *Frosts*, and *Tempests*, equall with a Gentleman; And there is strong reason

[18] The Netherlands.

for it, Because the *Clowne* is like a Carryers horse, Which can carrye a sore Burthen, a great waye, With a slowe pace, and a ful bellye; but alter the one, or abate the other, and the *Jade* presentlie tireth. The *Gentleman* is like the kings Courser, the more you Labor him, the more his Abillitie to Laboure increaseth, and nothing makes him mad, but spurning.

So that to conclude this point I would have our *Muster-maister* (27ʳ) since he is to chuse Souldiers, both from the Cittye, and the Cuntrye, not to be nice in his election, but to take the ablest bodies, Which are acompanied with the most generous minds; the better Education, the more excellent service, for beleeve it, there is no such Embleame of cowardise, as rudenesse, Nor no such displaye of true valor as civil conversation.

To this perfection of Bodye & mynd, you must add the strength and vigor of youthe. And therein you must not too strictlie hold the Roman precept, Which chose their Souldiers at the age of fourteene & sixteene, for that is too young; Nor yet the Græcians rule, Which desired to have every man graye headed. A meanes betwixt theis extreames is most expedient; for extreame young is onely (27ᵛ) for excercise; extreame old, onely for advice; and the middle ranke, onely for ———.[19]

Next to theis is to be observed, the S[t]ature, and proportion of mens bodies; and in them, you must Differ both from the Romans, Whoe would have all tall men, and from the Græcians, whoe would have all strong men; because the Warr hath employement, for men of all sizes, & all proportions, as I have shewed formerlye, in the *Accidence*.[20]

Nowe for the Complection, & favor of mens faces, that which is most manlye, is most hopefull; yet must you not refuse those, which are faire and effeminate.

For howesoever, *Mars* is feind *Blacke*, that is the God of Battaile, Yet was none more faire then *Phaebus*, and he Conquered the monster *Python*; (28ʳ) Soe that Complexions hurt not courages.

Yet those which are *Stigmaticall*, marked and pointed out by nature, are fitter to be preserved for Instruments of mischeefe, then reserved for excellent uses.

The Romans were Curious to observe from what Trades and occupations their Young Souldiers were chosen; disalowing all that Did savor of niceness, or softness; as if Trades did transforme Natures;

---

[19] *Excercise* has been crossed out and an illegible word in the first hand has been inserted; see Introduction, p. 49, note 3.

[20] See *The Souldiers Accidence, or an Introduction Into Military Discipline* . . . (London, 1635), pp. 1–2.

or that the handling of soft & nice Commodities, should make a man of a Cowardlie Disposition. This Principle is too much over-streind.

I doe confes, Manly, vigorous, and fearce imployements make men fitter for great Actions; but Let the imployement be what it will, (*28ᵛ*) if the Mynd have any height, or Largenesse, it may easily be made fitt for any Warrlike, or Martiall atcheivement.

When our *Muster-maister* hath thus chosen men likelye, and hope-full, it is then meete that he Dispose & prepare them, for the manage, use and ordering of their Weapons.

And herein he shall observe, not to stand to punctuallye, or pre-ciselie, upon anye one Weapon onely; but first to see his Souldiers use Diverse; and to that which he useth with the greatest Dexteritie, Nimblenes & Delight, to that to knitt him, and therein to traine him up to perfection. And yet not soe constantlie, to knytt him there-unto, but that now and then, he make him excercise, all manner of other weapons; because he is no good schollar, which cannot (*29ʳ*) reade of other Bookes, as well as his owne.

After the Souldier is expert in the manage, and use of his weapon, whether it be shott or Pike, he shall then be excercised, in all manner of Marches, and by the Beating of the *Dromme*, or other Comaund, howe to alter, mend, or Decrease his pace, even from the slowest motion of the foote, to the swiftest ronning, that can be expressed. And that this maye be the better effected, the Souldier shall be excercised in ronning of *Races*; and that it may be done with greater cheerefullness, it is expedient to propose certaine prizes, or prittie Triffles, Which the swiftest, or best Deserver may carrye awaye. For there is no activitie in a souldier more Necessarie, then this Action of ronning; (*29ᵛ*) especially, when either an enimye is to be charged furiouslye; or a place of advantage is to be gotten suddaine-lye; or any Retreyt to be made, upon speciall Discoverie.

As this Action of Ronning, soe it is good to excercise Your young soldiers in Leaping, Jumping & vaulting: the first twoe Motions that they maye with greater dexteritie mount over Ditches, small Rivers, Railes, Poles, hedges, and all other hinderances which may give them Impeachement, either in their Marches, or anye other pursuite of the Enimie, As allsoe, to keepe their Arms and Furniture cleane, and drye, which throughe Wading, might otherwise be indangered.

And that the Souldiers maye be inflamed the more unto this action it should not be amisse, to have small (*30ʳ*) prizes, and Rewards, for those which are best Deserving.

The Last motion (which is vaulting) is no Lesse necessarie, then any before named, for thereby the Souldier is made able and nimble, to mount, or Dismount, to or from his horses backe, at his pleasure, Without the aid of sturrop, Saddle, or other Implement.

And this the Romans held of such worrthye account, that they caused wooden horses (which we call vaulting horses) to be sett up; on which the Souldiers did daiely use to practise themselves. And for mine owne part, I wish the like Custome were with us, amongst our horse-troopes; for I can speake that by experience, that there is not a grosser fault amongst our horsemen, then their unnimble, and uncomely Mounting and Dismounting (*30ᵛ*) to and from their horses. Whereas, if they use of the Vaulting horse, & good instruction thereunto, being first taught to vault in theire Apparrell, and after in their Armor, there would not be any thing soe Difficult, which would not become most facile & easie.

For in this practise, they are not to bind themselves strictlie, to the observation of sides, or hands, as Riders doe, but to practise mounting and Dismounting, on both sides, sometime with their swords drawne, sometimes with their Pistolls charged, and sometimes with other more combersome Burthens, as weightes of Iron, Or Led, Gamelocks, *Chambers* or the like, that if they were compeld at any time to carry Armor, munition, victuall, or the like, the Burthen (*31ʳ*) might not be offensive to them.

As theis, soe it is verye necessarie, that the Souldier be taught the Art of Swimming, either by their owne practise, or the help of others, that are skillfull therein; for it is of a great availe, and bringeth much safetie to the Armie, and preserveth many a soule, that would else perrish.

And the Romans were soe careful to advance this action, that they chose the place, in which they used to excercise, and Traine their Soldiers, close by the River of *Tiber*, and called it *Campus Martius*; observing allwaies, after the excercise of Weapons was finisht, to incite the Souldiers (being in the Sommer Season) to fall to the practise of Swimming and this brought them, to great perfection therein.

(*31ᵛ*) It is a Laudable Custome, and woorthie the cherrishing, to instruct Soldiers in the art of *Fencing*. Which howsoever of Late Daies (Not for the Art, but for the Professors Sake) it be drawne into some Contempt, Yet is it right necessarie in the Warres; and he that is a good Swordman (in the Daye of Battaile, and in the houre of execution) will not onely save himself, but many others.

And this excercise, Was soe well allowed of, by the Romans, that they invented certaine wicker Targettes, that were Massie, and heavie, and Cudgells of great Weight with which their Souldiers used to playe & fence, against certaine wooden *Statues*, or Stakes of wood, and found it brought them to great skill & activitie.

But for mine owne part (*32ʳ*) I rather allowe, that they should practice one against another; because theis Dead, and unmoving Images, doe teach them but a falce art, and when they come in opposition with that, Which is equall in skill, equall in strengthe, and equall in Danger, they are soe Lost in their Judgements, that they knowe not which Waye to turne them.

And in this Excercise, I would have the Souldiers apply themselves, rather to the practice of the Backsword, and Rapier playe, then to the Sword and Targett, Sword and Buckler, or Sword & Dagger, for it is more Dangerous, more Deadly, and more swift in execution.

Lastlie, and not Inferior, but rather (*32ᵛ*) superior to any Excercise I have foreshewed, I wold recomend to this officer, the practise of the Long Bowe; either simple of itself, or else annexed to the Pike. For, in a Daye of Battaile (at which our English Discipline onely should Looke) there is no doubt, but it will do infinite service.

And me thinkes, it would prove both pleasing to the souldiers, & profitable to the kingdome, if all the supplies, Which are registred in the severall Counties, and are to take Trained mens places as they fall (being nowe, all together without Arms, and without Excercise) were Armed with Bowes and Arrowes and trayned to the Perfection (*33ʳ*) of that Discipline.[21]

But the Wisdome of the State can better point at this, then mine Imagination, and soe for them I Leave it, and soe finishe my praeceptis.

(*33ᵛ*)   *blank*

(*34ʳ*)   *The Office, Place & Dutie*
                         Of the Muster-master in
                            the Land of Warre
                              Chapter 4

It may apeare unto those which are not muche Conversant in the affyres of the Warres a matter somewhat straunge and (as it were) overstrayned that I make these greate differences & distinctions betwene these twoe places, as if they were (as allmost they are) meare Contraries; whereas they are nowe in parte generallye receyved and exercyssed as thinges of one and the selfe same Nature, which is a Faulte bothe in the doer & Sufferer.

For the *Muster-master* in the lande of Warre is nothinge ells but an excellent, Contionable and honest Auditor, keepinge faythfull and Just accountes betwene the kinge and his Captaines & the Captaines

---

[21] See Poynter, *Bibliography*, p. 186.

and their Souldiers, so that Righte may be (*34ᵛ*) doone on every syde, and the kinge neyther defrauded in his paymentes, nor the Hyerlinge robde of his Wadges; And With this hathe the *Muster-master* in the lande of Peace, nothinge to doe. For in the lande of Peace amongst the Cautionarie or Trayned Bands, there is no pay payed from the kinge nor any pay due, and so no Necessitie for anye Auditor; And if there be any time any Gratuitie given to the Souldiers, The Highe-Constables themselves (who are the Collectors) are sufficient Treasurers and the *Deputie-Liuetenantes* ever keepe the Audite. So that if the *Mustermaster* doe but medle therewith he is an Intruder.

As thus in this one thinge so in manie thinges ells the *Mustermaster* in the land of Peace and the Mustermaster in the Land of Warre are Contrarie one from another.

But to Come to the Nature and Duties which belonge to this *Muster-master* in the land of Warre, You shall understand that he ought to be a man of good Reputation and greate Integritie (*35ʳ*) of life; Learned in the Lawes and Ordinances of the Warres, But above all thinges an excellent Accountant and Prompte & Readie in all manner of Recconinges.

He ought to stand upon highe and Nyce Terrmes bothe touchinge hys owne Meanes and Entertaynment, and the Meanes and Enter-taynment due for his *Comissaries, Clarkes* and all other Inferior *Substitutes* and shall see that it be Competent and Convenient, for by that meanes he shall scorne Brybes and Benevallences & standing uprightlie on his one Integritie; he shall not neede to layne to any Supporte —————————²² then the kinge or his Generall, For Wante is ever founde the first Ingredian to Compound a knave. And there-fore that it may not by any meanes Come Within his *Potion*, It is meete that this *Mustermaster* be exceedinge Temperate & Sparing in his Expences and rather haveinge his hande a littill toe Closse, then anythinge at all toe much dylated.

It is the dutie & Office of this *Mustermaster* to keepe a true Booke, Lyst or Rolle of every Captaines Companie (*35ᵛ*) throughe the whole Armie as well horsmen as Footemen accordinge to their true strengthe, Number and Abillitie for service and accordinge to theire Allowance or Warrante of Entrye; And to that ende shall Register and sett downe everie Mans Name & Surname; The Armor and Weapon wherewithe he standethe charged, and the deffectes and Insufficiencies with which he shall encounter; And that there may not be Chopping & Chaungeinge, Borrowinge of Men for days or howers & other like Jugglinge Tryckes with which many Captaines

²² Illegible word inserted over a caret.

are frequent, It is verie meete that the Mustermaster Conceyve unto himself divers hydden and Mysticall Charracters Some sygnifyinge the proportion & Composition of Men as Heighte, Breadthe, Thycknes or Shortnesse, Some their Complections, Collours of Hayres, and Comelynesse or deformitie in Cariage; and Some to signifie eyther Markes naturall as are Moales, Wartes, Wenns, and the like, or Markes unnaturall as Woundes, Scarres on the face, Blemisshes in the Eies or the like; And these Charracters shall be (36^r) added and sett to everie Mans Name, that if any alteration be, the Error will soone be apparant.

As thus of Men, so he shall have espetiall Charracters for the Collours of horses, their outward Markes & other proportions; And accordinge to theis viewe or Muster taken by the Muster-master or his Comissaries (And it ought to be so ofte as Convenientlie their Affayres will give them leave; But espetiallie before and Imediatelie everie day of Battayll or Service performed) So he shall without all partiallitie returne his Certifycates unto the Treasurer.

It is the dutie and Office of this Mustermaster to urdge and Importune the *Generall* for the establishing of Lawes and Ordinances by which all Enterances and discharge of Souldiers may be registred playnlie and publiquelie & not kept in Cloudes and acted after an obscure fashion; For this cannot chuse but be an abuse to the kinge & to the Souldier halfe an undoeinge. And these Lawes and Ordinances once made the Mustermaster (36^v) shall deliver them to his Comissaries and all other his Inferior Substitutes together with many other seavere & particular Instructions of his owne touchinge the puttinge of the same in execution, and shall not fayle to call them many times to an accounte howe they have discharged their duties in the same. And where he fynd ethe[r] Neglect or Remissnesse, there to make his punishment Witness hys owne Integritie.

It is the dutie of this Mustermaster to be exceedinge carefull; Nay he must not at all sett downe anye Pennye certaine upon any Captaine or Bande whatsoever without most apparante, Certaine & due proofe, And to that ende, If the Controversie be doubtfull and uncertaine, He shall rather respite the Cause to a further examination; then by a rashe Certificate to defraud the Souldier of one pennye Meanes; For this is no good husbandrie for the kinge, But an Injurie to him & hys Service.

It is this Mans Office, if anye Captaine can shewe good and lawefull cause; or if (37^r) it be but Reasonable; Why he should be Releived out of the Checkques as eyther in respecte of his losses in Service, as Where Horse are taken or Slayne, Armor or Munition Woone or surprised by the Enemie, with thinges of like Nature and

Condition, which are woorthie of Consideration. In this case the Mustermaster shall presente both the Captaines prooffes and his owne Checkques unto the *Generall,* beceechinge him to have Noble Consideration of the same and playinge the Faythfull and Honest Advocate without Fee; He shall frame his Certificate accordinge to the *Generalls* pleasure.

It is the dutie of this Mustermaster (If he doe perceyve toe muche familiaritie to growe betwixte any of his Comissaries and the Captaines, If he finde the devill Temptinge, and the Man but leaneinge to Temptation) presentlie to growe Jealious of the same, and to call them to accounte, and overlooke their passadges; And if he fynde that his Comissarie have a daubd up Eie or an Eare that loves the sound of *Chinke, Chinke;* He shall presentlie displace him; Nay if there (37^v) be no proofe but onlie the Strengthe of his owne Suspition, Yet shall he remove him to another Quarter or another Garryson, and place such an one in his steade as shall throughlie examine all his former passadges.

Nowe as this Offycer is thus Seaverelie carefull of all thinges betwene the kinge and his Souldiers, and would not to gayne a Million deprive the Captaine of a due pennye, Nor for any favor of Greatnesse, frendship of Intymates, or touche of Bloode would strayne his Contience to beguyle the kinge; So he will be more then ordnarilie watchfull to present his Checques truelie & faythfullie as he findes leaveinge all Favor, Pardon & Excuse to him unto whom it Justlie & onlie belongethe; that is the kinge hymselfe or ells hys *Generall.*

It is the dutie of this Offycer to solicite the Generall and othe[r] superior officers to establishe Orders for the Trayninge of Souldiers; And it is his parte to sterre up the Captaines to performe the same; And where he fyndethe ethe[r] a well deserveing Souldier, if eyther by (38^r) gracefull wordes or some smale Reward he give him incouragement the Action will apeare noble & Woorthie in him.

It is against the honour of this Offycers place to take the valewe of a Pennye from any Captaine or Souldier more then the Fees due unto his place, Neyther may he Receyve that privatlie and Concealed, as thoughe it brought a Benevollence with it; But publiquelie and in open shewe that the world may say, This he deservethe.

To conclude; This Mustermaster ought so to fixe and settle himselfe onlie upon God and the clearnesse of hys owne Contience, That he neede not Relie on any Friendes more then the Kinge and his *Generall;* And as he must be most precysse and Curyous in himselfe neyther to give Penny far this Office nor to receyve Bribe or Benevallence, more then his due Fees; So ought he to make it a verie princypall matter of Contience (As longe as he is [o]wner of anye such place) not to present to any of his honourable Friendes, kins-men, or indeede anye that bearethe Aucthoritie above him any Giufte (*38ᵛ*) Remuneration or Remembrance whatsoever Greate or Littill, least it should drive into their Mindes or the Mindes of suche as should behold suche thinges (thoughe a farre of) some vehement Suspition that his Pathes were not straight, and that such Guiftes were an Insynuation to supporte or deffend some unjust Action.

Thus in fewe wordes I have shewed you the true Nature and dutie of these twoe Offycers, which beinge kepte in their Mindes & practised in their Imploymentes, No doute but they will bringe to their Cuntries muche Profitt and to themselves a never dyinge Reputation.

Finis

IV

A BOOK OF ALL THE SEVERAL OFFICERS OF THE COURT OF EXCHEQUER TOGETHER WITH THE NAMES OF THE PRESENT OFFICERS, IN WHOSE GIFT, AND HOW ADMITTED. WITH A BRIEF COLLECTION OF THE CHIEF HEADS OF WHAT EVERY OFFICER USUALLY DOETH BY VERTUE OF HIS OFFICE ACCORDING TO THE STATE OF THE EXCHEQUER AT THIS DAY, JANUARY 1641.

by

LAWRENCE SQUIBB

edited by

WILLIAM HAMILTON BRYSON, B.A., LL.B., LL.M., Ph.D.

CONTENTS

Introduction[1]

In January 1642 Lawrence Squibb, a man with exchequer connections, composed a succinct tract which described the duties and gave the names of most of the exchequer officers at that time. This short treatise is very helpful to our understanding of the procedures for the gathering of the English royal revenues in the first half of the seventeenth century. Until now it has never been printed, but its contemporary value is attested by the existence of at least sixteen manuscript copies. Since this work was considered useful in the seventeenth and early eighteenth centuries and since its accuracy

[1] The editor would like to acknowledge the generosity of Clare College, Cambridge, in meeting the expenses which he incurred in the preparation of this edition and of the Bodleian Library, Oxford, in giving permission to publish their manuscript Rawl. C 715.

is corroborated by its acceptance for copying and circulation by exchequer officials, it is a tract which cannot be entirely ignored by modern scholarship. An edition is therefore here presented for the use of institutional historians and for anyone else who might be interested.

I. Lawrence Squibb[2]

Lawrence Squibb was born in 1604[3] in Winterborne-Whitechurch, Dorset. The earliest traces of him in the records of the times are a warrant dated 21 March 1631/32 for £100 for the king's secret service[4] and a grant dated 27 October 1632 for protection from arrest on the grounds that he was a servant of lord Cottington, the chancellor and undertreasurer of the exchequer (freedom from arrest being the customary privilege of the servants of exchequer officers).[5] It appears from the records that he remained in the service of lord Cottington at least until August 1645.[6] Cottington left England in the following year and died still in exile in 1652. It is most likely that the money for the secret service was received on behalf of or in connection with Cottington, who was active at the time in diplomatic manœuvres with Spain.

Squibb's patron, Francis Cottington, lord Cottington,[7] was a native of Somerset, and it may have been their common west country origins which brought them together. In 1629 Cottington was made chancellor of the exchequer and in 1635 master of the court of wards. He was in the treasury commission of 1635 to 1636. However, he was disliked by the members of the Long Parliament and was forced to surrender the mastership of the wards in 1641 and the chancellorship of the exchequer in January 1642. Nevertheless, in 1643 he was made lord high treasurer by the king. Three years later he went into exile, and he died in Spain in 1652.

The other likely patron in the exchequer was Lawrence Squibb's kinsman, Arthur Squibb, who had been a teller in the exchequer

[2] The editor is indebted to Mr. G. D. Squibb, Q.C., for pointing the way to much of the biographical information in the Public Record Office which is to follow.

[3] He was 60 in 1664: Squibb v. Hales, P.R.O., E.113/116/50 & 51 (1665).

[4] P.R.O., S.P. 39/30, pt. 85.

[5] S.P. 16/224, pt. 53.

[6] S.P. 16/364, pt. 15 (1634–35); S.P. 16/488, pt. 87 (24 Jan. 1641/42); S.P. 16/489, pt. 6 (3 Feb. 1641/42); S.P. 16/491, pt. 61 (10 July 1642); *Cal. of the Committee for Advance of Money*, i, p. 122 (10 Jan. 1643/44), ii, pp. 578–80 (Aug. 1645); see also Cottington v. Squibb, C. 33/221, f. 474 (1663).

[7] *D.N.B.*; M. J. Havran, *Caroline Courtier. The Life of Lord Cottington* (London, 1973).

from 1624.[8] It is safe to assume that it was through the efforts of lord Cottington or Arthur Squibb or both of them that Lawrence Squibb received a patent to the reversion of a tellership dated 9 June 1635,[9] and it was, no doubt, Cottington who obtained for him the grant of the reversion to the office of clerk of the court of wards.[10] On 29 April 1637 Lawrence Squibb, Robert Squibb, and others were granted the office of sealer of playing cards and dice.[11] Judging from the amount of litigation which this latter office involved, it must have been reasonably profitable. The records show that Squibb was busy in this office from the time he received it until at least 1641.[12]

In January 1642 Squibb wrote the tract here presented. It is most unlikely that it was written for Cottington since his patron had been chancellor and undertreasurer of the exchequer for many years and no doubt knew as much or more about the subject than Squibb. But, owing to his lack of popularity with the House of Commons, Cottington was forced to resign these offices, and on 2 January 1642 John Colepeper[13] (later first lord Colepeper) was made chancellor and undertreasurer of the exchequer. They were both royalists and there was no enmity between them. Colepeper had come into favour with the king as a result of his support for crown policies in Parliament; he had had no previous exchequer experience. Although no direct evidence has been discovered, it does not seem too farfetched to suggest that the inexperienced Colepeper upon entering into his official exchequer duties asked his friend and predecessor, Cottington, for advice; whereupon Cottington had his faithful servant, Squibb, who was intimate with the intricacies of the exchequer, compose this treatise for Colepeper. The tract was written, or at least begun, within a few weeks of Colepeper's admission to office. Moreover, no other important person had come to office in the exchequer in this period. It is to be noted that Squibb did not comment upon the duties of the chancellor or undertreasurer of the exchequer. Colepeper was, no doubt, more interested in his

---

[8] P.R.O., E. 36/266, f. 81; see also H. S. London and G. D. Squibb, 'A Dorset King of Arms: Arthur Squibb, Clarenceux, 1646–1650,' *Procs. of the Dorset Nat. Hist. & Arch. Soc.*, lxviii (1947), pp. 54–65.

[9] P.R.O., P.[atent] R.[oll] 11 Car. 1, pt. 18: C. 66/2701.

[10] Dated 15 Jan. 1637/38; *Cal[endar of] S[tate] P[apers] Dom[estic]*, *1637–38*, p. 160. This court ceased to exist before Squibb's reversion fell in.

[11] P.R.O., Cal. Patent Rolls, 12 & 13 Car. 1, f. 209; C. 66/2759.

[12] See *Cal. S.P. Dom.*, *1637–38*, pp. 149, 322, 378, 610; *1638–39*, p. 143; *1639–40*, pp. 70, 245; *1640*, p. 101; *1640–41*, pp. 283, 284, 322, 511; *1641–43*, pp. 167, 300; *addenda 1625–49*, pp. 635, 637, 638.

[13] *D.N.B.*

rights of exchequer patronage than in his duties as an exchequer official. At this time the chancellor and undertreasurer of the exchequer were always the same person; the general nature of the duties of these two offices was only supervisory. If this officer did not act, for whatever reason, then these functions could be performed by the treasurer or the barons of the exchequer. When Cottington was in Spain, there is no evidence that he appointed a deputy.

During the civil war Squibb was with the king in Oxford.[14] This and his connections with Cottington were probably the reasons for the lack of success of his petitions in May and June of 1654 to be admitted as teller.[15] In 1653 Squibb married Anne, daughter of Sir Henry Leigh of Eggington, Derby, and widow of Sir Simon Every, baronet.[16] They were resident in the parish of St. Martin's in the Fields, Middlesex, as well as at 'West Farm', Winterborne-Whitechurch, Dorset. Squibb was sworn into office as one of the four tellers of the exchequer in July 1660.[17] He died between 4 and 7 December 1674.[18]

II. The Manuscripts and their Descent

A major part of the preliminary work for this edition was the collecting and collating of the various manuscripts in order to determine which should be the basis for the transcription. Over the past few years sixteen copies have been located; this was the result of a systematic search through the various catalogues and indexes to the manuscript collections, the vigilance and kindness of friends, and a great deal of luck. Perhaps there are other copies extant; if so we must rely on the latter two sources of information, since the time for further searching has come to an end.

The manuscripts are now located in a large number of libraries, and they have passed through a large number of interesting collections. This section, therefore, discusses as far as possible the descent and the migrations of all of the known copies of this tract. Since the work dates from only the seventeenth century, the gaps in many cases are not very great.

The following list of the manuscripts assigns a letter of the alphabet to each. This letter will be used to refer to each manu-

---

[14] Cal. of the Committee for Compounding, ii, p. 1558.

[15] S.P. 18/73, pts. 77, 78.

[16] For litigation by Squibb on his wife's behalf, see Squibb v. Tredder, C. 7/445/73 (1658); Squibb v. Robinson, C. 7/444/86 (1659). Squibb v. Lambert, C. 6/48/112 (1660).

[17] See Squibb v. Hales, E.113/116/50 & 51 (1665); see also S.P. 29/24, pt. 48 (26 Dec. 1660), and C[alendar of] T[reasury] B[ooks], i, pp. 50, 182.

[18] See his will: P.R.O., PROB. 11/346, pt. 148; C.T.B., iv, p. 638; [The] Stat[utes of the] Realm (London, 1810–1828), v, p. 851.

script as it is then separately discussed. The conclusion will give a tentative chart of descent and make a few generalizations as to why and for whom the copies were made.

A—Public Record Office, S.P. 16/488, part 103, and S.P. 16/406, part 22.

B—Bodleian Library, MS. Rawl. C. 715, ff. 1–30.

C—House of Lords Library, Exchequer MS. 4º, ff. 1ʳ–34ᵛ.

D—British Museum, MS. Eg. 2436, ff. 4ʳ–27ʳ.

E—British Museum, MS. Harl. 3278, ff. 1ʳ–33ᵛ.

F—London University, MS. 57, ff. 3–39.

G—Lincoln's Inn, MS. Hill 86, pp. 1–27.

H—Valence House, Dagenham, MS. 54, ff. 1ʳ–18ᵛ [1st copy]; ff. 91ʳ–111ᵛ [2d copy].

I—House of Lords Library, Truro Exchequer MS. 2º, ff. 6ʳ–21ʳ [1st copy]; ff. 80ʳ–96ᵛ [2d copy].

J—British Museum, MS. Add. 30216, pp. 1–101.

K—Public Record Office, A.O. 16/196, pp. 1–103.

L—British Museum, MS. Stowe 327, ff. 19ʳ–31ᵛ.

M—British Museum, MS. Add. 24689, ff. 16ᵛ–36ᵛ.

N—British Museum, MS. Add. 38419, ff. 26ʳ–58ᵛ.

Manuscript A is in two parts. The first part, S.P. 16/488, part 103, [A1] is a quire of six sheets. There is only a short title at the beginning of the text: 'Officers of the Court of Exchequer'; but on the 'dorse' of the quire (i.e. sideways on the last page) is written:

January 1641. A Booke of all the severall Officers of the Court of the Exchequer, together with the names of the present officers, in whose guift, & how admitted, with a breife Collecion of what is done by each Officer According to the State of the Exchequer at this day January 1641.

per Law. Squibb

with a briefe Collecion of the cheif heades of what every officer usually doth by vertue of his Office according to the State of the Exchequer at this day.

A2, *i.e.* S.P. 16/406, part 22, has no title at the head of the text, but there is written on the 'dorse': 'Officers of the Receipt their duty & place.'[19] A2 was originally a quire of three sheets, but the first sheet has been torn in half along the fold. Although A1 and A2 are not on the same type of paper, they are in the same hand and layout; they were no doubt composed at the same time. A1 contains notes for the

[19] The editor would like to thank Professor G. E. Aylmer for bringing A2 to his attention.

chapters on the officers of the upper exchequer (or 'exchequer of account'); A2 for the chapters concerning the lower exchequer (or 'exchequer of receipt'). Thus can one easily understand how the two parts of the tract became separated before they were bound into two different composite volumes of state paper miscellanea at some later date.

Manuscript A is clearly only a rough draft or collection of notes from which to make the final version of the tract. It is not very neat or clear; often the sentences are not even complete. Where the author did not know the names of the officers, blank spaces were left, and the information was discovered and given in the final version. For example, in the section on the king's remembrancer, the first names of the sworn clerks were added later and their names were rearranged so as to be in order of seniority. Also the order of several paragraphs was rearranged. Moreover, the final version is significantly larger than A.

It appears from a comparison of A with Squibb's autographs in E.402/249 that this manuscript is in his own hand.[20] Since Squibb's name appears on the rough draft of the tract, it is obvious that it was composed by him rather than merely transcribed by him.

How A got into the state paper office is anyone's guess. Perhaps Squibb's papers were confiscated during the civil wars; perhaps he lent it to a friend. It is more likely that the state paper office was given it along with a batch of miscellaneous exchequer papers in the seventeenth century. The state papers were transferred to the Public Record Office in 1852.[21] The two parts of A are mentioned in *Cal. S.P. Dom., 1638–39*, p. 198, and *Cal. S.P. Dom., 1641–43*, p. 272.

Before leaving A we should briefly mention S.P. 16/488, part 104. This is a fair copy of the first two sections of A1, *i.e.* the discussions of the king's remembrancer and the lord treasurer's remembrancer. This is in a different hand and on different paper from A1. It is a copy of A1 rather than the final version and so is of little interest. The existence of this manuscript suggests that A or at least A1 was borrowed to be copied and that it came to the state paper office with the other papers of whomever it was that borrowed it. This may have been the moment when A1 and A2 became separated. Perhaps after having copied the first two parts, it was discovered that A was not the final and complete version and that a better exemplar was available elsewhere. Of course the transcriber may have just lost interest in his task and not made a complete copy.

[20] Cf. also S.P. 16/449, pt. 16; S.P. 16/485, pt. 108; S.P. 16/489, pt. 6; S.P. 16/501, pt. 27.

[21] *Guide to the Contents of the Public Record Office*, ii (London, 1963), p. 3.

Manuscript B is a copy of the complete version and is the one chosen to be transcribed. Its title is an abbreviated version of that of A1 and includes the date January 1641/42. There is no clue as to who made this copy or when. It is now bound up with a tract entitled 'The Case of the Earle of Northumberland touching a Reliefe demanded of him', which concerns the inheritance of Algernon Percy, earl of Northumberland. His father died in 1632 and he died in 1668;[22] so this must have been written between these two dates. It was probably made only shortly after 1632. This portion of this book, however, has nothing to do with the tract by Squibb. It is in a different hand and on different paper from B. Clearly these two were bound together some time after they had been written. The probable reason that they are now between the same boards is that they both concern the exchequer.

B might be as old as 1642 whereas none of the other copies of the complete version can possibly be so old. It is a clear and reasonably neat copy, but it is not ornate. One is therefore led to the conclusion that this is not Squibb's presentation copy to Colepeper or whomever.

B belonged to Richard Rawlinson (1690–1755), the eccentric antiquarian book-collector.[23] When Rawlinson died in 1755, he bequeathed his manuscripts to the Bodleian Library, and B has been there ever since. It is noted in W. D. Macray, *Catalogi Codicum Manuscriptum Bibliothecae Bodleianae*, part 5, fasc. 2, Rawlinson MSS., class 3 (Oxford 1878), col. 362.

In the House of Lords Library is a quarto manuscript book (pressmark L. 25) containing copy C of Squibb's tract. It begins with the tract by Squibb and then gives a memorandum from Samuel Edwards to George, viscount Dupplin, composed in 1711. This latter memorandum or communication consists of four parts. It begins with a note entitled 'Orders, Rules, and Instructions to be Observed and Executed by the Remembrancer of his Majesty's First Fruits, the Comptroller of the Same Revenue, the Receivers, the Auditors, and All Others who are or may be Concerned in Relation to the Said Revenues of First Fruits and Tenths'. It was signed at the end by John Lowther, Richard Hampden, and Stephen Fox and dated Whitehall, Treasury Chambers, 5 September 1690. The next part is a note: 'An Order of the Treasury for Locking Up the Out Cash in the Tellers' Office'. The third part has no title but begins: 'The whole revenue of the crown is or ought to be paid at

[22] *D.N.B.; G.E.C.*, ix, pp. 732–8.
[23] *D.N.B.;* W. Y. Fletcher, 'The Rawlinsons and their Collections', *Trans. Bibliographical Soc.*, v (1899), pp. 67–84.

the receipt of the exchequer to the four tellers. . . .' This part includes lists of fees and forms for various revenue instruments; the samples are dated 1692. The last part is a memorandum which begins: 'To the Rt. Hon. George, lord viscount Dupplin, one of the four tellers of the receipt of her majesty's exchequer. Samuel Edwards, whom your lordship has been pleased to appoint your first clerk in the said office, in obedience to your lordship's command humbly presents to your lordship's consideration the following particulars. Her majesty having been pleased to appoint your lordship a teller in the room of the Rt. Hon. Peregrine Bertie, Esq., by letters patent bearing date the 3rd of September 1711. . . .' Edwards goes on to give notes, fees, and forms, which are dated 1711. Edwards' entire memorandum concerns the office of teller, and it appears to have been compiled in 1711 for viscount Dupplin upon his appointment as a teller.[24]

Since the entire book is in the same hand, C cannot have been made before 1711. It is a beautifully transcribed copy with ornamental titles; probably it was made for some important exchequer or treasury official. The date in the title of the second section of Squibb's tract which deals with the officers of the exchequer of receipt has been changed from 1641 to 1642. In 1752 the first day of the legal year was moved from 25 March to 1 January; this change in the title suggests that this manuscript was made after 1752. It could, of course, be a scribal error; but C appears to be a careful copy. Nevertheless, the case for the scribal error is supported by the fact that E, which was made before 1719, has the 1642 date.

The earliest known owner of C was Isaac Reed, the Shakespeare critic and editor, who died in 1807. He gave it to Edward Roberts, who was clerk of the pells from 1823 to 1825. On 25 November 1829 it was given by Roberts to Spencer Percival, who was one of the four tellers from 1813 to 1834. A descendant of Spencer Percival, Mr. J. Percival, presented it to the House of Lords on 24 October 1932. It is described in M. F. Bond, *Guide to the Records of Parliament* (London 1971), p. 286.[25]

Copy D is now in the British Museum as a part of the Egerton collection. On one of the blank pages in the front of the book is written 'Sh.G.A.' (or 'Sh.G.H.') and a note that the book was pur-

---

[24] George Hay, lord Dupplin (d. 1758), was a political associate of Harley; in 1709 he married one of Harley's daughters; he was a teller from 1711 to 1714; in 1719 he became 8th earl of Kinnoull: *D.N.B.*; *G.E.C.*, vii, pp. 321, 322.

[25] The editor is grateful to Mr. J. C. Sainty for bringing this MS. to his attention before Mr. Bond's book was published.

chased by the British Museum from J. Harvey on 26 January 1878.[26] In addition to Squibb's essay, it contains Edwards' memorandum on the office of a teller. The fourth part has, however, been altered so that it is addressed to Thomas lord Mansell[27] by Lionel Herne; it also states than Mansell had been appointed a teller in the place of John Smith on 23 July 1712. Obviously Herne copied Edwards' notes for his own superior and substituted the appropriate names and dates.

The entire manuscript is in the same hand. Moreover, Squibb's tract ends on the recto of a leaf, and on the verso of the same folio is the beginning of the Edwards memorandum. D therefore cannot have been made earlier than 1712. The date of the second title of Squibb, like C, was changed to 1642. D is a neatly copied book with elaborate titles.

E, the Harleian manuscript, has exactly the same content as D, i.e. Squibb plus Herne; also the date of the second title is 1642. These tracts were copied into a blank book in the same professional hand, which is clear but not ornate. In the front of the book, before the text begins, is written: 'This account of the exchequer was drawn up by Mr. Lionel Herne, first clerk to one of the tellers. He gave this account to my Lord Dupplin, and from him I had this copy. Mr. Herne had the reputation of being a most exact clerk and excellent officer. He died in 1714, I think.' This note was written by Robert Harley, first earl of Oxford and Mortimer (1661–1724).[28] Not only was Harley a great collector of manuscripts, but he also had exchequer interests, having been lord high treasurer from 1711 to 1714. From this note we might think that it was Herne who composed the memorandum about the tellers' office and copied Squibb's tract with it. However, we know from C that the credit should go to Samuel Edwards. It is interesting to note that lord Dupplin had two copies of this tract: one given to him by Edwards, C or the exemplar therefor, and one from Herne which was the exemplar for E. Dupplin was Harley's son-in-law[29] and this provided a natural point of contact.

The inclusion of Edwards' and Herne's memorandum dates the making of this manuscript after 1712. It cannot be known exactly when Harley made the note in it; this was probably done as a part

---

[26] See also *Catalogue of Additions to the Manuscripts in the British Museum* (London, 1882), p. 293.

[27] Thomas, 1st lord Mansell (d. 1723), was a treasury commissioner in 1710 and a teller from 1712 to 1714: *G.E.C.*, viii, pp. 384, 385.

[28] *D.N.B.*; *G.E.C.*, x, pp. 263–6.

[29] See above, p. 84.

of the cataloguing of his library after his retirement. In any case it must have been after 1714. In 1719 lord Dupplin became the earl of Kinnoull; that Harley continued to call him lord Dupplin is not likely. This puts the making of this copy before 1719.

Thus E was made for Harley between 1712 and 1719. Harley died in 1724, and his son kept his manuscript collection together. In 1753 his heirs sold the collection to Parliament, and it became a part of the foundation collection of the British Museum.[30] E is mentioned in *A Catalogue of the Harleian Manuscripts*, iii (London, 1808), p. 14, and in C. E. Wright, *Fontes Harleiani* (1972), p. 184.

Copy F has the same contents as D and E and the date of 1642 in the second title. It is listed in R. A. Rye, *Catalogue of the Manuscripts . . . of the University of London* (London, 1921), pp. 29, 30. It was first discovered in the collection of books relating to economics assembled by Professor Hubert Somerton Foxwell (1849–1936).[31] Foxwell sold his collection to the Worshipful Company of Goldsmiths in 1901, and in 1903 the collection was given to the University of London.

G, the copy in Lincoln's Inn, is an interesting one. The first two parts of this book are the same as D, E, and F. They are the tracts by Squibb and Herne. The date of 1642 is also found here in the second title of Squibb's work. Furthermore, a third part was added to G; this is the so-called Lowndes memorandum. All three works were copied into a blank book in the same hand.

The Lowndes memorandum consists of four parts. The first is entitled 'The Report Made by Mr. Lowndes to the Rt. Hon. Lawrence, Earl of Rochester, Lord High Treasurer of England, about Methods in the Exchequer'. It is signed by William Lowndes and dated 11 October 1686. The second section is entitled 'The Orders Made by the Earl of Rochester, Lord Treasurer of England, Upon the Aforegoing Report and Now Remaining and Practised in the Receipt of Exchequer are as Follows, which were Also Approved by Mr. Attorney General, viz.' This is signed by Rochester and dated 28 October 1686. The third part is only a short note about a statute of the year 1696. The last part is a memorandum on the exchequer, which has four short sections: 'Of the Receipt of the Exchequer', 'The Method of Payments in the Receipt', 'Matters in the Receipt Relating to Accounts', and 'The Nature of Tallies'. This is signed by Lowndes and dated 1691. Other copies of this collection of exchequer information by Lowndes are to be found in P.R.O.,

---

[30] A. J. K. Esdaile, *The British Museum Library* (London, 1946), pp. 231–9.

[31] For a sketch of Foxwell's life, see M. Canney, D. Knott, and J. H. P. Pafford, *Catalogue of the Goldsmiths Library*, i (Cambridge, 1970), pp. x–xviii.

T.48/6; British Museum, MSS. Add. 36107, ff. 47–65, and Add. 36108, ff. 39–47; Duchy of Cornwall Record Office MS. (a small paper quarto which belonged to James Rowlands in 1736);[32] British Museum, MSS. Add. 15898, ff. 102–109 [part 4 only], and Harl. 6838, ff. 78–80 [part 2 only]; P.R.O., E.36/266, ff. 87–88 [part 2 only].

The title of the entire book is as follows: 'A Book Concerning the Exchequer Copied from the Manuscript Thereof Formerly Lord Mansell's but Since in Lord Onslow's Possession. To Which is Annexed a Report of Mr. Lowndes to the Earl of Rochester, Lord High Treasurer, with his Lordship's Orders Thereon, &c.' Thus the first two parts of G were copied from an exemplar in the possession of a lord Onslow, perhaps D or F. There are two Onslows who might have been the person mentioned: Richard Onslow, first lord Onslow (1654–1717), who was chancellor and undertreasurer of the exchequer from 1714 to 1715 and a teller from 1715 to his death in 1717,[33] and his son Thomas, second lord Onslow (1679–1740), who was a teller from 1718 to 1740.[34]

This manuscript was owned by Serjeant George Hill (1716–1808).[35] In the front of the book Hill wrote a memorandum of the payment of his salary as the king's first serjeant-at-law in 1802, and there is another note at the end which includes the form of a warrant dated 15 August 1791. This suggests that this manuscript was in Hill's possession as early as 1791. Hill died in 1808, and his manuscripts were purchased by the Honourable Society of Lincoln's Inn.[36] G is mentioned in *The General Report of the Commissioners on the Public Records* (London, 1837), App., p. 384, and in J. Hunter, *A Catalogue of the Manuscripts in the Library of the Hon. Soc. of Lincoln's Inn* (London, 1838), p. 130 (see also p. xv).

H, the manuscript at Valence House, Dagenham (which is now a part of the public library system of the London Borough of Barking), is one of the most interesting books in the manuscript transmission. The first part of the book consists of a copy of Squibb's tract, copy H1, plus the Herne memoranda. H1 is the same in content as D, E, and F and could quite possibly have been copied from one of them. To this was added a short essay on the pells of receipt and issue,

[32] The editor would like to thank Miss M. Randall for bringing this MS. to light.
[33] *D.N.B.*; *G.E.C.*, x, pp. 66–8; R. Sedgwick, *The House of Commons 1715–1754* (London, 1970), ii, pp. 310–11.
[34] *G.E.C.*, x, p. 69; Sedgwick, *op. cit.*, ii, pp. 311–12.
[35] *D.N.B.*
[36] See the order of 6 July 1808 in *The Records of the Hon. Soc. of Lincoln's Inn*, 'The Black Books,' ed. W. P. Baildon, iv (London, 1902), p. 113.

which is dated Michaelmas 1597. It has no title but begins: 'King Henry the Seventh your majesties most noble grandfather of worthy memory being . . .' There is no signature upon it. Part one is ff. 1–44.

The second part of this manuscript book, ff. 45–90, contains Peter Osborne's *The Practice of the Exchequer Court* plus the articles for uniting the courts of augmentations and of first fruits and tenths to the exchequer. This treatise was written in 1572; when it was printed for the first time in 1658, the publisher mistakenly attributed it to Thomas Fanshawe.[37]

The third part, ff. 91–111, is a second copy of Squibb's tract, H2. But this copy is a very sloppy transcription of the work. Since the entire book is in the same hand and since the first two parts were carefully and accurately executed, it is obvious that the scribe was copying an inaccurate exemplar which is now lost. H2 gives the date of 'January 1641' at the end of the title for the first part of the tract but gives no date at all in the title to the second part.

These tracts were copied into a blank book sometime after 1712. In 1902 Arthur Reader, a London bookseller, sold this book for two pounds to Basil T. Fanshawe of Bratton Fleming, North Devon. His descendant, Captain Aubrey Fanshawe, R.N., bequeathed it and others along with the Fanshawe family portraits to Valence House, which had for several centuries been the seat of one branch of the Fanshawe family (other branches had lived nearby in Dagenham). The physical transfer took place in March 1963.[38] H is mentioned in *The Memoirs of Ann Lady Fanshawe*, ed. H. C. Fanshawe (London, 1907), p. 263; and in H. C. Fanshawe, *History of the Fanshawe Family* (Newcastle-upon-Tyne, 1927), p. 24.

Copy I appears to be a faithful transcription of H. This gives us two additional copies of the tract by Squibb. It was given by the widow of Lord Chancellor Truro (1782–1855) to the House of Lords in 1856 along with his law library.[39] The present shelf mark of this very attractive copy is 101.L.

Copies J, K, L, M, and N form a group which is clearly distinct

---

[37] W. H. Bryson, 'Exchequer Equity Bibliography,' *American Journal of Legal History*, xiv (1970), pp. 333–9, 348; since this article was written the following additional copies have been discovered: Bodleian, MS. Rawl. C 180; University College Oxford, MS. 126; British Museum, MSS. Lansd. 649, ff. 8 ff., and Harl. 5169; Duchy of Cornwall Record Office, 2° MS., ff. 96–133; House of Lords Library, Truro Exch. MS., ff. 48–74.

[38] The editor is indebted to Mr. J. Howson, reference librarian at Valence House, for this information.

[39] C. S. A. Dobson, *The Library of the House of Lords* (London, 1960), p. 11.

from all of the above-mentioned copies. But J and K are so significantly different from L, M, and N that one is forced to postulate a
missing exemplar which must be the common link to the other
copies. All five have enough similar variations to preclude the
possibility that they might have come from different exemplars.

The postulated exemplar must have made the following alterations to the original, which might have been B. It was made in 1692,
and this date was substituted for the date of 1641/42 in the original
titles to the two parts of the tract. It was more or less a new edition
of the tract in that the names of the current office holders were
substituted for the old and out of date names and minor enlargements were made to the text. The editor, however, abandoned his
task about nine-tenths of the way through. The last bit was only a
mechanical transcription. The order of the paragraphs of the section
on the lord treasurer's remembrancer was rearranged; four paragraphs from the middle were put at the end. This was probably the
result of a slip in copying; when it was discovered, the four omitted
paragraphs were then copied at the end of the section.

J completes the work of substituting the names of the 1692
officers. It also makes significant additions to the sections on the
auditor of the receipt and the clerk of the pells. This copy is legible
but far from elegant; the hand is more likely that of some exchequer
official than that of a professional copyist. Squibb's tract covers the
first 101 pages plus five unnumbered pages, which contain the table
of contents. On pp. 102-75 is 'The Returns of the Fees and Commissions of the Officers of the Court of Exchequer,' and on pp.
176-219 'The Returns of the Fees and Commissions of the Receipt
of Exchequer.' The dates of these last two items is 1692. On pp.
230-64 in a different hand and probably at a later date is the fourth
part of the Lowndes memoranda. It is therefore possible that J was
made as early as 1692.

The earliest known owner of this manuscript was Thomas Jett,
who was one of the auditors of the exchequer. His grant is dated
20 June 1706.[40] He was admitted to the Middle Temple on 13 April
1705 and was called to the bar on 27 May 1715; on 6 June 1722 he
was admitted to Gray's Inn.[41] J was bought out of Jett's library on
7 October 1736 by James West (1703-72), a lawyer, politician, and
antiquary, who was joint secretary to the treasury from 1741 to

[40] P.R. 5 Ann. pt. 4: C.66/3456; the editor is grateful to Mr. Sainty for this
information.
[41] H. A. C. Sturgess, *Register of Admissions to the Hon. Soc. of the Middle
Temple*, i. (London, 1949), p. 257; J. Foster, *Register of Admissions to Gray's
Inn 1521-1889* (London, 1889), p. 365.

1762.[42] West died in 1772 and the following year his manuscripts were sold to William Petty, second earl of Shelburne and first marquess of Lansdowne (1737–1805).[43] Shelburne's descendant, the fifth marquess of Lansdowne (1845–1927)[44] sold J to the British Museum on 9 December 1876. It is mentioned as Shelburne MS. vol. 174 in *H.M.C. Rept.*, v (1876), p. 259, and is described in the *Catalogue of Additions to the Manuscripts in the British Museum* London, 1882), pp. 48, 52.

The next item to be considered is K, which is now in the Public Record Office among the miscellanea of the records from the exchequer and audit office of the treasury. This volume bears the armorial bookplate of 'William Bromley of Baginton in the County of Warwicke Esq.' This was probably either William Bromley, M.P., (d. 1732) or his son William Bromley, M.P., (d. 1737).[45] In 1871 it was in the library of W. Bromley-Davenport at Baginton Hall, Warwickshire,[46] and on 9 May 1903 it was sold for nineteen shillings to A. Carter.[47] Somehow this book got into the exchequer and audit department, and it was transferred thence in 1937 to the Public Record Office.[48]

All of the tracts in K were copied into a blank book in the same hand. The latest date mentioned is 1702; so it must have been made thereafter. The first 220 pages are the same as the original part of J: Squibb's tract plus 'The Returns of the Fees and Commissions of the Officers of the Court of Exchequer'. Then follows the 'Orders and Instructions Appointed by the Earl of Rochester When Lord High Treasurer of England to be Observed by the Officers Following'. This was dated 28 April 1685 and was copied on 1 May 1702. This latter date is more likely the date of the exemplar than the date of K. The final section of this manuscript book is the second part of the Lowndes memorandum.

The copy of Squibb's tract appears to have been taken from J. One noteworthy difference is that K has in addition to the old out-of-date section of the clerk of the parcells a new description in a

---

[42] *D.N.B.*; L. Namier and J. Brooke, *The House of Commons 1754–1790* (London, 1964), iii, pp. 624–6.

[43] *D.N.B.*; *G.E.C.* vii, pp. 436–8; see also Esdaile, *The British Museum Library*, pp. 248–50; N.B. that J is not part of the 'Lansdowne MSS.'

[44] *G.E.C.*, vii, pp. 441, 442.

[45] *D.N.B.*; Sedgwick, *The House of Commons 1715–1754*, i, pp. 493–5.

[46] *H.M.C. Rept.*, no. 2, p. 79 (1871).

[47] Sotheby, Wilkinson, and Hodge, *Catalogue of the Library from Baginton Hall* . . . [of] *William Bromley Davenport, Esq.* (1903), p. 26, lot. 325; see also London, *Daily Telegraph*, 11 May 1903.

[48] *D.K. Rept.*, no. 99 (1938), p. 13.

different hand. This new section was probably copied from L, M, or N.

L and the two following copies differ from the postulated 1692 exemplar in that they substitute an up-to-date account of the office of the clerk of the parcells, which had by then been suppressed. These three also put the section on the clerk of the pells before that of the auditor of the receipt.

This book contains many tracts in different hands, but all of the exchequer material appears to have been written by the same scribe. Ff. 11–14 are the fourth and third parts of the Lowndes memorandum; ff. 14–18 are the 'Instructions proposed by the Lord Rochester for Accompting. Anno 1685', which was copied on 1 May 1702. This last bit is the same as in K. Then follows the copy of Squibb's tract. The first and third parts of the Edwards–Herne memorandum were copied on ff. 32–41. The rest of this book consists of several maritime tracts and Hale's *History of the Common Law*. The latest date on any of these is 1702. At the end of the book are bound in some loose notes, letters, printed Acts of Parliament, etc. Of interest to us are ff. 276, 277. This is a letter from Edward Roberts to Thomas Astle in regard to a collation of their two copies of Squibb's tract, i.e. L and M; it is dated from the exchequer, 11 September 1802.

L was number 389 in the collection of Thomas Astle (1735–1803), the antiquarian.[49] Astle was patronized by the Grenvilles, a family with exchequer connections. George Grenville was chancellor of the exchequer and first lord of the treasury from 1763 to 1765, and his son, the first marquess of Buckingham, was one of the tellers of the exchequer from 1764 until his death in 1813.[50] By means of this connection Astle became keeper of the records in the Tower of London. When Astle died in 1803 he offered in his will to sell his manuscript collection for the token sum of £500 to the Grenville family out of gratitude for their patronage. The sale took place in the following year, and L along with the other books were taken to Stowe House, Buckinghamshire, the seat of the Grenvilles. In 1849, the Stowe manuscripts were sold to Bertram Ashburnham, fourth earl of Ashburnham (1797–1878),[51] and the British Museum in 1883 bought the collection from the executors of Ashburnham.[52]

This copy of Squibb's tract is noticed in C. O'Conor, *Bibliotheca*

---

[49] *D.N.B.*; see also his papers in P.R.O.: T.64/309.

[50] *D.N.B.*; *G.E.C.*, ii, pp. 406–8.

[51] *G.E.C.*, vol. i, p. 274; A. N. L. Munby, *Phillipps Studies, iv : The Formation of the Phillipps Library from 1841 to 1872* (Cambridge, 1956), pp. 24–8.

[52] Esdaile, *The British Museum Library*, pp. 257–9.

MS. Stowensis (Buckingham, 1818–19), ii, p. 341; W. J. S[mith], *Catalogue of Manuscripts from Stowe* (Sotheby's sales catalogues, 1849), p. 193, lot 815; *H.M.C. Rept.*, viii, part 3, 'Ashburnham MSS.' p. 23, col. 1, no. 6;[53] *Catalogue of the Stowe Manuscripts*, comp. E. C. L. Scott, i (London, 1895), pp. 370, 371 (see also pp. i–vi).

M has the same exchequer material as L but is a slightly more ornate copy; it is written throughout in the same hand. Perhaps someone was commissioned to copy out the exchequer parts of L for the use of some high exchequer official. As with L, the latest date mentioned in M is 1702.

This manuscript was owned either by Richard Gray, who was a deputy auditor of the exchequer from 1767 to 1826.[54] or by Richard Gray, deputy auditor of the exchequer, who died on 16 September 1781.[55] The younger man was probably the son or nephew of the older. The Richard Gray who owned M gave it to Edward Roberts sometime before 1802, when Roberts compared it with L. It is interesting to note that Edward Roberts, who was deputy clerk of the pells from 1795 to 1823 and clerk of the pells from then until 1825,[56] also owned copy C. M came into the possession of Charles Devon, a clerk in the Chapter House of Westminster Abbey, one of the record repositories of the exchequer. On 12 April 1862 he sold it to the British Museum. M is mentioned in the *Catalogue of Additions to the Manuscripts in the British Museum* (London, 1877), p. 98.

The final copy of Squibb's tract to be discussed, N, is the most recent of those so far discovered. This book, which is in the same hand throughout, contains the same material as M and the exchequer parts of L. But on the first folio of N is written the following title: 'An Account Of the Nature of the Receipt of the Exchequer And of the Methods Observed Therein. 1764'. The title is for the fourth part of the Lowndes memorandum which follows it. This tract was composed in the last quarter of the seventeenth century. The date of 1764 appears to be the date N was made rather than a copyist's error.

N is now in the British Museum as vol. 230 of the Liverpool Papers. It is a clear but inelegant copy. It was probably made for Charles Jenkinson, first earl of Liverpool (1729–1808), who was joint secretary to the treasury from 1763 to 1765 and one of the lords of

---

[53] Reprinted in H.C. sess. pap. 1883 (no. 282) vol. 38, pp. 133 at 179, col. 2, no. 6.

[54] The editor is grateful to Mr. Sainty for this information.

[55] *Gentleman's Magazine*, li (1781), p. 443.

[56] *Royal Kalendar* (1795–1825).

the treasury from 1767 to 1773.[57] Possibly, but less probably, it was acquired by his son, Robert Banks Jenkinson, second earl of Liverpool (1770–1828), who was first lord of the treasury from 1812 to 1827.[58] This manuscript was presented along with the rest of the Liverpool Papers to the British Museum in 1911 by the Hon. Henry Berkeley Portman. It is mentioned in the *Catalogue of Additions to the Manuscripts in the British Museum* (London, 1925), pp. 91, 92, 103, 104.

By putting together all of the evidence, both internal and external, we get the following chart of the descent of the manuscripts of Squibb's tract on the exchequer:

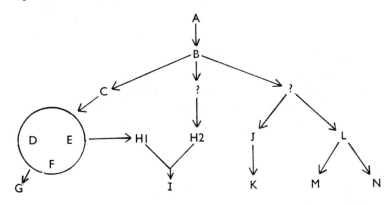

As to the questions of why and for whom these copies were made, it is interesting to note that most of them, C, D, E, F, G, H, I, N, were made seventy-five years after the dates on their exemplars. Although the constitution of the exchequer did not change significantly in the seventeenth and eighteenth centuries, its importance was considerably diminished during the second half of the seventeenth century. In 1660 an act of Parliament[59] abolished the ancient and antiquated feudal fees and dues connected with knight service and thus reduced the traditional occupation of the exchequer. Of greater significance was the rise and development at this time of more efficient revenue collecting machinery within the treasury but outside the exchequer.[60] In the eighteenth century the treasury was far more important than the exchequer.

[57] *D.N.B.*; *G.E.C.*, viii, pp. 86–7; Namier and Brooke, *The House of Commons 1754–1790*, ii, pp. 674–8.
[58] *D.N.B.*; *G.E.C.*, viii, pp. 87–9.
[59] Stat. 12 Car. 2 [1660], c. 24, *Stat. Realm*, v, pp. 259–66.
[60] See S. B. Baxter, *The Rise of the Treasury 1660–1702* (London, 1957).

Yet the exchequer retained a sufficient importance to make it lucrative to procure offices therein which could be exercised by deputies. New officials, especially the higher ones who had purchased their positions or acquired them through royal favour, had had no previous exchequer experience, and they needed to know what their duties were, how the exchequer operated, and what rights of appointment they had. These rights of patronage were of great value politically as well as financially. It is reasonably clear that copies were made for Harley, lord Dupplin, lord Mansell, and lord Liverpool; no doubt most of the copies were made to satisfy these needs.

It is unlikely that any trouble was taken to procure the best tract or the best copy of a particular one for transcription. Any convenient tract or copy which appeared to be reasonably competent would be borrowed from an acquaintance and given to a scrivener to reproduce. C, D, E, F, H, I, K, L, M, and N appear to be the products of professional copyists.

Yet if a systematic search for the best tract to read for these purposes had been made, Squibb's work would have been a likely choice. There was an anonymous sixteenth-century article entitled 'A Brief Collection of the Principal Under-Officers . . .'[61] but this was both older and shorter than Squibb's. The most likely rival was Osborne's *Practice of the Exchequer Court*. This treatise though longer was older, having been composed in 1572. Although it was printed in 1658, manuscript copies seem to have been made after its publication; this suggests that printed copies became scarce soon after publication but that demand was not great enough to justify a second edition.[62] C. Vernon's *Considerations Touching the Exchequer* (London, 1642) would have been a relevant book to have had if a copy was available. Although its prime object appears to have been the reforming of the exchequer, it does in the course of advocating changes mention the duties of the exchequer officers. It is of greater value to modern scholars than it would have been to eighteenth-century revenue officials. Moreover, it would not have been easy to use as a reference work for quick consultation. The Edwards–Herne and Lowndes memoranda were useful and often copied, as we have seen, but they are both scanty in comparison with Squibb's tract. The *Dialogue of the Exchequer* and the scholarship of Thomas Madox were too antiquarian for official eighteenth-century purposes.

The exchequer was at its height of importance as the collection

[61] See Bryson, 'Exchequer Equity Bibliography', *American Journal of Legal History*, xiv (1970), pp. 340, 341.

[62] *Ibid*, pp. 333–9, 348; and see above in the discussion of copies H and I.

agency of the national revenue at the time when Squibb wrote. The only other significant work on the subject, the treatise by Peter Osborne, was seventy years old. In the interim the offices of the receivers and auditors for recusants revenue were set up. In addition to describing the duties of these new officers, Squibb also added to Osborne's work by including sections on the clerk of the pipe, the surveyor of the green wax, and the usher of the receipt. Thus Squibb's tract was the most modern of the substantial tracts on the subject. Moreover, it was a comprehensive and competent compilation of exchequer information and was easy to use.

It is very fortunate for modern scholarship that once these copies had been made and used and had become antiquated they were still preserved rather than discarded. We have seen how two at least, E and N, can be traced back to their first owners. Probably J also was made by or for the man who was the earliest owner known to us, Thomas Jett. In addition it is likely that K was made for Bromley; however, it is unknown where this copy was after 1903 and before it came to the exchequer and audit department, which was sometime before 1937.

These copies of our tract were made primarily for exchequer purposes. They were preserved also by and for exchequer officials; however, their preservation is due as much or even more to persons who had no exchequer connections. To the antiquarians and manuscript collectors, Richard Rawlinson, Isaac Reed, Shelburne, Ashburnham, Professor Foxwell, is due the greatest share of praise. It was Rawlinson who rescued B, the earliest copy that we have. Serjeant Hill, William Bromley, M.P., and Lord Chancellor Truro apparently acquired their copies for legal purposes. It was family interest which led B. T. Fanshawe to purchase H, one of the more interesting ones. The place of family archives, the Public Record Office, the great libraries of the bibliophiles, the universities, and the Inns of Court is also forcefully brought to mind. And it is fitting and proper indeed to end this section with another refrain of praise for the British Museum, which has preserved six copies of Squibb's valuable work.

III. *Editorial Practice*

The conclusion of the examination of the manuscripts is that the proper exemplar for this edition is the copy in the Bodleian Library. Except for the rough draft in the Public Record Office, this is the only one which could have been made before 1692 or as early as 1642. The date of the manuscript is unknown save that it must have been made before 1755, when it was bequeathed to the Bodleian Library. Internal evidence suggests also that this is the earliest copy which we have in the descent of the tract.

The additions and corrections, which were made in 1692 and later, appear to have been made in three stages. They all seem to be the work of knowledgeable people, and all of the additions have therefore been included in this edition. They are in italics; since the copyist of B never used italics, there should be no danger of confusing the old and the new. The additions were made by several persons, and it cannot be said that one of these later manuscripts is much better than another; they have therefore been transcribed with modern orthography. The resulting edition thus comprises the Bodleian copy, printed in its entirety in roman type, together with enlargements from the several later sources in italic type. Where the 1692 material is a substitution rather than a mere addition, parallel columns have been used.

In general the principles of editing used are those suggested in the *Bulletin of the Institute of Historical Research*, i (1923), pp. 6–25. However, i, j, u, and v have been rendered in their modern form since this is a matter of calligraphy rather than linguistics.[63] Variant readings which are no more than scribal errors have been ignored. Mr. J. C. Sainty of the Institute of Historical Research in London has very generously allowed me to use his voluminous notes on the personnel of the treasury; wherever in the footnotes I am indebted to him, I have put his initials in brackets.

The apparatus can not and does not pretend to be complete. However, it is hoped that the notes given may be of use to aid further research in financial and administrative history.

[63] See H. Maxwell Lyte, ' "U" and "V"—A Note on Palaeography,' *B.I.H.R.*, ii (1925), pp. 63–5.

[*p. 1*] A Booke of all the Severall Officers of the Court of Exchequer, together with the names of the present officers, in whose guift and how admitted.

With a breife Colleccion of the cheife heads of what every officer usually doth, by vertue of his office, According to the State of the Exchequer at this day. January 1641.[b]

[a] In fact the references here are to pages.
[b] The date is omitted in C, D, E, G, and H1; '1692' is added in a different hand in F; 'at this day January 1641' is replaced by 'Anno domini 1692' in J, K, L, M, and N.

The Kings Remembrancer

Richard Fanshaw[1] esquire is the present officer and holdeth his place by lettres Pattents under the great Seale of England is in the Kings guift and admitted by taking oath in open Court before the Barons of the Exchequer. Hee hath two joyned in Patent[2] with him that are to succeede him Mr. William Litton & [   ] Ayliffe.

Henry Ayloffe[3] *Esquire is the present officer and holdeth his place by letters patent[4] of King Charles the Second under the Great Seal of England dated the 7th of August in the 12th year of his Reign to be executed by himself or his sufficient deputy or deputies. It is in the king's gift, And he is admitted by taking the oath in open court before the Barons of the Exchequer. And he hath a yearly fee out of the Receipt of the Exchequer of £55.17.4.*

It is said that Mr. Ayloffe hath this office in trust[5] for my lord Fanshawe[6] the youngest son of Sir Thomas Fanshawe his father who was made lord Fanshawe by King Charles the Second.[7]

Hee hath eight Clerkes or Atturnyes within his office, in his owne Guifte, which are admitted by him selfe and an oath administred before him, by vertue whereof they enjoy their places during their lives.

[1] Brother of Sir Thomas Fanshawe (later first viscount Fanshawe); Richard, a royalist and his successor as king's remembrancer, was appointed on 28 September 1644 (E.159/484, Mich. 20 Car. 1, rec. ro. 23); he was created a baronet on 2 September 1650 and died 16 June 1666: *D.N.B.*; A. Fanshawe, *Memoirs of Ann Lady Fanshawe*, ed. H. C. Fanshawe (London, 1907).

[2] Dated 5 August 1641 and enrolled at E.159/481, Trin. 17 Car. 1 rec. ro. 57; the reversioners were Rowland Litton and William Ayloffe; a blank space was left in the MS. because Squibb was confused as to their names. Ayloffe (later 3rd baronet Ayloffe) was a first cousin of Thomas and Richard Fanshawe: H. C. Fanshawe, *History of the Fanshawe Family* (Newcastle-upon-Tyne, 1927), pp. 33, 34.

[3] Brother of William Ayloffe; see note 2.

[4] Dated 7 August 1660 and enrolled at E.159/501, Mich, 12 Car. 2, rec. ro. 67; his predecessor Thomas Fanshawe, 2nd visc. Fanshawe, died in office in May 1674 (*D.N.B.*), and he died in office 13 September 1708: see E.159/553, Mich. 7 Ann., rec. ro. 122.

[5] There was a long and complicated lawsuit in the exchequer in regard to this trust: see W. H. Bryson, *The Equity Side of the Exchequer* (forthcoming), chap. 3, part 1, sect. F.

[6] This is an error; the beneficiary of the trust was Charles Fanshawe, 4th visc. Fanshawe, the next to youngest son of Thomas 1st visc. Fanshawe (see notes 1 and 2); when Ayloffe died Charles refused to act, and his younger brother Simon became king's remembrancer (and later 5th visc. Fanshawe): *G.E.C.*, v, pp. 255–6; *D.N.B.*; Fanshawe, *Hist. of the Fanshawe Family*, pp. 116–24.

[7] On 5 September 1661: *G.E.C.*, v, p. 255; see also notes 1, 2, and 6.

The present Atturnyes[8] are Martin Boothby,[9] Anthony Bourcher,[10] Nathaniell Hall,[11] Sir Symon Fanshaw,[12] Walter Hillary,[13] Ellis Young,[14] Edward Burgh[15] & John Payne[16] whereof the two first are called secondaries and have a small fee[17] from his Majesty. [*p. 2*] All English Bills[18] in the Exchequer are within this office, and the proceedings thereof much agreeing to that of the Chauncery, as by Bill, Answere, Replication and Rejoynder.

The Cause being at issue, wittnesses are examined in Court before the Barons[19] or by Comission[20] in the Country.[21]

And being ready for hearing is sett downe to be heard *in the Exchequer Chamber at Westminster in Court* by the Lord Treasurer Chauncellor of the Exchequer or Barons *& in the vacation at one of the Serjeants' Inns.*

The writts are first Subpena, upon not appearing affidavit is made of serving of the Subpena upon which an attachment[22] goes out of course,[23] then an alias and a Plures,[24] afterwards a writt of proclamacion[25] and lastly a Comission of Rebellion.[26]

Breife notes of all Orders pronounced either in the Exchequer

[8] In 1692 the attorneys were Thomas Hall, George Watts, Francis Butler, Gabriel Armiger, William Bathurst, William Walker, Thomas Eyre, and John Thompson.

[9] Boothby was in office from 1619 to 1648.

[10] Bourchier was in office from before 1630 to 1652.

[11] Hall was in office from 1622 to 1661.

[12] Sir Simon Fanshawe was in office from 1620 to 1647; he was the brother of Thomas and Richard Fanshawe: see notes 1 and 6.

[13] Hillary was in office from 1636 to 1655.

[14] Young (usually spelled Yonge) was in office from 1638 to 1659.

[15] Burgh was in office from 1639 to 1642.

[16] Payne was in office from 1638 to 1671.

[17] See below, p. 103.   [18] E.112.

[19] E.133.

[20] *I.e.*, commission or writ of *dedimus potestatem* to take the depositions of witnesses.

[21] E.134.

[22] *I.e.*, a writ of *attachiamento facias* to the sheriff to arrest the defendant who was in contempt of court for not obeying the original subpoena (*ad respondendum*) to appear and answer the bill of complaint.

[23] A writ of course was one which was issued by the court clerks automatically upon the request of a party; it was not necessary to have an order or to get permission from a judge.

[24] *I.e.*, an *alias attachiamento* and a *pluries attachiamento*, which were only repetitions of the original writ of attachment.

[25] If the defendant could not be found and so could not be arrested, a writ of proclamation was sent out by virtue of which it was proclaimed in the county that the defendant appear and answer upon his allegiance to the crown.

[26] This writ declared the defendant to be a rebel to be arrested by anyone anywhere; it was similar to the common law writ of outlawry.

Chamber upon hearings[27] or in the outer Court*c* upon Mocions,[28] are taken by the Kings Remembrancer himselfe, or such of his office as hee shall appoint to doe it And there upon the Atturnyes for the partie drawe the same up in forme,[29] either for *the* plaintiff or defendant and then they are entred into Bookes[30] by his Clerkes, which are accompted as Registers But are noe sworne officers. *whereof one is Mr. Henry Ayloffe, Register for the orders of the outward court and the other is Mr. George Morrison Register for the decretal orders who are accountable to the master*[31] *of the office.*

Att certaine dayes prefixed in the Terme he ought to call to accompt in open Court all the great accomptants, as [*the*] *treasurer of their majesties chamber, pay-master of the works, master of the robes,* the Cofferar, Master of the great Wardrobe, Clerke of the Hanaper, *treasurers of the navy and ordnance, pay-master general of the army and garrisons,* [p. 3] victualler of the Navy & such like, And all *cashiers, receivers, comptrollers, and* Collectors of Customes and Subsidies *and impositions,* And all Searchers for the moyety of all forfeitures.

Hee receiveth the *duplicates or rolls oj assessment or* Subsidie rolls[32] of all the Counties of England, and calleth to *an* accompt all *the receivers and* Collectors of Subsidies & fifteenes, as they are appointed and certified into his office by the *respective* Comission every where for the assessing and levying ot the same, according to their dayes of payment appointed them by *the respective* Statutes *whereby they are charged and payable.*

Hee receiveth the Certificates *half yearly* from *the writer of the tallies called* the Auditor of the Receipt of all monyes imprested out of the Exchequer for which men ought to come to *an* accompt.

Hee maketh out processe of Distringas[33] (or ought so to doe) against all accomptants that are slacke, to bring them in to accompt, and such as come not in upon the first processe, against them hee is to issue an alias Distringas, and then a Plures and then a Capias[34] to take the bodies to compell them to an accompt, and may also make out processe[35] against *the* Lands goods and Tenements where neede shall require *which is done by order of court.*

c 'Chamber' in C, D, E, F, G, and H1.

---

[27] Minute Books: E.162.   [28] Minute Books: E.161.

[29] The original, loose decrees and orders: E.128–131.

[30] The entry books of decrees and orders: E.123–127.

[31] The king's remembrancer was the master of the exchequer office.

[32] E.179.   [33] *I.e.*, a writ of distraint to seize chattels.

[34] *I.e.*, a writ of arrest.

[35] Probably a writ of *extendi facias* (extent) since the writ of *fieri facias* did not reach realty.

Hee only taketh all Bonds and Recognizances to the Kings use, of all Shereiffs, Customers, Comptrollers, *receivers of assessments or subsidies and all other* Receivors, Bayliffes, and all other persons what so ever that are bound in the Exchequer.

[*p. 4*] For monies due upon bond or Recognizances, he may ex officio send forth Extents,[36] *And* If the Condicions bee not absolutely for payment of monie, hee may send forth writts of scire facias[37] at first & afterwards Extents.

In his office are all manner of Informacions upon penall statutes[38] Intrusions, Concealment & the like, put in & sued *in the Exchequer and* with matters *as* Recognizances & bonds proceeding upon the same.

After every Bishopps death he maketh the Record of his Mulcture of his best house,[d] ring and Cupp &c seized to his Majestys use or of the fine made thereof.

Hee keepeth all Judgments, fines, Recoveries, Deeds, Charters & other evidences[39] whatsoever brougt into the Court by anie person for the assurance of anie Lands or tenements belonging to the Crowne.

He keepeth an entry of record of the accounts of the excise after they are declared before the chancellor of the exchequer and the lord high treasurer or commissioners of the treasury of the exchequer which are transmitted from them to the treasurers remembrancer.

Hee receiveth all Shereiffes forraine[40] accounts,[41] Accompts of Escheators,[42] *and accounts of* Customers[43] *Receivers and* Collectors of *assessments* Subsidies & fifteenes, *and other aids and impositions granted in Parliament,*[44] *post office,*[45] *wine license,*[46] *and coinage duty*

---

[d] *I.e.,* 'horse' as in G, H2, J, K, L, M and N; 'house' corrected in margin in F.

---

[36] *I.e.,* writs of *extendi facias* to seize the debtor's realty.

[37] The writ of *scire facias* lay to prosecute a debt or matter of record; it required the defendant or debtor to show cause why the debt should not be paid.

[38] *E.g.,* E.148; see also G. R. Elton, 'Informing for Profit', *Star Chamber Stories* (London, 1958), chap. 3.

[39] Perhaps E.118, E.210–214.

[40] For the foreign and declared accounts, see *Guide to the Contents of the Public Record Office*, i (London, 1963), pp. 50–4, 70–4; see also E.102 and below under the sections on the lord treasurer's remembrancer, the clerk of the pipe, the auditor of the imprests, and the seven auditors of the exchequer.

[41] E.364; see also E.199.

[42] E.357; see also E.136, E.153.

[43] E.351/607–1268; see also E.356, E.122.

[44] E.359; see also E.179.

[45] E.351/2731–2789.   [46] E.351/3153–3197.

&c. and of the treasurers of the navy[47] *and ordnance,*[48] *victuallers of the navy,*[49] *treasurer of the chamber,*[50] Cofferar, *master of the robes, master of the revels,*[51] *paymaster of the works,*[52] *master of the wardrobe,*[53] *hanaper,*[54] *and mint*[55] &c and taketh the totall of the debts due thereupon & putteth them to the Treasurers Remembrancer to be there likewise entred to the end *that* the debts may be put into the viewes of every yeares Remembrance, that he to whome it appertaines may make processe upon the same that noe super or debt be suffered to be out of processe untill it be discharged. This Article being performed is much for his Majestys service.

[*p. 5*]   Hee ought to informe the Lord Treasurer, *or lords commissioners of the treasury*, or Chauncellor or Barons *of the exchequer* or the Kings Atturny of all debts & arreages &c. & all suits and pleas in his office depending thereupon to drive thinges to an issue for the recovery of the Kings debt.

Hee sendeth every Hillary & Trinity terme severall parchment blancke bookes[56] to all the Customers, Comptroulers, Surveyors, Collectors & searchers of all the Ports of England *and Wales* for the entries of all the Customes & subsidies and afterwards receiveth the same againe, by the oath of the said officers in open Court or before one of the Barons, that they have made all true entries of the same as they ought to doe, *which are returned with all bonds*[57] *entered into with their majesties by any masters of ships in the said ports touching their trade from port to port and performance of the condition therein expressed.*

Hee readeth all the oathes that the officers of the Court of Exchequer doth take before the *lord chancellor or* Lord Keeper *or commissioners of the Great Seal, Chancellor* and Barons *of the Exchequer.*

Hee maketh the prerogative writt[58] of the Court for all officers & ministers of the Exchequer & receipt, that be sued els where to remove the plaint before the Barons or to surcease the suite.

Hee sendeth the redd booke[59] by one of his Atturnies with the

---

[47] E.351/2193–2598; see also E.101.
[48] E.351/2599–2713; see also E.101.
[49] E.351/2193–2598; see also E.101.
[50] E.351/541–568.
[51] E.351/1794–1948, 3024–3152.
[52] E.351/3199–3615; see also E.101/458–504, 667–683.
[53] E.351/1794–1948, 3024–3152; see also E.361, E.101.
[54] E.351/1591–1722; see also E.101/211–229, 619, 672, 673.
[55] E.351/2030–2192; see also E.101/288–307, 620, 667, 674.
[56] Port books: E.190.   [57] Coast bonds: E.209.
[58] *I.e.*, the writ of prohibition.
[59] E.164/2 (ed. H. Hall (Rolls Series, 1897)).

fifth Baron[60] to the Kings Bench or Common Pleas to remove anie matter sued there against anie officer, minister or accomptant that prayeth the priviledge of the Court, uppon which redd booke shewed & the parties so testified by the Baron to be [*p. 6*] of the Court his priviledge is thereupon ordinarilie allowed.

There is a fee of £45.12.0 payable every year to their majesties remembrancer out of the customs in lieu of the ancient fees for passing of the accounts of the customs of England and Wales out of which there is payable to the first secondary £7.0.0.

A yearly fee of £4 is payable out of the receipt of the exchequer unto each of the secondaries—£4.0.0.

A fee of £15.6.8 is payable every second year out of the receipt of the exchequer unto the eight sworn clerks in the office of their majesties remembrancer for charging of amerciaments, out of which there is due to the first secondary £3.0.0.

[*p. 7*]   Treasurers Remembrancer

The Lord Treasurers Remembrancer of the Exchequer is an office granted by patent under the great seale of England, & in the [   ][61] Guift.

Sir Peter Osborne[62] is the present officer and is admitted by taking oath in open Court before the Barons of the Exchequer.

Hee hath under him in his office Twelve sworne Clerkes or Attornies, *but the business of that Office being much diminished, by taking away the Court of Wards & Liveries by Act of Parliament*[63] *he hath now no more than six,* which are by him admitted & their oath administred before himselfe. The two aunscientest of them are called Secondaries of that office *and there is also a deputy remembrancer who is now Learned Diggs Esq.*

---

[60] The cursitor baron, a minor official who had no judicial functions; see E. Foss, *Judges of England*, (London, 1848–64), vi, pp. 16–27, ix, p. 109; E. Foss, 'On the Origin of the Title and Origin of Cursitor Baron of the Exchequer', *Archaeologia*, xxxvi (1855), pp. 23–32; *Procs. of the Soc. of Antiquaries*, iii (1856), pp. 118–23.

[61] Space left blank for 'king's': see 'A Brief Collection of the Principal Under Officers' (Brit. Mus., MS. Harl. 830), f. 218.

[62] Osborne received a grant in reversion for life by a patent dated 29 June 1605 (P[atent] R[oll] 3 Jac. 1, pt. 19: C.66/1681); he succeeded to the office 4 Nov. 1628 and died in March 1654. In 1692 this officer was Sir John Osborne bart., who received a grant in reversion for life by a patent dated 16 Apr. 1639 (P.R. 15 Car. 1, pt. 9: C.66/2849); he succeeded to the office in March 1654; he received new grants 27 May 1662 (P.R. 14 Car. 2, pt. 6: C.66/3008) and 20 October 1674 (P.R. 26 Car. 2, pt. 7: C.66/3162) [J.C.S.]; see also *D.N.B.*

[63] Stat. 12 Car. 2 (1660) c. 24, *Stat. Realm*, v, pp. 259–61.

The present Clerkes[64] are Henry Osborne, Thomas Gundry, William Wymondshall, William Tuthill, Thomas Stich, Nicholas Turbervile, Thomas Osborne, Edward Badby, Richard Dawson, Richard Barlow, John Tuthill & Edward Reynolds.[65]

To this office belongs the duty of execution upon the originalls[66] estreated to him yearely out of the chauncery which conteyne all graunts that passe under the great seale and all Commissions that passe under the great seale.

Upon those, where rents are reserved, he causeth the same to be prepared for the Clerke of the Pipe, & to be drawne downe into the great Roll,[67] from whence they are written have[e] yearelie to the Shereiffes [*p. 8*] to leavy in their respective Counties.

Where accomptes are to be rendred *by any sheriff, bailiff or farmer of liberties* he causeth processe to be made forth against the parties, ad reddendum Compotum.

Where anie tenure is reserved,[68] hee causeth processe to be awarded against the tenants to doe their service to the King be it homage or Fealty, as also for Releives where they are due.

To this office originals out of Chancery, being transcripts of all grants of lands, or offices which pass the great seal, wherein any rent is reserved to the Crown are to be triennially transmitted, to the end that those rents may be drawn in charge to the great roll of the pipe.

In this office is yearely made a Roll called the Roll of profferrs,[69] by which the Sheriffs every Easter & Michaelmas are called in the Exchequer to pay their profferrs, which is *a payment certain by advances out of* the proffitts of their Counties, *expressed to be de* [   ] *Balivi* being auntient Rents, & the somes certaine in every County & for nonpayment infra mensem Pasche & Michaeles they forfeite their Recognizances, & the default is to be certified by him to the Kings Remembrancer (where the Shereiffs bond remaines) who makes out processe thereupon.

In the same Roll is conteyned the Profferrs for Bayliffes of liberties, *which is also a sum certain and but small*, who making

[e] *I.e.,* 'half'.

---

[64] In 1692 they were George Blackwell, John Tayleure, William Scarborough, Ralph Butler, Charles Batley, and John Hamond.
[65] Wymondshall, Stitch, T. Osborne, Badby, Dawson, and Reynolds are mentioned in *Cal. S.P. Dom., Add. 1625–1649,* p. 754 (1643?).
[66] E.371.
[67] *I.e.,* the great roll of the pipe (pipe roll): E.372.
[68] *Re* rents reserved, see E.365, E.380, E.381.
[69] E.375.

default are amerced by the Court & a Record thereof made in that office, & from that Record drawne downe into the great Roll of the Pipe, & from thence written forth to be leavyed.

[*p. 9*] In this office is yearely made a Roll by which all accomptants are called at their severall dayes of prefixcion, *which are days certain and known,* to passe their accompts & their defaults *are* there entred, and soe they are proceeded against according to the Course of the Exchequer.

Into this office are transcripted out of the Petty bagge all Inquisicions taken post mortem,[70] from whence are abstracted all the Lands conteyned in them, which are holden of the king in cheife or by knights service of anie honors or Mannors, or of any mannor of the kings by rent, And are entred upon Record for preservacion of the kings tenures, And from thence is process awarded for the Releifes, Homage, & Fealties as the case shall require.

From hence all processe are made forth for all fines due to the king for Alienacions made of Lands holden with out licence, either by deed enrolled, Fines or recoveries.

From this office all processe issue against the kings tenantes to pay their respects*f* of homage, as also against all such as are intruders & purchase lands holden in cheife without the kings licence and those processe cease not but termely issue against them untill they have paid the fine for respect of Homage and the fine for Alienacion.

[*p. 10*] In this Office halfe yearely is made a Record of all issues forfeited for the Causes aforesaid, & by him delivered over to the Clerke of the Estreates, whoe writes them forth to the Sheriffe for the leavying the same.

Hee taketh all estreates[71] of fines issues & amerciamentes sent into the Court *of Exchequer* from the Kings Bench, Common Pleas, Justices of Assize & all Justices of peace through England which are by him delivered over by the rolls of streats, to the Clerke of the Extreates to write out, who setts his hand for the receipt of the same.

In this office is entred[72] the viewe of all Shereiffes accompts & of other Accomptants togeather with the some of each mans debt thereupon.

Out of this office issue all processe *of nomine destrictionis* against all such Shereiffes as passe not their accomptes in due time; *which is against body, goods and lands.*

f I.e., 'respites'.

---

[70] E.149, E.150.   [71] Probably E.137; see also E. 362.
[72] In the lord treasurer's remembrancer's memoranda roll (E.368) in the 'Status et Visus' section.

Hee makes entries[73] of all discharges for anie debts charged in the Sherieffs accounts either by vertue of the kings pardon, or privy Seale, or by warraunt from the Lord Treasurer *or commissioners of the treasury* or the Chauncellor of the Exchequer or by Judgment or order of the Court *of Exchequer.*

[*p. 11*] In this office an entry is made of all allowances given to Shereiffes by warrant of the Lord Treasurer, *Lords Commissioners of the Treasury* or the Chauncellor of the Exchequer for anie extraordinary expences.

From hence all proces issue for all debts that are charged in the great Roll of the Pipe[74] And for all debts in super before the Auditors which proces goes against the bodies, the goods & the Lands of debtors, & if anie leavy be made a Record is thereupon made up & the mony charged downe into the pipe upon the Shereiffe whoe is not discharged thereof untill he bring his Talley of the payment.

Out of this office issue all proces and Commicions against *all* Recusants for seizing of their goods & tow parts of their Lands to satisfye their xxˡⁱ per mensem for not coming to church according to the Statute.[75]

From hence speciall Comissions are awarded either for surveying of the Kings Lands or woodes or to enquire of concealements by warrant from the Treasurer *Commissioners of the Treasury* or Chauncellor *of the Exchequer* or by order of the Court.

In this office are made & kept upon Record all Liveries, Ousterlemaynes, & other pleadings that concerne and preserve the kings Tenures.

In this office abstracts are entered[76] *by the first secondary of the cash accounts of the subsidy of tonnage and poundage and of all duties and impositions upon merchandise granted to the Crown by act of parliament and of the commissioners and governors of excize, and of the general post office and penny post office and of the commissioners for managing the duty of wine licences and of the coinage duty and of the treasurers of the navy and of the victuallers of the navy and the pay master general of their majesties armies, forces, guards and garrisons and of the master of the ordnance and of the treasurer of the chamber and the cofferer of their majesties household and of the keeper of the great wardrobe and of the gentleman and master of the robes and of the paymaster of their majesties works and buildings and of the master and worker of the mint, all which*

[73] E.368.   [74] E.372.

[75] Stat. 23 Eliz. 1 (1581) c. 1, s. 4, *Stat. Realm*, iv, p. 657; Stat. 29 Eliz. 1 (1587) c. 6, ss. 2–4, *Stat. Realm*, iv, p. 771.

[76] Declared and foreign accounts: E.368 'States and Views of Public Accounts'; see also under king's remembrancer, clerk of the pipe, auditor of the imprests, and seven auditors of the exchequer.

are transmitted over by him to the clerk of the pipe, who makes forth a quietus to the several accountants respectively thereupon.
[p. 12 is blank]

[p. 13]   Clerke of the Pipe

Sir Henry Crooke knight[77] hath his place by letters Patents under the great Seale of England & of the kings guifte. Sir Robert Crooke[78] (his sonne) is joyned in Pattent with him, Hee is admitted & sworne in open Court before the Barons.

Reversion after them granted to Thomas Jermyn & Henry Jermyn esquires.

Robert Russell Esquire[79] is now clerk of the pipe. He hath his place by letters patent under the great seal of England dated the 31st day of August in the first year of their majesties reign to hold to him and his deputies during their majesties pleasure.[80] He is admitted and sworn in open court before the barons of the exchequer.

Hee hath power by his Patent to make a Deputy, *or deputies as aforesaid* & hath eight sworne Clerkes or Attornyes,[81] (whereof the 2 seniors are called Secondaries) sworne & given by him, vizt. Christopher Vernon[82] & William Gifford secondaries Richard Carrell Benjamin Wallinger John Billingsly, William Burnett, Francis Boyton,[83] & Nicholas Heymor.

John Burton & John Bonnett *are* called Clerkes of the Boards end[84] are the Masters Clerkes, & attend him but are not sworne.

Christopher Masters is his Deputy or Clerke for the Custodie of all the Records of the late Court of Augmentacions.[85]

In this Office is made a yearely charge of all the antient Revenues of the Exchequer which were before the late Court of Augmentacions & the first fruites & tenthes.

---

[77] His patent is dated 29 July 1616, and he was admitted 6 October 1616 (P.R. 14 Jac. 1, pt. 7: C.66/2096; K.R. memoranda roll Mich. 14 Jac. 1, recorda ro. 457: E.159/451); he died on 1 January 1660. [J.C.S.]

[78] His patent is dated 15 November 1632 (P.R. 8 Car. 1, pt. 1: C.66/2592); he succeeded to the office in 1660 and died 8 February 1681. [J.C.S.]

[79] Clerk of the pipe from 1689 to 1703; his successor's patent is dated 19 August 1703 (P.R. 2 Ann., pt. 4: C.66/3441). [J.C.S.]

[80] P.R. 1 Will. & Mar., pt. 5: C.66/3329. [J.C.S.]

[81] In 1692 they were Walter Wallinger, Thomas Cole, Joseph Cranmer, Charles Milbourne, Philip Tully, Simon Musgrave, Peter Froude, and William Wroth.

[82] Also surveyor of the greenwax; author of *Considerations for Regulating the Exchequer* (London, 1642).

[83] Vernon, Carrell, Wallinger, Burnett, and Boyton are mentioned in *Cal. S.P. Dom., Add. 1625–1649*, p. 754 (1643?).

[84] In 1692 they were Joseph Horneby and William Prowse; the former was also the clerk of the leases.

[85] In 1692 Simon Musgrave.

[*p. 14*] Hee putteth in charge yearely in his booke called the great Roll[86] all Accompts of Shereiffes & Escheators, all accompts of Bayliffes & men of certaine townes, that are called to accompt by the Treasurers Remembrancer.

Hee after the Forraine Apposer hath made up the some of the Greenewax of every Sherieffe & delivered the same into the pipe doth make the next charge of the Sheriffe (for the Greenewax) which riseth of the Estreats[87] of the fines, issues, & amerciaments, *and post fines*[88] that come from the Kings Bench, Common Pleas, Justices of assize, The Kings or Treasurers Remembrancers side.

Hee chargeth every Sheriffe with his casualties which are all manner of debts as Releifes, Fines, amerciaments, *or felons or outlawed men's goods when they happen concerning which a particular oath is made before a baron and transmitted to him.* Sheriffs debts recovered, & such like that are drawne downe either from anie Record or from the Remembrancers of the Exchequer, or from anie other ground, matter or seizure of the Court, and soe *are by him* brought together *and charged upon record.*

All fee farmes or anie rent reserved, or other farmes that are to be paid at the Receipt of Exchequer or to the hands of the Sheriffe are to be charged and accompted for in the Pipe office.

[*p. 15*] All manner of debts recovered by Judgement in the Kings Remembrancers office & the Treasurers Remembrancers office, are to be drawne downe into the Pipe.

Hee hath yearely a booke called the Customers Roll[89] into which every Customers charge is conveyed, & the debts & remaynes are from thence put into the great Roll, & summoned out from schedula Pipe, to be a ground for the Treasurers Remembrancer to make proces by.

Hee hath the like Rolls[90] for all *assessments, taxes, aids,* Subsidies & Fifteenes *granted to the Crown by act of Parliament,* the debts whereof are also conveyed into the great Roll to be charged and summoned out, [91] or *if not answered then* written forth by proces from schedula Pipe[92] by the Treasurers Remembrancer.

[86] The pipe roll: E.372.
[87] Probably E.137, see also E.362.
[88] E.374.
[89] Probably E.364, cf. customs accounts: E.351/607–1268.
[90] E.364, E.359.
[91] For examples of summonses of the pipe, see E.206, E.370/116–122.
[92] *E.g.*, E.370/106.

All accompts are to be ingrossed in the Pipe, & if anie debt remaine upon the accomptant, to be written out & likewise all under supers, that are sett of from any of the accompts are to be written forth in proces.

All accounts are to be engrossed in the pipe, and if any debts remain in super upon the accountant, or any other person, it is first to be written out in summons, and if not answered then transmitted to the treasurer's remembrancer in schedula pipae for process of extent against body, goods, and lands.

All such debtors as pay their monie into the Receipt are to have their Tallies Joyned *by the chamberlains* & allowed upon the Record in the Pipe office, & soe to be acquited.

The residue that stand undischarged are written out in proces by the Comptroller of the Pipe to the Sheriffe who coming [*p. 16*] to accompt, chargeth himselfe with as manie as are leavyable, & for such other debts, as he retornes the debtors to be dead having noe goods or chattells &c they are put into schedula Pipe for the Lord Treasurers Remembrancer to make out proces according to the auntient Course of thexchequer.

All conviccions of Recusants, certified by the Clerkes of Assize & Clerkes of the peace are presently conveyed into schedula pipe, for proces or Commissions to be made thereon, out of the Treasurers Remembrancers office to seize their goods, & tow parts of their Lands.

Hee hath the drawing & making of all leases of lands[93] that are to passe under the Exchequer seale, All Leases upon Extents & Outlawries, All graunts of Custodies, Stewardshipps, Bayliwickes & Gaugers.

[*p. 17*]   The particuler heads & Braunches of his Majesties Revenue certaine & casual charged in the Pipe.

Certainties

{
The vicontells, Custodies, feefarms.
The Minute farmes being rents reserved, Assart lands, Ulnages & new draperies, Farmers of Customes, *poundage and impositions upon merchandise when not in farm.*
Lands extended for debts & granted by Lease.
Lands extended for want of licence of Alienacion.
Rents reserved upon Lycences, & Farmes of Customes or imposicions.
Recusants Lands.
}

[93] *Cf.* drafts of leases: E.380.

Debts drawne
downe into
the Pipe
from the
kings
Remembrancers
office

{ Recognizances & obligacions recovered.
Forfeitures & Fines upon penall statutes.
Spoyle of Woods, Amerciaments of Sheriffs.
Enstalments of debts by the Court.
Goods retorned by fieri feci.
Fines in the Exchequer Chamber, Fines upon
   port Bonds, Composicions for the penaltie of
   bonds & Recognizances forfeited & the debt
   paid.
Composicion upon Redemcion of lands forfeited.
Composicions for nomine penes for nonpayment
   of rent, *cash accounts of the treasurer of the
   chamber, and cofferers accounts and master of
   the ordnance and of the general and cash account
   of the customs, and the cash accounts of all new
   impositions upon merchandise and of the pay
   master general of the garrisons and land forces,
   and of all commissioners and governors of the
   excise, and of the master of the robes, and the
   general post office and penny post office together,
   and of the master of the mint, and commissioners
   for wine licences, and of the victuallers of the
   navy and treasurer of the navy and of the great
   wardrobe and coinage duty.*[94]

[*p. 18*]
from the lord
Treasurers
Remembrancer

{ Releifes for lands, Fines for respit of Homage,
   Castleward rents of Dover.
Amerciaments of sheriffes, Debts recovered upon
   Sheriffes & other accomptants by way of writt
   of fieri feci.
Recusants Lands & goods found by Comission.

Greenewax
certified from
the forraine
apposer into
the Pipe

{ Fines for licence of Concord.
Yssues of Jurors before the Justices of Assize
   and pease.
Fines amerciaments & Recognizances before the
   Justices of Peace & before the Justices of
   Assize.
Fines & issues before the King *in the court of
   Kings Bench.*
Fines issues & amerciaments in the Chancery in
   the Common Pleas & before the Barons of the
   Exchequer.
Fines & amerciaments before the Clerke of the
   markett & before the Commissioners of Sewers.

[94] Declared and foreign accounts: E.351, E.364, E.356–361; see also under
king's remembrancer, lord treasurer's remembrancer, auditor of the imprests,
and seven auditors of the exchequer.

From the Remembrancer of the First fruites & tenths—Amerciaments of sheriffs.
From the Clerke of the pleas—Amerciaments of Sheriffs.
From the Clerke of the Nichells—Recognizances nichild before the
forraine Apposer.

the Sheriffes forraine account	{ Rents of lands seized for want of Lycence of Alienacion, Felons Fugitives & attainted mens goods. Rents of lands seised for debts in the Kings & Lord Treasurers Remembrancers office.

[p. 19 is blank]

[*p. 20*] Comptroller of the Pipe

Francis Vernon esquire given & presented by the Chauncellor of
the Exchequer and sworne in open Court.[95]

Hee is to be present in Court at the Apposalls of every Sheriffe
upon the farmes & debts by him written out to them, by the
Summons & is to marke the awards of the Court for every farme &
debte in his Roll[96] & to be made privy to all manner of discharges, &
to see that all Sheriffs & Accomptants be duely & justly charged by
the Clerke of the Pipe, & by the Auditors upon their casting out of
the Court.

Hee writeth twice a yeare the Summons of the Pipe[97] to every
Sheriffe in the Realme. His first Summons every Hillary Terme, of
their vicondells, Feefarmes & oblata or old debts. His second
Summons, every Trinity Terme, wherein hee writeth his nova oblata
and casualties.

[*p. 21*] Surveyors of the Greenewax

William Cholmely & Christopher Vernon esquires[98] holdeth their
places by letters pattents under the great Seale of England & of the
kings guift.

[95] Vernon was admitted to office on 28 November 1632 (E.368/625, m. 91;
K.R. memoranda roll, Mich. 8 Car. i, recorda ro. 91: E.159/472). In 1692 the
office was held by John Pottinger, who was admitted on 7 February 1677
and died on 18 or 19 December 1733 [J.C.S.]

[96] The chancellor's roll: E.352.

[97] E.g., E.206, E.370/116–122.

[98] In 1692 Nathaniel Booth held this office alone; his patent was dated
5 September 1689.

This is an office newly erected *in the reign of King Charles the first* for the taking a viewe of all the Greenewax monyes that it might be knowne how much that Revenue doth yearely amount unto, & was intended for prevention of the granting of it in farme. But since this hath bin farmed out at a certaine rent they have beene imployed by the farmors as Receivors of that Revenue as I have bin informed.[99]

[*p. 22*]   Office of Pleas

George Long esquire[100] Master in the guift of the Chaunncellor *of the Exchequer* & presented by him to the Court whoe admitts him by giving him his oath, by vertue whereof hee holds it during life & hath noe other graunt.

Hee hath under him in his guift 4 Atturneyes or Clerkes[101] which he himselfe admittes by giving them their oath namely Samuel Tovey, William Ball, Dixie Long & Richard Palmer, *whereof the first named is secondary and first attourney.*

There are pleaded in this office all Common Pleas of the Exchequer, according to the course of the Common Law.

The writts that issue originally from hence are Quominus which is a capias & a Subpena, upon either of which writts when there is an apparance made the proceedings therein are little different from the course of the kings Bench.

In this office all the officers of the Exchequer theire Clerkes and servants, All his Majesties Tenants & farmors of his landes & Tenements & all manner of accomptants of the Court of Exchequer should be sued in or may implead one another, or anie Stranger in any accion upon the Case or for trespasse debt ejectione firme and such like as are sued in the Kings Bench.

[*p. 23*]   Hee hath all suites presented in his office betweene party and partie, that are removed out of any Court at Westminster by the redd booke[102] or out of anie Court of Record elsewhere in England by anie writt of priviledge, for any of the said persons that are priviledged, as before to sue & to be sued only there in the said

[99] In 1692 this revenue was farmed out to Lord William Paulet, second son of the duke of Bolton, by a patent dated 27 May 1690 for 41 years at the annual rent of £500.

[100] Long was admitted to office on 8 May 1619 (E.368/573, m. 120; K.R. memoranda roll, Pasch. 17 Jac. 1, recorda ro. 120: E.159/456). Thomas Marriott held this office from 1690 to 1724. [J.C.S.]

[101] In 1692 they were Thomas Arden, Charles Haynes, Samuel Anderson, and David Feilder.

[102] See above under king's remembrancer.

accions and noe where els, if they will in time clayme[103] and sue out their priviledge.

[*p. 24*] The two Chamberlaines

The Chamberlaines of the Exchequer are Sir Nicholas Carye[104] & Sir Edward Bash,[105] They have their offices graunted by letters Patents under the great Seale, & of the kings guifte they are admitted & sworne in open Court before the Barons.

They have two deputie Chamberlaines *in the court side of the exchequer* (besides those in the Receipt side) namely Alexander Stafford[106] & William Page[107] (who last is also Cursitor Baron of the Court) Theise deputies are presented by the cheife Chamberlaynes & then sworne in Court and have an exemplificacion of their admission out of the Treasurers Remembrancers office under the Exchequer Seale, & by vertue hereof doe hold it during life.

The Chamberlaines have places in the Exchequer Chamber & may sitt at the hearing of Causes but doe not at all intermedle in anie Cause They have antiently bene of great authoritie & trust, but now have little to doe (in the Receipt) save only *what is done* by their deputies.

Their two deputie Chamberlaines of the Court side comonly called the Joyners of the Tallies doe fetch the foyles of the Tallies from time to time from the Tallie Court & doe keepe them in a Roome appointed for that purpose under the Exchequer Court. When the parties doe bring their Tallies they seeke out the foyles of them, &

---

[103] *I.e.*, before a general appearance or issue pleaded; the cases are not clear as to which.

[104] Sir N. Carew-Throckmorton was made king's chamberlain for life by a patent dated 11 January 1612/13 (P.R. 10 Jac. 1, pt. 24: C.66/1966) and his successor was appointed on 3 April 1644. In 1692 this office was held by Sir Nicholas Steward, bart., by a grant for life dated 1 October 1660 (P.R. 12 Car. 2, pt. 24: C.66/2939) and he died on 15 February 1709/10. [J.C.S.]

[105] Bash was made Maudit chamberlain for life by a patent dated 21 May 1625 (P.R. 1 Car. 1, pt. 11: C.66/2358) and died on 12 May 1653. In 1692 this office was held by Philip Hilliard by a grant for life dated 16 February 1674/75 (P.R. 27 Car. 2, pt. 4: C. 66/3171) and his successor was appointed on 26 May 1693. [J.C.S.]

[106] Stafford was the deputy of Bash; he was appointed by Young on 23 June 1603 (E.403/878) and by Poyntz on 12 May 1613; Stafford's successor was appointed on 27 July 1660 (E.36/266, f. 84). Hilliard's deputy in 1692 was Henry Ballow, who held office as early as 1688. [J.C.S.]

[107] Page was appointed deputy by Carew-Throckmorton on 24 January 1614. Steward's deputy in 1692 was John Ady, who was appointed on 23 November 1672 (E.403/2464, p. 91) and his successor was appointed on 13 August 1696 (E.403/2469). [J.C.S.]

Joyne them to see if they agree & then they [*p. 25*] marke them with a marking Iron & delivereth the Tally into the pipe office where the letter & summe thereof is entred together with the day of Joyning & there are filed allowed & kept, & then the debt is discharged, But this course of Joyning of Tallies is now but little used & Quietus est taken from the pipe office instead thereof, *which is a great abuse.*

[*p. 26*]   First fruites office

Remembrancer of the first fruites[108] William Lord Harvey granted by the king by letters patents under the great Seale of England is admitted by taking oath in open Court before the Barons.

Reversions hereof granted [   ] Rogers & [   ].[109]

Hee hath three Clerkes or Attornies granted sworne & admitted before himselfe, by vertue whereof they hold their places during life The present Attornyes are William Wheeler, Mathias Presse and Thomas Baker.	*He hath two clerks or attorneys granted, and sworn and admitted before himself by vertue whereof they hold their places during life and a deputy, the present deputy is Robert Butler[g] Esquire. Mr. William Pettyman and Mr. Walter Smith are the two attorneys.*
Theise doe take all the bonds of the Clergie for payment of their first fruites & gives them foure dayes of payment according to the Statute. They certifie the Receivor in the masters name from time to time what each Incumbent is to pay.	*These do take all the bonds of the clergy for payment of their first fruits and give them four half years from institution for payment according to the statute, and when bond becomes due, they certify the receivers in the master's name the living, sum, and payment.*

And where there is fayling of payment they make out proces or Sequestracions *to the sheriff* for recovery thereof.

Also they make out proces against Bishops & their Collectors that pay not their tenths at the times appointed *and make out sequestrations to the bishops for levying the arrears of tenths of the clergy.*

Receivors of the first fruites Henry Knollys esquire grant[110] by the

g 'William Porter' according to J and K.

---

[108] In 1692 Sir Charles Porter, who was granted the office by a patent dated 28 April 1670 (P.R. 22 Car. 2, pt. 8: C.66/3121). [J.C.S.]

[109] The names of the reversioners were left blank.

[110] Knollys' patent is dated 6 May 1633 (P.R. 9 Car. 1, pt. 17: C.66/2631). This office was held in 1692 by Robert Squibb, who had patents dated 5 March 1685 (P.R. 1 Jac. 2, pt. 6: C.66/3267) and 15 August 1689 (P.R. 1 Will. & Mar., pt. 5: C.66/3329); his successor was appointed on 4 October 1694 (P.R. 6 Will. & Mar., pt. 9: C.66/3375). [J.C.S.] Lawrence Squibb had two nephews named Robert (PROB. 11/346, pt. 148); this was no doubt one of them.

king by letters patents, puts in security by the appointment of the Lord Treasurer *or Lords Commissioners of the Treasury when there is no treasurer, and he together with the remembrancer* accounts[111] once a yeare in Easter terme for the yeare ending the last of December before which are made up by one of the Auditors of the Imprests, & declared before the Barons of the Exchequer. [*p. 27*] There is a Reversion granted of this Receivors place to John Houston esquire.

Forraine Apposer

George Evelyn,[112] in the guift of the Lord Treasurer *or Lords Commissioners of the Treasury when there is no Lord Treasurer* & presented by him *or them* he sitting with the Barons in Court where he hath his oath given him, when he is sworne the Lord Treasurer *or Lords Commissioners respectively* delivers him a patent under his *or their* owne hand and Seale *or hands and seals* which is Recorded in the severall offices & then endorsed on the backside & all the Barons setts their hands to it testifying the time he was sworne by virtue where of he holds it during life.

Hee causeth all Sheriffes to retorne their sommons of Greenewax (which are made out by the Clerke of the Estreates) & at their dayes of prefixion by him appointed he doth appose them thereupon & what he hath received he Tots *or allows* & thother he Nichells, & what belongs to particuler Bayliffes of Liberties is sett over to them.

After Apposall he casts up all the sheriffes Charge into a Scrow being fayrely engrosed in parchment & by him signed & then transcribed into the Pipe office there to remayne a debt upon the Sheriffe; which he must pay or otherwise discharge.

[*p. 28*] Hee maketh forth Schedules to all Bayliffes of liberties to collect such monies as were sett over to them at the Apposall of the Sheriffes, And what is not Totted or sett over to the particuler Bayliffes of Liberties, Hee delivers over to the Clerke of the Nitchills.

Hee likewise makes a Certificate[113] of all the Justices wages that were sitting at the severall Sessions which is by him engrosed in parchment & signed by one of the Barons & by him carried to the pipe office, where the Sheriffe hath so much discharged out of his debet as that allowance comes unto.

[111] E.351/1521–1555.
[112] Evelyn was appointed on 31 March 1627 (E.403/2456, p. 139). In 1692 this office was held by Charles Whitaker, Jr., who was appointed on 8 February 1666 (E.403/2468, p. 147) and who died on 7 March 1711. [J.C.S.]
[113] E.370/71.

[*p. 29*]   Clerke of the Estreates

Anthonie Williams,[114] Given by the Lord Treasurer *or the Lords Commissioners of the Treasury when there is not a Treasurer, and is* admitted & sworne before the Treasurer & Barons in open Court, by Grant under the hand & seale of the Treasurer *or Lords Commissioners of the Treasury respectively* and signed by all the Barons, & holds it during life in the same maner as the forraine Apposer.

This officer Receives from the Treasurers Remembrancer the Estreates[115] of all *post fines*, Fines issues & amerciaments that are Estreated from the Clerkes of the Assize & Peace, Fines from the Kings Bench & Comon pleas, Clerke of the markett & Commissioners of Sewers Issues and amerciaments for not paying of Respits of Homage.

Out of every of theis he Extracts what is for every Countie, which he writes out in Sumons of Greenewax to the severall Sheriffes at the end of Hillary *term* and Trinity Terme.

[*p. 30*]   Clerke of the Nitchells

John Loope[116] is the present officer, This *office* is given & *the officer* presented by the Chauncellor of thexchequer & he takes his oath in open Court before the Barons and hath an Exemplificacion of his admission under the Exchequer Seale, by vertue whereof he holds it during life.

Hee repayreth to the Forraine Apposer & Clerke of the Estreates every yeare & seeth what nichills be marked in the whole liberate of the Greenewax sent out that yeare which nitchells be yssues that the sheriffe *that* is apposed doth say be nothing worth & illeviable for the insufficiency of the parties that should pay the same. Whereupon he drawes them downe into Schedules, or Rolls of parchment & delivers them over to the pipe office from whence proces is againe issued for the Recovery and leaving thereof.

[114] Williams' grant is dated 12 June 1627 (E.403/2456, p. 151). This office was held in 1692 by John Hastings by a grant dated 10 March 1690; his successor's grant is dated 11 May 1699 (E.403/2469, p. 185). [J.C.S.]

[115] E.137; see also E.362.

[116] Loope or Loup was admitted on 7 May 1636 (E.403/2459, p. 37) and was still in office in July 1668. [J.C.S.] In 1692 this office was held by Thomas Squibb according to J, K, L, M, and N; by Arnold Squibb according to Mr. Sainty and Wentworth *v.* Squib, 1 *Lutwich* 43, 125 *Eng. Rep.* 23 (C.P. 1701).

[p. 31] Clerkes of Parcells

John Taylor & Henry Coveny in the guift of the Lord Cheife Baron & sworne in open Court. They are to take the casuall accompts of Revenue of all Sheriffes, Escheators, Bayliffes of liberties & Mayors of Corporacions, for all waives,[h] Strayes, Fellons goods, Fugitives Outlawries, Treasure trove &c. And theis doe send out proces to cause these Accomptans to come & accompt before them.

They are to receive out of the Treasurers Remembrancers office sett downe in the Roll of Streates[117] there all Transcripts of offices sent yearely thither out of the Chauncery that be found by an Escheator through the Realme.

They make up the whole charge of the Escheators & other accomptants, & doe deliver the same to the Auditor that is assigned to engrosse & cast up the Accompt which is done verbatim according to the parcells by them delivered.

The parcel maker is an ancient office ordained in the time of King Richard the Second to make the parcels of all escheators' accounts and were used to receive out of the treasurer's remembrancer's office all the transcripts of offices sent thither yearly out of the chancery, which were found by an escheator throughout the realm, and out of those they were to collect into a particular roll the parcels wherewith every escheator was to be charged by the auditor to be assigned to engross and cast up the account which was to be done verbatim according to the parcels by them delivered but the escheators were in the time of Queen Elizabeth discharged from making accounts for any new escheats the same being put in charge in the court of wards, so as there was little or no use of their offices, and now that the court of wards is taken away by Act of Parliament[118] there is no such officer continued.

[p. 32] Auditors of the Imprests

John Worfeild[119] & George Bingley[120] esquires are recomended by the Lord Treasurer *or Lords Commissioners of the Treasury* & graunted by his Majestie under the great Seale of England during Life they are sworne in open Court before the Barons or out of Terme before the lord Treasurer *or Lords Commissioners of the Treasury, when there is no Lord Treasurer.*

[h] *I.e.,* 'waifs'.

---

[117] E.362.

[118] Stat. 12 Car. 2 (1660) c. 24, *Stat. Realm*, v, pp. 259–61.

[119] Worfield's grant is dated 1 March 1632 (P.R. 7 Car. 1, pt. 2: C.66/2561); he was still in office on 13 June 1643 (see *Docquets of Letters Patent*, ed. W. H. Black (London, 1837), p. 360). In 1692 this office was held by Thomas Done whose grant is dated 4 December 1677 (P.R. 29 Car. 2, pt. 9: C.66/3196) and who died before 16 January 1703 (*C.T.B.*, xviii, p. 111). [J.C.S.]

[120] Bingley's grant is dated 7 March 1632 (P.R. 7 Car. 1, pt. 11: C.66/2570); he succeeded to office in 1634 upon the death of Sir Richard Sutton (PROB. 11/165, part 53); he was still in office in 1643 (see *Docquets of Letters Patent*, p. 360). In 1692 this office was held by Brook Bridges whose grant is dated 21 May 1672 (P.R. 24 Car. 2, pt. 1: C.66/3134); he surrendered the office on 5 May 1705 (*C.T.B.*, xx, p. 247). [J.C.S.]

John Wood[121] hath a Revercion granted to succeed the first of theise that shall next fall voyd, & [   ] Beale[122] hath another Revercion to succeede that of John Woods.

Theis doe take the accompts of all persons that receive anie of his Majestys monies upon accompt to be disbursed for anie particuler service. They also take the accompts of all the great Accomptants *except of the excise for which an auditor is established by act of parliament.*

For every *great* accomptant they make three accompts[123] which are by them engrossed & signed by the Lord Treasurer *or Lords Commissioners of the Treasury* & Chauncellor whereof one is for the partie, another for themselves & the third [124] to be delivered into the pipe office, where it is to remayne for a Record & if anie monie be fond due upon anie accompt delivered, proces issues from thence for the recovery thereof.

The yearely accompts[125] by them taken are the Cofferar of his Majestys houshold, Treasurer of the Chamber, Treasurer of the Navy, Victualler of the Navy, Master of the great wardrobe, Master of the Robes, Wardens of the Minte, Master Workers of the monyes, Paymaster of the workes, Clerke of the Faculties, Clerke of the Hanaper, Receivor of first fruites, Cheife Butler of England, Liuetenante of the ordinance, Master of the Armoury, Master of the Posts, Master of the Tents & pavilions, Master of the Revells, Farmors & Collectors of the Customes Subsidies and Imposts.

[*p. 33*]   The seaven Auditors of thexchequer[126]

There were established upon the granting abbey lands to the crown and setting up the Court of Augmentations, but though that court was suppressed[127] these officers continue their places.

[121] Wood had a grant for life in reversion by a patent dated 24 July 1640 (P.R. 16 Car. 1, pt. 6: C.66/2873); he succeeded to the office before December 1660 (*C.T.B.*, i, p. 111); he died before 17 October 1670, the date of the warrant for the admission of Wilde, his successor (*C.T.B.*, iii, p. 672). [J.C.S.]

[122] Bartholomew Beale had a grant for life in reversion by a patent dated 17 August 1641 (P.R. 17 Car. 1, pt. 1: C.66/2890); he succeeded to the office before December 1660 (*C.T.B.*, i, p. 111); he died before 11 May 1674 (*C.T.B.*, iv, p. 520). [J.C.S.]

[123] The declared accounts; see *Guide to the Contents of the Public Record Office*, i, pp. 70–72.

[124] This copy passed through the king's remembrancer's and the lord treasurer's remembrancer's offices and is now E.351; see above under king's remembrancer, lord treasurer's remembrancer, and clerk of the pipe.

[125] A.O.1; see also A.O.3.

[126] They were also known as the 'auditors of the land revenues': *Guide to the Contents of the Public Record Office*, i, pp. 47, 89.

[127] It was annexed to the exchequer in 1554; see generally W. C. Richardson, *History of the Court of Augmentations* (Baton Rouge, 1961)

Their places are granted by Letters Patents under the great Seale of England recommended by the Lord Treasurer *or Lords Commissioners of the Treasury when there is no Treasurer* & sworne in open Court before the Lord Treasurer *or Lords Commissioners* and Barons.

A Revercion is granted to William Hill[128] to take place upon the first avoydance of anie of the seaven in being.

There is another Revercion graunted to John Phillips to succeed next after him, & a Third granted to Robert Worrell to take place after Mr. Phillips.

The present Auditors together with the Receivors are here under mencioned according to their severall Counties.

They take the accompts[129] of the severall Receivers according to their divisions, which are engrossed[130] in paper & brought in yearely before the xx[th] of March, & signed by the Lord Treasurer *or Lords Commissioners of the Treasury* or by the Chauncellor of the Exchequer which remaynes with the Senior Auditor Hill for a Comptrollment for the yeare following.

The account it selfe is afterwards engrossed[131] in parchment & declared before the Barons, which remaines with the severall Auditors according to theire divisions.

Aboute Michaelmas yearely they all goe their Circuits and keep their Audits in their severall Counties to take the accompts of Collectors, Bayliffes, Farmors & Feefarmes of his Majesties Lands, or of his Casuall Revenue within that Countie *to which they are appointed and of subsidies, monthly assessments, and other public aids granted in parliament by special direction.*

They also take the accounts of the Bishopps lands & rents (sede vacante) & of all Collectors of Subsidies & fifteenes of the Clergie & laytie granted by parliament.

And of all [*p. 34*] Sheriffes & Escheators & all other Revenue accompts, All seizures made and conveyed into the forraine accompt are engrossed by the severall Auditors.

The Sheriffes for wales are charged by that Auditor for all Greenewax totted there.

[128] A William Hill is listed below as auditor for Wales, and his name is not mentioned at the end of the list as a reversioner; thus it appears that his reversion fell in while this tract was being written. Mr. Sainty's notes show that a William Hill received a grant for life in reversion dated 21 May 1603 (P.R. 1 Jac. 1, pt. 18: C.66/1624); this was our Hill's father, see *Cal. S.P. Dom., 1637–1638*, p. 6.

[129] L.R.5, L.R.8, L.R.12; see also under king's remembrancer, lord treasurer's remembrancer, and clerk of the pipe.

[130] L.R.7.   [131] L.R.6.

And the Sheriffes of Chester before the Auditor of the Countie.

And the Sheriffes of Lancaster & Durham the like *manner in the reign of King Charles the First* by a late order made by the lords of his Majesties privy Councell.

[Receivors generall]

The Receivors generall are granted by the Lord Treasurer *or Lords Commissioners of the Treasury for the time being* & hath letters Pattents under the great Seale & hold their places during life. They put in Security in the Kings Remembrancers office at the appoint-ment of the Lord Treasurer *or Lords Commissioners of the Treasury* by warrant under his *or their* hand *or hands* & are not sworne.

There are noe revercions of their places at this present but some of their pattents are granted for two lives.

These goes their Circuits twice a yeare at our Lady day & Michaelmas, before which they send out their precepts to his Majesties fermors tenants Collectors & Bayliffes to attend at a certaine time & place by them (therein) appointed for the paying of his rents & duties within their severall Counties.

They are to accompt for the yeare ended at Michaelmas before the xx[th] of March following, & to pay all their monies due upon the determinacion of their accompt according to the Statute[132] 7° Ed. 6. *chap. 1st.* otherwise they & their suerties may be extended, & they forfeit the offices besides.

[*p. 35*]

Auditors	Counties	Receivors
	Kent Surrey Sussex	Henry Sandford[133] & Sir Richard Gurny[134] Lord Maior
	Bedford Buckingham	Thomas Daniell[136]
Sir Edmund Sawyer knight[135]	Oxford Berkshire	Michell Holman[137] & Mark Cottle[138] in trust for Richard Holman[139]
	Windsor Castle	Sir Robert Bennet[140] by order of thexchequer only Mr Windsor the present receiver by Patent put out by the Earl of Holland[141] for misdemeanors. Sir Charles Howard hath a revercion of this.

Auditors	Counties	Receivors
William Hill[142]	North Wales South Wales	Humphrey Jones[143] William Watkins[144]
Justinian Povey[146]	Essex Hertford London Middlesex Suffolke Cambridge Norfolke Huntington	Richard Abbott[145] Richard Miller[147] & [ ] Miller[148] Gilbert Havers[149]

[*p. 36*]

Auditors	Counties	Receivors
William Guyne[150]	Terra Lenox in comitatu Eborum Inheritance of King James before he came to the Crowne	Robert Grymes
	Lincolne	John Harvey[151] Daniell Harvey[152]
	Nottingham Derby Chester	Edward Basse[153] & Edward Darling[154] Humphrey Jones[155] who is also receivor for North wales

132 Stat. 7 Edw. 6 (1553) c. 1, s. 9, *Stat. Realm*, iv, p. 163.

133 Sandford had a grant dated 3 July 1622 (P.R. 20 Jac. 1, pt. 6: C.66/2274); his successor had a grant dated 20 July 1660 (P.R. 12 Car. 2, pt. 27: C. 66/2942). In 1692 this officer was John Evelyn, Jr., who had a grant dated 25 February 1690 (P.R. 2 Will. & Mar., pt. 1: C.66/3334). [J.C.S.]

134 Richard Gurnard, Esq., had a grant dated 3 July 1622 (P.R. 20 Jac. 1, pt .6: C.66/2274); his successor was appointed on 20 July 1660 (P.R. 12 Car. 2, pt. 27: C.66/2942). [J.C.S.]

135 Sawyer had a grant for life in reversion dated 9 Dec. 1611 (P.R. 9 Jac. 1, pt. 41: C. 66/1938). In 1692 this officer was John Shales, who had a grant for life in reversion dated 21 Mar. 1677 (P.R. 29 Car. 2, pt. 3: C.66/3190). [J.C.S.]

136 Daniell held by a grant dated 24 May 1623 (P.R. 21 Jac. 1, pt. 1: C.66/2295). In 1692 this officer was John Duncombe, who held from 1690 to 1705. [J.C.S.]

137 Michael Holman had a grant dated 28 May 1637 (P.R. 13 Car. 1, pt. 46: C.66/2795). [J.C.S.] In 1692 this officer was William Roberts.

138 Mark Coltell had a grant dated 23 June 1637 (P.R. 13 Car. 1, pt. 46: C.66/2795); he remained in office until 1670 when the beneficiary of the trust received a grant of his own. [J.C.S.]

139 Richard Holman himself received a grant dated 26 September 1670 (P.R. 22 Car. 2, pt. 8: C.66/3121). [J.C.S.]

140 In 1692 this office was held by William Roberts.

Footnotes to page 121 overleaf

[141] Henry Rich was created earl of Holland on 24 September 1624 and was executed on 9 March 1649: *G.E.C.*, vi, pp. 538–40.

[142] Hill had a grant for life in reversion dated 6 December 1637 (P.R. 13 Car. 1, pt. 24: C.66/2773). In 1692 this office was held by Ralph Grey, who had a grant during pleasure dated 18 March 1692 (P.R. 4 Will. & Mar., pt. 2: C.66/3350). [J.C.S.]

[143] Jones held by a patent dated 1 February 1632 (P.R. 6 Car. 1, pt. 6: C.66/2538). In 1692 this office was held by Roger Whitley, who had a grant dated 24 September 1675; his successor was appointed on 21 February 1708 (P.R. 6 Ann., pt. 3: C.66/3459). [J.C.S.]

[144] Watkins held by a patent dated 13 November 1639 (P.R. 14 Car. 1, pt. 38: C. 66/2833); his successor was appointed on 10 July 1662 (P.R. 14 Car. 2, pt. 5: C.66/3007). In 1692 this office was held by Bevis Lloyd; his successor was appointed on 16 June 1696 (P.R. 8 Will. 3, pt. 8: C.66/3389). [J.C.S.]

[145] Abbott held by a patent dated 10 October 1637 (P.R. 13 Car. 1, pt. 46: C.66/2795). In 1692 this office was held by John Smith, who was appointed in 1676 (*C.T.B.*, vi, p. 402, vii, p. 341); his successor was appointed in 1698. [J.C.S.]

[146] Povey received a grant for life in reversion dated 26 May 1606 (P.R. 4 Jac. 1, pt. 1: C.66/1691). In 1692 this office was held by John Philips, who had a grant for life in reversion dated 12 January 1638 (P.R. 13 Car. 1, pt. 24: C.66/2773). [J.C.S.]

[147] Richard Miller held by a grant dated 28 Feb. 1617 (P.R. 15 Jac. 1, pt. 21: C.66/2150); his successor was appointed on 14 December 1642 (P.R. 18 Car. 1, pt. 4: C.66/2903). In 1692 this officer was John Smith, who held between 1676 and 1698. [J.C.S.]

[148] A blank space was left for 'Isaak', who was appointed jointly with Richard.

[149] Havers held by a grant dated 2 July 1639 (P.R. 15 Car. 1, pt. 20: C.66/2860). In 1692 this officer was John Smith, who held between 1676 and 1698. [J.C.S.]

[150] Gwyn held by a grant for life in reversion dated 1 February 1612 (P.R. 9 Jac. 1, pt. 9: C.66/1906). In 1692 this officer was William Aldworth; he received a new patent to hold during pleasure dated 23 April 1697 (P.R. 9 Will. 3, pt. 4: C.66/3393). [J.C.S.]

[151] John Harvey held by a grant dated 31 March 1624 (P.R. 22 Jac. 1, pt. 6: C.66/2329); his successor was appointed 20 Aug. 1667 (P.R. 19 Car. 2, pt. 4: C.66/3091). In 1692 this officer was Samuel Finnes, who held between 16 May 1684 and 28 September 1694. [J.C.S.]

[152] Daniel Harvey held by a grant dated 31 March 1624 (P.R. 22 Jac. 1, pt. 6: C.66/2329); his successor was appointed 13 January 1644 (*Docquets of Letters Patents*, p. 373). [J.C.S.]

[153] Bass held by a grant dated 17 May 1640 (P.R. 16 Car. 1, pt. 12: C.66/2879); his successor was appointed 15 December 1660 (P.R. 12 Car. 2, pt. 30: C.66/2945). In 1692 the receiver for Nottingham was Samuel Finnes, who held office from 1675 to 1701. In 1692 the receiver for Derby was William Chambers, who held office from 1675 to 1698. [J.C.S.]

[154] Darling held by a grant dated 17 May 1640 (P.R. 16 Car. 1, pt. 12: C.66/2879); his successor was appointed on 15 December 1660 (P.R. 12 Car. 2, pt. 30: C. 66/2945). [J.C.S.]

[155] In 1692 this office was held by Roger Whitley, Jr., see above 'Roger Whitley' [Sen.?]

Auditors	Counties	Receivors
Richard Kinsman[157]	Southampton Wiltshire Gloucestershire	Robert Scawen[156]
	Somersett Dorsett	Francis Croffts[158]
	Devon Cornewall	[Godolphin[159]
Francis Phillips[162]	Lancaster Westmoreland Cumberland	John Braddill[160]
	Northampton Rutland	Sir George Benyon[161]
	Warwicke Leicester	William Green[163]
	Stafford Hereford Shropshire Worcestershire	William Geere[164]

[156] Scawen held by a patent dated 16 July 1638 (P.R. 14 Car. 1, pt. 26: C.66/2822); his successor, Simon Smith, was appointed on 17 August 1677 (P.R. 19 Car. 2, pt. 4: C.66/3091). [J.C.S.] Smith was still in office in 1692.

[157] Kinsman held by a grant for life in reversion dated 23 May 1625 (P.R. 1 Car. 1, pt. 2: C.66/2349); in 1692 this officer was Anthony Parsons, who held by a grant for life in reversion dated 15 March 1643 (P.R. 18 Car. 1, pt. 4: C.66/2903). [J.C.S.]

[158] Croft held by a patent dated 19 May 1641 (P.R. 17 Car. 1, pt. 2: C.66/2891); his successor was appointed on 25 July 1660 (P.R. 12 Car. 2, pt. 20: C.66/2935). In 1692 this officer was Simon Smith, who was appointed on 23 March 1677. [J.C.S.]

[159] Francis Godolphin held by a grant dated 10 June 1640 (P.R. 16 Car. 1, pt. 12: C.66/2879); his successor was appointed on 2 May 1667 (P.R. 19 Car. 2, pt. 6: C.66/3093). [J.C.S.] In 1692 this officer was Simon Smith.

[160] Braddill (or Bradwell) held by a grant for life in reversion dated 13 July 1606 (P.R. 4 Jac. 1, pt. 2: C.66/1692); his successor was appointed on 16 August 1660 (P.R. 12 Car. 2, pt. 22: C.66/2937). [J.C.S.] In 1692 this officer was Richard Rivington.

[161] Benion held by a grant dated 20 June 1631 (P.R. 7 Car. 1, pt. 18: C.66/2577); his successor was appointed in December 1669 (C.T.B., iii, p. 316). In 1692 this officer was Samuel Finnes, who held from 1685 to 1693. [J.C.S.]

[162] Phillips held by a grant for life in reversion dated 28 June 1604 (P.R. 2 Jac. 1, pt. 5: C.66/1635). In 1692 this officer was Sir Joseph Seymour, who held by a grant for life in reversion dated 10 September 1641 (P.R. 17 Car. 1, pt. 1: C.66/2890). [J.C.S.]

[163] Green held by a grant for life in reversion dated 3 February 1641 (P.R. 16 Car. 1, pt. 21: C.66/2888); he received another grant on 3 August 1642 (P.R. 18 Car. 1, pt. 4: C.66/2903); he was out of office in 1672. In 1692 this officer was Samuel Finnes, who held from 1685 to 1694. [J.C.S.]

[164] Geere (or Geers) held by a grant dated 13 March 1639 (P.R. 14 Car. 1, pt. 41: C.66/2836); his successor was appointed on 13 August 1660 (P.R. 12 Car. 2, pt. 21: C.66/2936). In 1692 this officer was Samuel Finnes, who was in office by 28 September 1671 (C.T.B., iii, p. 938) and whose successor was in office in 1698. [J.C.S.]

[*p. 37*]

Thomas Brinley[168]	Eborum	{ Thomas Bland[165] & John Bland[166]
	Northumberland Archdeconry of Richmond & Bishoppricke of Durham	{ John Braddill[167] patentee for Thomas Clopton Recusant Executed by Commission by Maior Norton[169]

Revercions Robert Worrall Mr Phillipps.

[*p. 38*]   Revenewe of Recusants

Receivors of this Revenue Sir George Wentworth knight for the eleaven Counties beyond Trent. Robert Long esquire for all England on this side Trent. Theis places are granted by his Majesty by letters Patents & hold during life. They are to put in security into thexchequer for their due accompting & answering this Revenue as the Lord Treasurer shall appoint.

This office was first erected about 15 years since the Earl of Marleburgh[170] being Treasurer before which tyme this Revenue was paid immediatly into the Exchequer without anie charge to his Majestie for the Receiving thereof.

The accounts of those Receivors were taken by the Auditors of the Imprests untill about 3 or 4 years since.

Auditors of this Revenue lately erected Henry Stanley & Phillip Darrell & the longest liver of them by Letters Patents under the great Seale in his Majesties guift.

John Pulford appointed Agent by warrant under his Majesties signe Manuall for the indictments & conviccions of Recusants and

[165] Thomas Bland held by a grant dated 23 June 1640 (P.R. 16 **Car.** 1, pt. 12: C.66/2879). In 1692 this officer was William (or Richard) Aldworth, who held from 1680 to 1697. [J.C.S.]

[166] John Bland held by a grant dated 23 June 1640 (P.R. 16 Car. 1, pt. 12: C.66/2879); he died in 1680 (*C.T.B.*, vi, p. 663). [J.C.S.]

[167] Braddell held by a grant for life in reversion dated 7 February 1622 (P.R. 19 Jac. 1, pt. 9: C.66/2253); his successor was Major Norton (see below). In 1692 this officer was William (or Richard) Aldworth. [J.C.S.]

[168] Brinley held by a grant for life in reversion dated 24 October 1617 (P.R. 15 Jac. 1, pt. 1: C.66/2130). In 1692 this office was held by Anthony Stephens, who had a grant for life in reversion dated 6 January 1679 (P.R. 30 Car. 2, pt. 5: C.66/3205). [J.C.S.]

[169] Norton received a grant dated 3 August 1642 (P.R. 18 Car. 1, pt. 4: C.66/2903); he was out of office in 1669 (*C.T.B.*, iii, pp. 278, 667). [J.C.S.]

[170] James Ley, earl of Marlborough, was lord high treasurer from 1624 to 1628.

for the Inquisitions and Composicions for the 2 thirds of their estates, & for their goods.

John Sompner was appointed by the late Commissioners for Recusants in the North, for the indictment, conviccion & prosecucion of the Recusants in the eleaven Northerne Counties and to draw them in to Compound.

[*p. 39*]   Duchy Revenue

[   ] Receivor of the Revenue of the Duchy of Lancaster, holds by letters Patents under the *great seal.*

[   ] Napper Receivor of the Revenue for the Duchy of Cornewall.

Auditor for this Revenue [   ] Downes.[171]

William Loving hath a Patent granted him for the Reversion of this place.

[*p. 40*]   Marshall of the Exchequer

Edmund Thorould[172] is the present officer by guifte of the Earle Marshall, & holds by letters Patents under the great Seale during life & is admitted & sworne by the Barons in open Court. Nathaniel Thorould[173] joyned in Patent with him (vacante Earl Marshall in the Kings guift.)

Hee is an officer to whom the Court of Exchequer Sometimes comitts the Custody of such as they will not for the tyme send to the *prison of the* Fleet but doe thinke fitt in that wise in some cause to be Comitted.

Hee assigneth in open Court all Sheriffes Escheators Customers Collectors of Subsidies *and Receivers General of assessments and*

---

171 In 1692 this office was held by William Harbord.

172 Edmund Thorold held by a patent dated 9 July 1609 (P.R. 7 Jac. 1, pt. 27: C.66/1815); he received a new patent on 12 September 1616 (P.R. 14 Jac. 1, pt. 15: C.66/2104); his successor received a patent on 15 August 1660 (P.R. 12 Car. 2, pt. 23: C.66/2938). In 1692 this officer was Richard Baker (according to the manuscripts of this tract) or Michael Baker, Sr. (according to Mr. Sainty) who received patents dated 13 February 1681 (P.R. 33 Car. 2, pt. 2: C.66/3220), 7 May 1685 (P.R. 1 Jac. 2, pt. 1: C.66/3262), 14 June 1689 (P.R. 1 Will. & Mar., pt. 4: C.66/3328), 21 July 1702 (P.R. 1 Ann., pt. 11: C.66/3434), and 10 March 1715 (P.R. 1 Geo. 1, pt. 10: C.66/3507); his successor was appointed on 10 November 1727 (P.R. 1 Geo. 2, pt. 4: C.66/3569) he held office jointly with his son from 1689 until his death which occured between 1715 and 1727. [J.C.S.]

173 Nathaniel Thorold held by a patent dated 12 September 1616 (P.R. 14 Jac. 1, pt. 15: C.66/2104); his successor received a patent on 15 August 1660 (P.R. 12 Car. 2, pt. 23: C.66/2938). [J.C.S.]

public taxes & such like Accomptants to such of the Auditors as he thinkes fitt for the taking of their Accompts.

Hee receiveth all offices[174] that Escheators doe find (virtute officii) & delivereth them in Court into the Treasurers Remembrancers office to be delivered by the Roll of Streates[175] there to the Parcell makers to charge the same in the Escheators Accompts & takes a note under the hand of the Clerke that Receiveth the same.

[*p. 41*]   Usher of the Exchequer

Clement Walker[176] hath his place by Inheritance from Edward the seconds[i] time. Hee hath fower ushers under him & by him presented & sworne in open Court which doe hold their places during life namely[177] Richard Bankes Thomas Colchester William Over & Christofer Vere.

These attend on the Barons & officers of the Court at their coming and going & are in the nature of Cryers of other Courts. They call all Juries, witnesses & persons appointed to attend the Court. They make in open Court all Noyses Silence and *make* proclamacions calling of Sheriffes and other Accomptants, both at & after their dayes of prefixion and times appointed them by law & course of the Court, & whatsoever else the Court shall Comand them.

The Cheife usher hath six Messengers presented by him & sworne in open Court, for the carrying of all proces Convicions port books &c to all parts of England and Wales which also hold their places during life Namely William Over Thomas Colchester, Christofer Vine, John Harris, Charles Bright & Richard Banckes.

Hee hath also a Chamber Keeper & Court Keeper[178] Christofer Vine but hee is noe sworne officer.

The Cheife usher hath the Custody of the Court Exchequer Chamber, & house with all the appurtenances & hath the generall keeping of all the Records there and waites upon the Lord Treasurer & Chauncellor when they come thither, & serves the Court & all the officers, with all kind of necessaries as paper Incke, Standishes,

[i] 'Henry II' according to J, K, L, M, and N; see also Note, 2 *Dyer* 213, 73 *Eng. Rep.* 472 (1562) and the references cited there.

---

[174] Probably E.357; possibly E.136 which are king's remembrancer's records.

[175] Probably E.362; possibly E.137, which are king's remembrancer's records.

[176] In 1692 this officer was John Walker.

[177] In 1692 they were Samuel Brewster, Augustine Brewster, William Ballow, and Walter Price.

[178] In 1692 this officer was Richard Crew.

Statute bookes &c for which he hath his liberate each Terme for the allowance & payment thereof signed by the Chauncellor of the Exchequer.[179]

And his six Messengers as they performe their service in carrying of proces &c. hath likewise their bills signed by the Chauncellor.[180] [*p. 42*] They are from time to time to deliver to the severall sheriffes and all others whome it concernes the Kings proces &c. and are to take bills subscribed by them or their undersheriffes for the Receipt thereof, which the cheife usher at their returne doth examine by his booke that he keepes of all the Kings proces that are delivered out every Terme wherein is sett & totalled upp the number of writts & proces that goeth out, & to what sheriffe & from what office they are sent.

[*p. 43*]   The Two Appraysers

Hugh Hobart & Robert Neale are in the guift of the Chauncellor of the Exchequer by him presented & admitted by taking oath in open Court by vertue whereof they hold their places during life.

Theise officers praise all goods & merchandize that anie informacion is put against in the Exchequer as seized by vertue of the Statute.

They have first a writt of appraisment directed unto them from the Court under the Exchequer Seale by vertue whereof they weigh number & value the Comoditie so seezed & doe then returne the writt backe againe togeither with their valuacion in an Indenture under their hand & Seale annexed thereunto.

And when the goods are condemned proclamacion is made in open Court of the value by them appraysed at, & if noe man comes in & gives more the goods are sould at the same rate according to which his Majestie is answered his moyetie of the seizure.

[*p. 44*]   Surveyors Generall

Sir Charles Harbord knight[181] in his Majesties guift by letters Patents under the great Seale of England.

Stewards of his Majesties Honors, Lordshipps, & Mannors.

Collectors of the dispersed Revenues in the several Counties.

Baylifes of his Majesties honors, Manors &c, in several Counties.

---

[179] E.5.   [180] E.5.

[181] Harbord held by a patent dated 19 June 1632 (P.R. 7 Car. 1, pt. 2: C.66/2561); he received another patent on 16 June 1660 (P.R. 12 Car. 2, pt. 20: C.66/2935). In 1692 this officer was William Harbord, who held by a patent in reversion dated 25 August 1662 (P.R. 14 Car. 2, pt. 5: C.66/3007); his successor was appointed during pleasure on 22 April 1693 (P.R. 5 Will. & Mar., pt. 4: C. 66/3362. [J.C. S.]

Woodwards of the severall Counties.

Gaugers of the severall Ports.

These officers abovemencioned are granted by patent under the Exchequer Seale during pleasure by warrant of the Lord Treasurer & Chancellor of the Exchequer & those that are to have charge of anie of his Majesties Revenue doe first put in securitie into the Kings Remembrancers office before their grant do passe the Seale.

[pp. 45-48 are blank]

[*p. 49*]   The Severall officers of the Receipt of Exchequer in whose guift & how admitted with a breife Collection of the cheife heads of what every officer usually doth by vertue of his office According to the State of the Receipt at this day January 1641.

Chamberlaines of the Exchequer

The 2 Chamberlaines are Sir Nicholas Cary & Sir Edward Bashe mencioned before in folio 24: These officers have antiently been of great authoritie and trust & have had the Chesting & Custody of the Treasure (as is informed) but now have little to doe save only by their deputies.

Their Deputies or underchamberlaynes of the Receipt are Scipio le Squire[182] & Thomas Fawconbridge[183] which are in their guift & nominacion and by them presented they are sworne.

The two underchamberlaines in the Receipt of Exchequer have each of them a key, & the Lord Treasurers Clerke *now writer of the tallies and counter tallies* another & doe keepe The Records of State, Arcana Imperii as golden Leagues Contracts Wills[184] and Joyntures of Kings and Princes All Leagues & principal Negotiacions of State forraine & domestickes[185] Till the lord Treasurer Salisbury[186] tooke the papers of his time & erected an office of Clerke of the papers,[187]

[182] LeSquire was admitted to office as deputy to Carew-Throckmorton on 30 November 1620: E. 36/266, f. 93. In 1692 this office was held by John Lowe who was admitted as deputy to Sir Nicholas Steward on 19 March 1666: E.36/266, f. 86.

[183] Fawconbridge was admitted to office as deputy to Bash on 28 September 1633: E.36/266, f. 82; he was dead before 27 July 1660 when his successor was admitted: E.36/266, f. 84. In 1692 this office was held by Peter LeNeve who was admitted as deputy to Philip Hilliard on 15 December 1684: E.36/266, f. 86.

[184] E.23.   [185] E.30, E.36/186-192, E.39.

[186] Robert Cecil, earl of Salisbury, lord high treasurer from 1608 to 1612.

[187] In 1610: see F. S. Thomas, *A History of the State Paper Office* (London, 1849), p. 7.

for his Secretarie Sir Thomas Wilson with a charge upon the King of 100^{li} per annum for the keeping thereof which hath so continued ever since.

[*p. 50*] They ought to receive by Indenture of the Secretary of State all leagues & Contracts of forraine princes, the last being that of Denmarke, the rest ought to bee but are not brought into the Sanctum Sanctorum *which is the repository of them* where they ought to be kept.

There also they have the Assayes of Gold & silver Comonly called the triall peeces, whereby the Mint is Comptrolled with which they waite on the Lords at the tryall of the Pix.

There are also divers Regalities of the kingdom as the Staffe of the Constabulary, Seales of Aulnage &c.

In the Abbey Treasury being late the Chapter house are the Plea Rolls & Fines[188] & other Records of the law from the Conquest to King Richard the thirds time which the vicechamberlaines exemplifie and transcribe to the Subject & retorne them upon *writs of* Certiorarie under their hands as occacion requires.

In the Pallace Treasury they have Cardinal Woolseys papers,[189] Traytors Evidences the old Stamps for Coyne,[190] pells of Exitus & Introitus[191] Bookes of victualling[192] & building, Orders of St. George[193] & St. Michell,[194] Henry 8^{ths} divorce & manie other Records of Remarkable consequence.

They have alsoe the keeping, sizing, and delivering to the Subject all the Standards of weights and measures of England.

[*p. 51*] They have also the keeping of all the Records of law vizt. Coram Rege,[195] De Banco,[196] Justiciarii Itinerant,[197] Justiciariis ad forestis,[198] Justiciariis ad Assisas[199]&c. which they Coppy & transcribe as well to the Subject as the king.

They have the 2 most antient & most used Records of England vizt. the booke of Doomesday[200] & the blacke booke,[201] the first being a Survey in the 20th yeare of the Conqueror. The second is de Necessariis Scaccarii observantiis *made in the reign of Henry II* and the originall & ground of the establishing & the mannor & proceedings of all the officers of the Exchequer, Wherein the oathes of all the

---

[188] C.P.25.

[189] E.24, see also E.21.

[190] E.29; D. Allen, 'Dies in the Public Record Office, 1938,' *British Numismatic Journal*, xxiii (1938), pp. 31–50.

[191] E.36/123–136; see also E.401/1794–2348, E.403/1693–2146.

[192] E.36/1–15.

[193] E.36/92, 113.

[194] E.36/276.

[195] K.B.26, K.B.27.

[196] C.P.40.

[197] Just. 1.

[198] E.32; see also E.146.

[199] Just. 1.

[200] E.31.

[201] E.36/266, 267.

officers of the Receipt are also enrolled, which the Senior vice Chamberlaine usuallie administreth to them in presence of the Lord Treasurer Chauncellor or Comissioners when they are sworne. There are also letters of Priviledge & exemcion graunted from hence for the Freeing of all those that are resident at the Exchequer from publike service in person, or by finding men Armes or monie they being to attend the Lord Treasurers comands in wayting upon the Treasury with their men, horses & Armes when occasion shall require.

They have also the keeping of the Seale of the Court of Receipt which hath bin of use in former times but not of late.

They doe cleave & examine all Tallies with the entry of the Clerke of the Pell, & the Clerke or writer of the Tallies by the Tellors bill in whose Custody it remaynes & then they deliver the Tallies to the parties & doe keepe the foyles[202] in a Chest (to which each of them hath a severall locke & key) untill the Joyners of the Tallies which are the other deputie Chamberlaynes *on the court side* doe fetch them away *and to that purpose they always attend in the tally court when business is to be done, viz. at six of the clock in the morning in summer and nine of the clock in winter on all days but holidays and sundays and are the principal officers there; and till of late years the chamberlain's deputies or clerks were comptrollers of the pells for the introitus and entered in a book[203] all the tellers bills after they were marked recordatur by the clerk of the pells.*

[*p. 52*]   *Writer of the Tallies and Countertallies*
              Sometimes Called Auditor of the Receipt

Sir Robert Pye knight[204] in the Lord Treasurers guift & hath a grant under the Lord Treasurers Seale, & of late times *is pretended to be* granted by letters Patents under the great Seale of England, *but not allowed by the lord treasurer* & is admitted by taking oath before *the lord treasurer or lords commissioners of the treasury and the chamberlains, or the eldest deputy chamberlain in the exchequer.*

This officer hath bin heretofore accompted noe other then the Lord Treasurers Clerke, & scriptor Talliarum *et contratalliarum* &

---

[202] E.402.   [203] Perhaps E.401.

[204] Pye was admitted on 25 January 1618/19 (E.36/266, f. 95) and his successor was appointed on 6 August 1642 (*Docquets of Letters Patents*, p. 348). In 1692 this office was held by Sir Robert Howard, who had a grant dated 13 March 1673 (P.R. 25 Car. 2, pt. 11: C.66/3153) [J.C.S.], was admitted on 14 July 1673 (E.36/266, f. 86); he was dead before 5 September 1698 when his successor was admitted (E.36/267, f.1).

now lives in that house which Sir Walter Mildmay[205] possessed as undertreasurer of thexchequer *which hath been since granted by letters patent to Sir Robert Dingley writer of the tallies and is now granted to Sir Robert Howard the present officer by like letters patent.* His Clerke that attends in the Tally Court *about six of the clock in the morning in the summer and nine in the winter on all days but Sundays and holy days* takes the Tellors Bill *thrown into the tally court* & the Tally[206] (that is squared & notched by the Tally Cutter) & writes the words of the Bill verbatim upon two oposite sides thereof, which being cleaven, the one makes the Tally & thother makes the foyle, which being examined he keepes the Tellers Bills & enters all of them fayre into a booke.[207]

Hee keepes the Lord Treasurers *or lords commissioners'* key of the Records remayning in the Treasury whereof the underchamberlaines hath likewise keys.

His Clerke that attends in his office, Enters all letters patents for all fees & annuities & all privy Seales[208] for payment & issuing of all monies out of the Receipt & now makes all debentures for fees and Annuities which are signed & directed to the Tellers (to be paid) by the Auditor alone And also draweth up all orders[209] upon privy Seales *as the lord treasurer's clerk* for the Signature of the Lord Treasurer *or lords commissioners for executing the office of treasurer* & under Treasurer *and when such orders are signed and returned to him, he receiveth now a letter or directive from them for payment*. And doth now direct at the lower end of each order, how much & by which of the Tellers anie monies shalbe paid upon the said orders.

[*p. 53*] Hee also now takes the Tellers Certificates & accounts *of money received* weekely[210] or as often as is required, severally & drawes up all into one Accompt.

Hee (with the Clerke of the Pells) strikes all Tallies of assignment & pro (whereof their are manie now a dayes, besides those settled by act of parliament) & takes the acquittances of the parties as accomptants themselves & noe man to Comptroll them, the Tellors being not charged therewith or made privy thereto and then they involve all together, adding those things into the Certificate amongst the Tellers Receipts & payments which Certificates are weekely delivered *or certified* to the Lord Treasurer *or lords commissioners of the treasury* & Chauncellor of the Exchequer.

Hee makes out Imprests certificates *to the king's remembrancer* for all Accomptants to charge them with all, which also is a ground for

205 *D.N.B.*; S. E. Lehmberg, *Sir Walter Mildmay* (Austin, 1964).
206 E.402. 207 E.401/2349–2476. 208 E.403.
209 E.404. 210 E.405/222–240.

proces to issue (if neede require) out of the kings Remembrancers office to compell them to accompt.

[p. 54]   Clerke of the Pells

Sir Edward Wardour & Edward Wardour his Sonne[211] Joyned in Patent with him in the Lord Treasurers guift *or lords commissioners of the treasury when there is no treasurer* & graunt under his *or their* seale *or seals* & is admitted by taking oath before the Lord Treasurer *or lords commissioners as aforesaid* or under Treasurer & holds *his place* during life.

The Clerke of the Pell is called in Record Clericus domini Thesaurarii & Scriptor Pellium.

It is the office appointed for recording all Receipts & payments made by the Tellors in the Receipt & hath severall Clerkes under him one that enters[212] all warrants orders & debentures for the issuing of monies & writes Recorded upon them before the Tellors makes any payment thereof.

Hee hath also another Clerke in the Tally Court that enters[213] all the Tellers bills & writes Recordatur upon them & examines the Tally with his booke before it passe with *the writer of the tallies now called* the Auditor of the Receipt *he* strikes Tallies of assignment & pro, without the Tellers privity or warrant as before is expressed.

Hee hath another Clerke that makes out Constats of all Receipts to be sued out before the allowing of anie Tallies & granting anie quietus est from the Pipe office.

Hee also enters all letters Patents *of offices of the exchequer or otherwise out of which any fee or salary is paid by their majesties* & privy Seales[214] for issuing of monies out of the Receipt. And makes up Certificates[215] of all Receipts & payments of the Tellers to which he adds Tallies of assignment & Pro in like forme as the Auditors doth & delivers one to the Lord Treasurer *or lords commissioners of the treasury when there is no treasurer* & another to the undertreasurer of the Exchequer *and his office is esteemed of record.*

[211] The Wardours were admitted on 25 April 1637 (E.36/266, f. 82); they were no longer in office on 7 July 1660 when William Wardour was admitted (E.36/266, f. 83); in 1692 this office was held by a William Wardour who was no doubt either the same as the above or his son. On 1 February 1697 Henry Pelham was admitted to this office (E.36/267, f. 1).

[212] E.403.

[213] E.401/1–2279.

[214] E.403.

[215] E.405/213–221.

[p. 55]   The Fower Tellers of the Exchequer

John Brooke,[216] Arthur Squibb,[217] Edward Pitt & John Savile.[218] They[219] hold their offices by letters Patents under the great Seale of England, by the Kings guift. They give bond with suerties for performance of their duties, & are admitted by taking oath before the Lord Treasurer or under Treasurer of the Exchequer.

There are three Revercions namely Lawrence Squibb,[220] Lawrence Swetman[221] & Arthur Squibb[222] to succeed in the next places that shall fall voyd.

They are to receive all monies payable in the Receipt of Exchequer, & hath the Revenue devided & assigned to each Tellor according to the Counties & quality of the Revenue.

They attend constantly every morning throughout the yeare (except on Sundayes & the great festivalls) & in the afternoones when neede requires for the Receiving & paying of his Majesties Treasure there.

When anie monie is brought, they imediately tell the same, & forthwith thereupon doe make a Bill[223] in parchment under their

[216] Brooke held office by a patent dated 6 March 1614/15 and was admitted 10 January 1622/23 (E.36/266, f. 81).

[217] A. Squibb, sr., held office by a patent dated 5 December 1623 and was admitted on 10 July 1624 (E.36/266, f. 81); he was no longer in office on 3 July 1649; he was a kinsman of Lawrence Squibb (H. S. London & G. D. Squibb, 'A Dorset King of Arms: Arthur Squibb, Clarenceux, 1646–1650,' *Procs. of the Dorset Nat. Hist. & Arch. Soc.*, lxviii (1947), pp. 54–65).

[218] Savile held office by a patent dated 23 December 1623 and was admitted on 9 May 1636 (E.36/266, f. 82).

[219] In 1692 these officers were John Loving (or Lovaine), Francis Villiers, Thomas Howard, and Henry Maynard. Loving held by a patent dated 14 December 1642 (*Docquets of Letters Patents*, p. 346) [J.C.S.] and was dead before 18 July 1693 when his successor was admitted (E.36/266, f. 86); see also Dennis v. Loving, Hardr. 424, 145 Eng. Rep. 529 (Ex. 1666). Villiers held by a patent dated 2 January 1672 (P.R. 23 Car. 2, pt. 8: C.66/3131). [J.C.S.] Howard held by a patent dated 11 February 1675 (P.R. 27 Car. 2, pt. 2: C.66/3169) [J.C.S.] and was admitted on 16 January 1688/89 (E.36/266, f. 85); he was dead before 11 July 1701 when his successor was admitted (E.36/267, f. 3). Maynard held by a patent dated 12 February 1675 (P.R. 27 Car. 2, pt. 2: C.66/3169) [J.C.S.] and was admitted on 16 April 1689 (E.36/266, f. 85), his successor was admitted in 1694 (E.36/266, f. 85).

[220] This was the author of this tract; for his life and career, see the Introduction.

[221] Swetman (or Swetnam) had a patent dated 31 October 1635 (P.R. 11 Car. 1, pt. 10; C.66/2693). [J.C.S.]

[222] A. Squibb, jr., had a patent dated 29 January 1640 (P.R. 15 Car. 1, pt. 2: C.66/2842) [J.C.S.]; see also *Cal. S.P. Dom., 1639–1640*, p. 151 [7 December 1639].

[223] E.402/4–344.

hand expressing the name of the partie & the County & the somme
& for what cause the same is paid, which bill is then throwen downe
to the Tally Court, whither the partie repayres to receive his Tally.

They pay noe monies upon anie order debenture or warraunt
unlesse it be signed or directed by the Auditor of the Receipt & also
recorded in the office of the Clerke of the Pells & Recordatur written
thereupon.

[p. 56] They weekely (or as often as is required) doe make up an
exact account or certificate[224] with the Auditor of the Receipt (which
formerly hath bin done with the undertreasurer) of all Receipts &
payments in their severall offices, Whereby is certaynely knowne the
particuler remayne in every Tellors hand upon all occasions.

They keepe every of them a fayre booke of every dayes Receipt,
out of which halfe yearely at Easter & Michaelmas they engrosse the
same in a nother booke, collecting & sorting every Branch of the
Revenue to their severall heads & titles which afterwards is by them
fayrely engrossed in parchment together with the issues & payments
& thereof making a true & exact account for the halfe yeare which
formerly hath usually delivered over to the Pipe office there to
remayne a Record for his Majestie.[225]

[p. 57]   The Tally Cutter

John Elston[226] in the Lord Treasurers guifte & holdeth his place
by grant under the Lord Treasurers hand & is admitted by taking
oath before the Treasurer or undertreasurer of the Exchequer by
vertue whereof hee holdeth his place during life.

Hee provideth seasoned wood of Hasell for Tallies[227] & Squareth
them, & when anie bill[228] comes downe from the Tellors he first takes
the same & cutts notches upon the Tallie according to the somme
mencioned in the bill having a certaine rule of proporcion for the
bignes & faishion of the notches of every denominacion of 1000li·
100li· 20li· pounds shillings pence and farthings.

And having fitted the Tally he doth wreath the Bill about it, &
then doth cast the same into the Court to the Clerke that writes the
Tallies.

---

[224] E.405.

[225] Probably E.405/477–561.

[226] Elston, a royalist, was restored to office in 1660 (E.36/266, f. 93). In
1692 this officer was Joseph Bark, who was admitted on 1 January 1690/91
and who was dead before 2 September 1692 when his successor was admitted
(E.36/266, f. 85, where they are called ushers).

[227] *E.g.* E.402/1–3g.

[228] E.402/4–344.

[*p. 58*]   Usher of the Receipt of Exchequer

Robert Bowyer[229] by letters Patents under the great Seale of England by the guifte of [   ][230] & is admitted by taking oath before the Lord Treasurer *or lords commissioners of the treasury* or undertreasurer of the Exchequer & holds it during life.

Hee hath the keeping & locking of the outer doores & passages of the Receipt, the Treasury Chamber & the Court of Starr Chamber, & hath the charge of repayring & keeping them cleane. And is to attend the Lord Treasurer & undertreasurer whensoever they come there, & waytes upon the Tally Court, & all the officers of the Receipt & provides & furnish them with all kind of necessaries belonging to their offices As paper, Incke, Bookes, Baggs, Standishes &c. and of late times doth also provide paper & Incke for the two Secretaries of State.

He hath also by another Patent (which formerly hath bin a distinct office from the other) the providing of parchment & parchment bookes for all the officers of the Receipt.

And is to carry the keys of the Treasury house of Records when the Lord Treasurers Clerke & Deputy Chamberlaines doe goe thither to make anie Search.

[*p. 59*]   Fower Messengers of the Receipt

Robert Bemboe,[231] Thomas Bemboe,[232] Robert Johnson[233] & Richard Aymys which[234] doe hold their places by letters Patents

229 Bowyer held office by a patent dated 25 June 1604 (P.R. 2 Jac. 1, pt. 8: C.66/1638) [J.C.S.] and was admitted on 5 June 1641 (E.36/266, f. 83); he was dead before 6 February 1663 when his successors were admitted (E.36/266, f. 83). In 1692 this officer was John Packer (or Parker) who held by a patent dated 22 February 1666 (P.R. 18 Car. 2, pt. 3: C.66/3083) [J.C.S.] and who was dead before 16 March 1698 when his successor was admitted (E.36/267, f. 1).

230 A blank space was left for reference to the king, as in Brit. Mus., MS. Add. 30216, f. 42, and P.R.O., A.O.16/196, p. 101.

231 R. Bemboe (or Benbowe) had patents dated 1 September 1615 and 18 September 1617 [J.C.S.] and was admitted in August 1635 (E.36/266, f. 82).

232 T. Bemboe (or Benbowe) had a patent dated 1 July 1625 [J.C.S.] and was admitted on 23 June 1635 (E.36/266, f. 82).

233 Johnson had a patent dated 9 September 1629 [J.C.S.] and was admitted on 3 December 1636 (E.36/266, f. 82).

234 In 1692 these officers were Benjamin King, William Wickett (or Workes or Werket), William Barnet (or Barret), and Joseph Ricard (or Richards). Wickett and Barnet were both admitted on 1 November 1689 (E.36/266, f. 85). Barnet was dead before 13 February 1698 when his successor was admitted (E.36/267, f. 1). Wickett and Ricard appear to have been readmitted on 10 June 1709 (E.36/267, f. 6).

under the great Seale of England of the Kings guift, & are admitted by taking oath before the Lord Treasurer & under Treasurer of the Exchequer.

William Cox hath a Revercion granted to succeed the first of these that shall next fall voyd and Henry Davison hath a graunt of the next.

Theis did antiently attend the Lord Treasurer and under Treasurer & the officers of the Receipt, where they now have but little imployment.

They have the charge of carrying of all Proclamacions to all partes of the Kingdome, & for all letters & precepts to the Customers & officers of the Ports & are to goe & Ride whensoever the Lord Treasurer & *chancellor of the exchequer* undertreasurer shall comand them.

V

THE LETTERS OF HENRY ST. JOHN
TO THE EARL OF ORRERY 1709–1711

edited by

H. T. DICKINSON
B.A., Dip. Ed., M.A., Ph.D., F.R.Hist. S.

CONTENTS

Introduction

These fifty-three letters, written by Henry St. John to Charles Boyle, Earl of Orrery, between July 1709 and October 1711, reveal much about St. John's growing determination to bring an end to the War of the Spanish Succession, about his activities as Secretary of State, and about the increasing friction between the allies as they manœuvred to secure their own particular interests before peace was made with France.

The letters start when St. John was in temporary and enforced political retirement, having failed to find a seat in the general election of 1708. It was during these two years, 1708–1710, that his sympathy with the plight of the Tory squires was re-awakened. Months before his return to office, in 1710, he had become convinced that a peace was essential, in order to reduce the tax burden on the squirearchy, and that a good peace settlement might have been made already if the allies had not sought to impose impossible terms on Louis XIV. Having returned to power in 1710, as Secretary of State for the Northern Department, he was determined that a peace should be made which would protect British interests. These, he felt, had been neglected in the past,[1] while the Dutch had sought the security of a barrier of fortresses to protect them against further French attacks and the Austrians had deployed much of their army in Hungary. Such selfishness, he maintained, had left Britain to bear

---

[1] *Letters and Correspondence of Bolingbroke*, ed. Gilbert Parke (London, 1798), i, pp. 26–7. To Drummond, 17 Nov. 1710.

a disproportionate share of the allied effort to place the Austrian claimant on the throne of Spain.

St. John's early correspondence as Secretary of State, even before he had recognized that it might be necessary for the Tory ministry to sacrifice the interests of the allies in order to secure the most advantageous terms for Britain, is full of complaints against the allies. As early as 1710–11 he was convinced that Britain should no longer continue her efforts to secure the particular interests of the Dutch and Austrians. Long before he attacked the Barrier Treaty in parliament, on 14 February 1712,[2] St. John had denounced it as inimical to Britain's own interests. The Barrier Treaty, which had been agreed upon by the British and Dutch in 1709, proposed to allow the Dutch to garrison a number of important fortresses in the Southern Netherlands, as a safeguard against future French attacks, and to grant the Dutch special trading privileges in this territory. The terms of this treaty, negotiated while the Whigs were in office, had been kept secret because of the fear of arousing resentment in Britain. St. John was well aware of this likely reaction when he wrote to Lord Raby, on 19 April 1711, protesting that 'if the Barrier-Treaty comes to be publickly known and considered in parliament, it will be absolutely impossible to keep the ferment down. All ranks, all parties of men, will unite in their protestations against it'.[3]

St. John was not prepared to let the terms of the Barrier Treaty stand between Britain and peace with France. He was even less willing to continue the war in order to put an Austrian on the throne of Spain. Even before he learned of James Stanhope's defeat in Spain, at Brihuega on 9 December 1710, N.S., St. John was ready to abandon Spain. In a letter to Drummond, the ministry's agent in Amsterdam, he confessed:

> We feel by experience, how insupportable an expence it is to carry on a regular war with great armies in Spain; we see, besides, how little hopes there are of any assistance from the good-will of the Spaniards to our cause; . . . in short, not to enumerate too many particulars, we think, that either there should have been no war in Spain, or another sort of one . . . we exhaust ourselves insensibly; and a million and a half is given to no purpose by us, when a very small addition to this on the part of our allies would perhaps have been decisive.[4]

---

[2] *The Wentworth Papers, 1705–1739*, ed. J. J. Cartwright (London, 1883), pp. 266–7 and B.M. Add. MS. 22227, f. 12. Peter Wentworth to Lord Strafford, 15 February 1712.

[3] *Letters and Correspondence of Bolingbroke*, ed. Parke, i, p. 154.

[4] *Ibid.*, i, pp. 44–5. 20 December 1710.

When the Emperor Joseph I died on 6/17 April 1711, and the Archduke Charles succeeded him, St. John was even less ready to continue a war in Spain which might enable Charles to re-create the Austro-Spanish Empire of Charles V. Even if the Austrians only secured part of the Spanish inheritance, they might be so strengthened that they would endanger the balance of power in Europe and threaten Britain's commercial interests in the Mediterranean. It was these two considerations which encouraged St. John to prefer the interests of one of Britain's minor allies, the Duke of Savoy. In contrast to his readiness to sacrifice Dutch and Austrian interests, he worked hard to promote Savoy's ambitions in Italy.[5]

St. John's attitude to Britain's allies is reflected in his letters to Orrery, published here. These letters also throw light on other aspects of St. John's activities in the first year of the new Tory administration. They reinforce the well-established view of St. John as a hardworking Secretary of State, who had a firm grasp on all aspects of his official duties. His particular department was responsible for Northern Europe and it clearly emerges that he was well-informed on the disputes between the Scandinavian powers, but, it is also apparent, that he was familiar with the affairs of Southern Europe, which were the responsibility of his fellow-Secretary of State, the Earl of Dartmouth. St. John's letters to Orrery show his constant concern to be fully informed by Britain's ambassadors, envoys and agents in Europe and the care he took to instruct them in their respective duties. These letters also illustrate some of St. John's particular interests in 1710-11. His efforts to mount an expedition against Quebec, which he pushed through the cabinet while Robert Harley was still absent from duty, suffering the ill-effects of Guiscard's attempts to assassinate him, are revealed in his attempts to find an engineer among the troops in the Netherlands. There are frequent references to the Pretender and his supporters in these letters, but they all suggest that St. John had, at this stage, little sympathy for the Jacobite cause.

As might be expected, however, these letters deal primarily with the affairs of the Southern Netherlands. Early in 1711 Orrery replaced General Cadogan as Britain's envoy-extraordinary to the States-General in The Hague and to the Council of State of the Southern Netherlands in Brussels. His main task was to act as Britain's envoy in the recently conquered Netherlands. He held this appointment until October 1711, and the majority of these letters by St. John are addressed to him during his stay in Brussels. Political

---

[5] H. N. Fieldhouse, 'St. John and Savoy in the War of the Spanish Succession', *Eng. Hist. Rev.*, l (1935), pp. 278–91.

and military developments in the Netherlands during 1711 reveal
the growing friction between Britain and her allies. After the allies
had conquered the Southern Netherlands in the name of Charles III,
the Austrian claimant to the Spanish inheritance, they had restored
the Council of State in Brussels. Details about the conduct of the
allies in the Southern Netherlands and their relations with this
Council of State fill much of the correspondence between St. John
and Orrery. The new Tory administration was already dissatisfied
with the military concessions granted to the Dutch in the Southern
Netherlands by the terms of the Barrier Treaty, but it was even
more alarmed by the commercial advantages which the Dutch were
enjoying. Article VIII of the Barrier Treaty allowed the Dutch to
send goods to their garrison towns in the Southern Netherlands duty-
free. This concession enabled the Dutch to bring their manufactures
into the Netherlands and to sell them underhand to the local
inhabitants. British goods, on the other hand, had to pay heavy
duties if they entered the Southern Netherlands. Furthermore, the
Dutch claimed the sole right of administering the territory captured
from France. This allowed them to collect import duties on goods
coming from the Southern Netherlands into the towns taken from
France. Dutch manufactures were sold in these towns free of any
duty, but British goods had to pay one duty when entering the
Southern Netherlands and a second duty when transported into the
towns captured from France.[6] As St. John makes clear in these
letters to Orrery, he was determined that not only would the terms
of the Barrier Treaty be revised, but Britain would no longer allow
the Dutch alone to reap the commercial advantages of the successful
prosecution of the war in the Low Countries.

From Orrery[7] and from prominent citizens of the Southern
Netherlands,[8] St. John received complaints about the way the Dutch
were executing the provisional administration of the Spanish
Netherlands. The Dutch were accused of subjecting the Southern
Netherlands to heavy exactions in money and provisions to help
meet their own military expenses and to provide for the upkeep of
the Imperial and Palatine troops garrisoned in the area. General
Cadogan, Orrery's predecessor, also came in for heavy criticism,

---

[6] For Britain's reaction to the commercial advantages of the Dutch in
the Low Countries see Roderick Geikie and Isobel A. Montgomery, *The Dutch
Barrier 1705–1719* (Cambridge, 1930), pp. 187–214.

[7] Orrery's letters, chiefly between April and June 1711, are in the Public
Record Office, State Papers Foreign, Flanders, vol. 60.

[8] See the letter of complaint sent by the citizens of Gand (Ghent) to St. John,
19 March 1711, in the Appendix to this correspondence.

because of his support for the exactions levied by the Dutch. When Orrery began to take the side of the Council of State in Brussels, he met hostility from the Dutch, Cadogan and the Duke of Marlborough. St. John, at first, refused to countenance these objections and gave Orrery his full support. He made this clear to Drummond, his agent in Amsterdam, when he wrote to him on 27 April 1711:

I cannot agree that Lord Orrery is so much in the wrong, or that there is so much danger of losing the subsistance of the Imperial and Palatine troops as Mr. Watkins seems to believe. My Lord has the Queen's positive and repeated orders to insist, in the first place, that the Spanish Provinces should furnish all the expenses charged upon them for the service of the war; but he is directed, at the same time, to act the part of an advocate and a protector, when any unreasonable proposition is by other people pressed upon them. Nay, in such cases, the common necessity will oblige him to yield, and where he knows beforehand that he is to do so; the Queen will, however, approve his conduct, if he shows a reluctancy to enter into oppressive measures, and if, at the time he consents to load them on one account, he endeavours to ease them in some other respects. These unhappy countries have found the government of those who pretend to be the assertors of public liberty so tyrannical and barbarous, that you know better than I how near they are driven to despair. The Queen's servants have, to the reproach of our government and nation, been, in great measure, the instruments of all these vile proceedings. Something, therefore, must be done to relieve the miserable people, and something to redeem the honour of the British name.[9]

This admirable concern for the liberties of the people of the Southern Netherlands was, of course, far from disinterested. It was to Britain's advantage to undermine Dutch influence in the region in order to pave the way for a peace settlement which would secure commercial privileges for her merchants at the expense of the Dutch. This concern for the liberties of the Southern Netherlands could not be taken too far, however. It could not be allowed to jeopardize relations between the British and the Dutch. A rupture in the alliance had to be avoided before the Tory government had secretly nego-tiated peace terms with the French. Moreover, both Orrery and St. John came to appreciate that the Council of State in Brussels was doing little to support the allied interest and that a policy of un-limited support for the Council against the Dutch would only make the dual control of the Southern Netherlands impossible.[10]

9 *Letters and Correspondence of Bolingbroke*, ed. Parke, i, pp. 168–9.
10 Duncan Coombs, *The Conduct of the Dutch* (The Hague, 1958), p. 245.

The friction between the Dutch and the Council of State in Brussels was not the only factor preventing the allies exerting maximum pressure on the French in the Low Countries during 1711. Although the Tory ministry was already embarked on separate peace negotiations with the French, it could not secure the best terms unless the allies continued to pose a serious threat to France's northern frontier. As St. John's letters to Orrery make abundantly clear, this proved very difficult in 1711. The allies had never been so disunited. This was not just due to the Tory government's readiness to open peace negotiations with France; negotiations which were designed to put Britain's interests before those of her allies. The affairs of the Holy Roman Empire distracted the attention of many of the allies away from the Low Countries. The death of the Emperor gave France the opportunity of intervening in the affairs of Germany. Suspecting that the French might launch a surprise attack across the Rhine, Prince Eugene marched off into Germany, in June 1711, with all the Imperial troops in the allied army. At the same time the King of Denmark and Augustus II, who was both Elector of Saxony and King of Poland, threatened to take their troops out of the allied camp in order to meet a potential Swedish attack. In 1710 the Hague Convention had guaranteed the neutrality of the Empire in order to prevent the German princes, needed to support the allied cause against France, joining in a free-for-all to partition Sweden's German provinces. A second convention, in December 1710, had proposed a Corps of Neutrality of 21,000 men to maintain the peace within the Empire. Charles XII of Sweden, however, had refused to accept this neutralization of the Empire, since this tied his hands. Denmark and Saxony, therefore, wanted the Corps of Neutrality to protect them from a Swedish expeditionary force and, perhaps, to assist them in their own plans to attack Swedish territory. The British and Dutch refused to support their proposals, but they feared that the Danish and Saxon troops would abandon the allies during the 1711 campaign. To make matters worse, the King of Prussia also threatened to withdraw the 20,000 Prussian troops serving in Marlborough's army. He made this threat in an effort to force the British and Dutch to support his claim to the family inheritance of William III, the former King of England and Stadholder of Holland. His threat might well have had the desired effect in the long-run, but the allies were saved from the embarrassment of a prolonged dispute by the sudden death by drowning of the rival claimant to the inheritance, the young Prince of Orange. In view of these disputes in the allied camp, the consequent reduction in the size of the allied army in Flanders, and the Tory ministry's evident desire for peace, Marlborough's success in 1711 is astonishing. In a brilliant campaign he managed to breach the formidable French defences, the *ne plus ultra* lines, and to capture the important fortress of Bouchain.

*   *   *

These fifty-three letters of Henry St. John to the Earl of Orrery were copied into two letter-books which are now deposited in the Bodleian Library, Oxford. It is not possible to say, with any certainty, when or by whom they were copied. The Bodleian Library bought the two letter-books from two different booksellers on two separate occasions and, unfortunately, their earlier provenance is no longer known.[11] All that can be offered therefore is conjecture. The two letter-books, though later separated, clearly belong together. The letters run on in chronological order from one letter-book to the other and, together, they probably make up all or most of the letters sent by St. John to Orrery while the latter was serving on a diplomatic mission to the Spanish Netherlands. The letters were not copied into the letter-books by Henry St. John himself, but they are the product of the same eighteenth-century hand. Because of the heading on the first page of each letter-book, it appears that the letters were copied some short time after they were written. Moreover, since the first letters were personal rather than official correspondence, it is unlikely that the letters were copied by a secretary in St. John's office *before* they were sent off to the Earl of Orrery. St. John may, however, have had them copied by one of his secretaries, perhaps Thomas Hare, *after* Orrery had been recalled from the Spanish Netherlands. This hypothesis is supported by the fact that the last letter in the collection, which is published below as an appendix, was from Thomas Hare to Orrery.

The first thirty letters constitute MS. Eng. misc. e. 180 and the remainder are MS. Eng. lett. e. 4. Each page of the letter-books is numbered, but the letters were copied onto the recto pages only. Ten of these letters were published in the first volume of Gilbert Parke's edition of *The Letters and Correspondence of Bolingbroke* (London, 1798), and these have therefore not been printed in full below. The original spelling and punctuation, including the idiosyncratic placing of accents in the letters written in French, have been retained, but abbreviations have been expanded and many

---

11 MS. Eng. misc. e. 180 was bought for two guineas from the bookseller, P. Dobell, on 17 October 1927. MS. Eng. lett. e. 4 was bought for £1 2s. 6d. from the bookseller, C. Radford, on 15 April 1933. These booksellers are no longer in business.

capital letters have been put in a lower case. The dating of the letters has been standardized, but they are still all dated according to the Old Style. The notes are an attempt to identify the important individuals mentioned in the letters.

I am most grateful to the Bodley's Librarian for permission to edit these letters for publication.

Copies of letters from Henry St. John Esqr to the Right Honourable Charles Earl of Orrery, in the years 1709, 1710, and 1711.

1. [*p. 1*]   Bucklebury.[1] 9 July 1709
  My Lord,
           What you excuse as a trouble, I must begin my letter with thanking you for as the greatest pleasure I have received since the time I enjoyed your conversation last. I have learnt to desire very few things, and by consequence shall never want many. Amongst those which I desire most earnestly, are [a] few friends; and nothing can give me greater joy than to find in any particular instance that my expectations on that side do not fail me.
  [*p. 3*] My health, which you are so kindly concerned for, is extreamly good. Those opportunities of spoiling it are at a distance: and to own the truth, as I have them seldomer, so I want them less. You see, my Lord, one effect of my retreat. The men of profound wisdom form to themselves a scheme of life; and every action is preceded by a thought. We, who are of a more ordinary size of understanding, act by chance at first, and by habit afterwards.
  Peace and fair weather follow health in your Lordship's letter, as they do in Sir Wm. Temple's[2] wish. The latter we are at last so happy as to enjoy: and I hope that you, who want it more, have your share of it.
  The other is, I fear, still a great way off. At least, it is to our eyes the more remote now, by how much the nearer we thought it some weeks ago.
  Since you engage me in this subject, I own to you, my Lord, that my judgment concerning our conduct at the Hague depends and turns on a fact, which we on this side, I mean, we who follow the [*p. 5*] plow, are not, I beleive, very exactly, nor very authentically informed of.
  If France chicaned about the evacuation of Spain, if they would not consent to withdraw their troops in two months, which troops then were and still continue within a much less march of their own country, my poor opinion would incline me to think that the French King intended nothing more than to take breath: to gain a summer, and by consequence a winter, and then to have it in his power, as he found his circumstances mend, or grow worse, to submit to your terms, or to carry on the war.
  If, on the other hand, he would have consented to the preliminaries

[1] St. John's country house in Berkshire.
[2] Sir William Temple (1629–99), statesman, diplomat and author.

in such manner, as might evidently have secured Spain to that miserable Lord Mayor of Barcelona,[3] and have given a reasonable Barrier to Holland, in such case our rigid insisting on every article of those preliminaries seems unaccountable. Especially, if those refiners judge right, who pretend to say that the advantages stipulated for Britaine bear no proportion to the part she has had in the war: and that Holland by [*p*. 7] the articles would not only have been rendered safe, but formidable. But I, who have not the necessary materials of thinking upon this subject, am very impertinent to say so much upon it.

Your Lordship hints at another thing which I know more of: the spirit of our gentlemen, and what is to be expected from it. Alas, my Lord, nothing. Examine a little this chain of causes. We have been twenty years engaged in the two most expensive wars that Europe ever saw. The whole burthen of this charge has lain upon the landed interest during the whole time. The men of estates have, generally speaking, neither served in the fleets nor armies, nor meddled in the public fonds, and management of the treasure.

A new interest has been created out of their fortunes, and a sort of property, which was not known twenty years ago, is now encreased to be almost equal to the terra firma of our island. The consequence of all this is, that the landed men are become poor and dispirited. They either abandon all thoughts of the publick, turn arrant farmers, and improve the [*p*. 9] estates they have left: or else they seek to repair their shattered fortunes by listing at court, or under the heads of partys. In the mean while those men are become their masters, who formerly would with joy have been their servants. To judge therefore rightly of what turn our domestick affairs are in any respect likely to take, we must for the future only consider, what the temper of the court, and of the Bank, is.

You see, my Lord, the effect of provoking an idle fellow. It costs you dear. At least, I doubt you will think so, before you get thus far.

That I may not, like the facheux in Moliere, encrease my impertinence by excusing it, verbum non amplius addam.

Ever most faithfully
Your humble servant
H. St. J.

[PS] I beg leave to assure the Duke of Argyll[4] of my humble service.

---

[3] Archduke Charles of Austria (1685–1740), the Habsburg pretender to the Spanish throne as 'Charles III'. He had little support in Spain beyond Barcelona. In 1711 he succeeded his brother to the Habsburg territories as the Emperor Charles VI.

[4] John Campbell, 2nd Duke of Argyll (1680–1743).

2. [*p. 11*]   Bucklebury. 1 September 1709

My dear Lord,
                    Those few people in the world, who have your good
sence and your knowledge, should never make that apology, which
begins your last letter. Your expressions of kindness are more agreeable to me, and your thoughts upon any subject more entertaining,
than the journals of your armies, or the minutes of your councils.

Whether it is owing to constitution or to philosophy I can't
tell, but certain it is, that I can make myself easy in any sort of life.
Nil admirari prope res est una, Numice, Solaque, quae possit facere
et servare beatum.

Happiness, I imagine, depends much more on desiring little, than
enjoying much; and perhaps the surest road to it is indifference. If I
continue in the country, the sports of the field and the pleasures of
my study will take up all my thoughts, and serve to amuse me as
long as I live. If any [*p. 13*] accident should call me again to the
pleasure and business of London, I shall be as eager as ever I was in
the pursuit of both.

This, my Lord, is an honest account of my system, which your
letter gave me occasion to mention.

Though the condition of France by evident tokens appears to
be miserable, yet their ill circumstances are certainly exaggerated in
our accounts. I doubt, we may add that our own state is not much
better than our enemy's, and that an unseasonable harvest would
reduce our people to the same misery as we triumph over.

Peace is as much our interest as theirs. I am so firmly persuaded of
this, that I will continue to hope the winter may ripen this glorious
fruit, which the summer could not.

As to the conditions of this peace, it is melancholy to reflect, that
those articles you speak of, which will in their consequence devolve
so prodigious a power on Holland, seem to be agreed on all sides;
whilst the single principle on which we engaged in the war, remaines
the only point in dispute.

[*p. 15*] You cannot think too meanly of our people. No man looks
on things as they really are, but sees them through that glass which
party holds up to him. I agree with you that it is happy our libertys
and propertys are in safe hands. There never was in any nation a
time, when to wrest both away was so easy an enterprise.

How great were the convulsions in Rome, before that government
was overturned? The Gracchi first, and multitudes after them, dyed
in the struggle. On these ruines victorious tyranny stalked in. But
Britons might be driven like a flock of turkeys: nay, we are tamer
still, for by my soul we should not cackle.

My dear Lord, adieu. Let me hear from you whenever you have a minute to spare; and believe this truth, that no man loves or honours you more than

Your ever faithfull
H. S.

3. [*p. 17*]   22 August 1710
I am just come home to write, and my servant tells me that Capt. Middleton[5] has been here, that he has letters for me, and that he will call tomorrow morning. For this reason, perhaps, my epistle may not prove so pertinent as I might have made it, if yours had come to my hands in time.

I begin now to see my way; and though in every respect it will not be possible, for reasons which I gave you in my last, and for some which I will give you by the first conveyance that offers itself safer than the post, to play the game just as we would wish to do, or as we at first proposed, yet certainly with common address, and uncommon steadiness, we may be able to build up as well as we have been to pull down.

It is incredible to what a degree 353 [the Whigs] are united in opposition; but their numbers will soon diminish if the 400 [the Tories] can be made to proceed reasonably; which I do not really much doubt, though I must think [*p. 19*] that we do not take these in with the best grace, and with the greatest advantage to ourselves. Several persons imagine that the new measures of 100 [Robert Harley][6] cannot last; these will come over, as soon as they see a firm foundation of strength layed. Others are alarmed and expect the utmost violence of a contrary extream; these will likewise be recovered, when they find 400 [the Tories] kept in order, and the true interest pursued.

28 [Lord Rivers][7] is gone, but to tell you what must go no further than yourself and 200 [the Duke of Argyll?], not absolutely so well instructed as we endeavoured he should be. However, we hope to supply this defect, and to prevail to send that after him, which we hoped he would have carried with him. 44 [the Duke of Somerset][8]

[5] John Middleton of Aberdeenshire, a captain in the Duke of Argyll's regiment of foot. He later reached the rank of Brigadier General and was elected M.P. for the Aberdeen burghs.

[6] Robert Harley (1661–1724) had been largely responsible for engineering the recent downfall of the Godolphin administration.

[7] Richard Savage, 3rd Earl Rivers (1654–1712), had just been sent as envoy to Hanover in an effort to convince the Electoral family that it had nothing to fear from the recent change of ministry.

[8] Charles Seymour, 6th Duke of Somerset, had been prepared to accept the

is out of Town, but I think he is to return towards the end of this week. I expect him to be very much out of humour. Its prodigious to see a man so zealous for a proposition, and so averse to everything necessary to support and make that good.

I will add no more now, but write to you by [*p. 21*] the next post.

I am ever entirely and zealously

Yours

[unsigned]

[PS] My best respects attend 200 [Argyll?]

4.   Friday, 29 December [1710]

My Lord,

I shall not be able to wait on you today, as I hoped to have done; but will endeavour to call upon you tomorrow morning when I go out.

If your Lordship has an inclination to serve the Queen at Brussels, as you once expressed yourself to me to have, your Lordship might now be appointed to that employment. In the other particulars relating to yourself, I hope Mr [*p. 23*] Harley has given you satisfaction. My Lord Ilay [Islay][9] writes to me about Desney's[10] commission, about which I do not remember whether I might speak to you or no. The Queen did order me, I think at Hampton Court, to prepare it; supposing that the Duke[11] had agreed with my Lord Ilay; from that time to this it has layn by, unfilled up till I should hear from my Lord.

I should be under the last concern if I imagined he could think me capable of doing the least thing, which was not perfectly agreeable to that respect and friendship which I have for him.

Think between this and tomorrow what you would have me do in your own affairs, and I will not fail to call to receive your orders.

I am, my dear Lord, ever inviolably yours

H.S.

---

recent changes in the administration, but he was bitterly opposed to the proposal to dissolve Parliament a year early and to call a general election which might result in a Tory landslide.

9 Archibald Campbell, Earl of Islay (1682–1761). The younger brother and eventual successor to the Duke of Argyll.

10 Colonel 'Duke' Desney or Disney was a great friend of St. John, Orrery, Swift and other Tories. He served under Colonel Hill on the expedition against Quebec in 1711.

11 John Churchill, Duke of Marlborough, was Captain-General and very jealous of his influence over army promotions.

5. [*p. 25*]   Whitehall. 10 January 1710 [/11]
    My Lord,
                By letters which I received yesterday I find that the
state of affairs in the Low Countrys requires on many heads immediate care to be taken of them, and the Pensionary[12] is very
desirous to have your Lordship dispatched.
    In respect to the preparations for the campagne, I am sure if you
are not in time at Brussells, the backwardness thereof, and any
failure therein, will infallibly be layed at your door, and at the doors
of your friends.
    I send you this note, because tomorrow I shall be obliged to speak
to the Queen upon this subject. The contract for the Imperialists
and Palatines bread and forage ends in February; and must be
renewed immediately. Cadogan[13] is coming to England. Adieu;
believe me to be with [*p. 27*] true respect and friendship.
                         Your Lordship's most obedient humble servant
                                                        H. St. John

6.   Whitehall. 1 February 1710/11
    My Lord,
                This is to acquaint your Lordship that there is a council
to meet this evening at St. James's, and that it is her Majesty's
pleasure that your Lordship should attend about six of the clock in
order to be sworn one of her Privy Councill.
    I am, my Lord, your Lordship's obedient most humble servant
                                                        H. St. John

7. [*p. 29*]   Whitehall. 9 February 1710/11
    My Lord,
                I am to acquaint your Lordship that there will be a
General Councill at St. James's at six of the clock this evening; and
it is her Majesty's pleasure that your Lordship do attend there at
that time in order to be sworn one of the Privy Councill.
                    I am, my Lord,
                        your Lordship's obedient and most humble servant
                                                        H. St. John

[12] Anthonie Heinsius (1641–1720) was Grand Pensionary of the province of
Holland and Keeper of the Seals (first minister) of the States General.
[13] William Cadogan (1675–1726) was Quarter-Master General and Adjutant
to Marlborough. He had just been replaced by Orrery as envoy to Brussels
and The Hague.

8. [*p. 31*]   Whitehall. 20 February 1710[/1
My Lord,
               Though the wind is high, yet it is fair, and I hope your
Lordship is safely arrived in Holland.
    I have yet no point of business to speak to your Lordship upon,
more than what we talked over when I last had the honour of seeing
your Lordship at my office.
    There is however one matter, which I will not lose a post in
advising your Lordship about. The Queen has a service extreamly at
heart,[14] which will from the nature of it require a very good Ingenier,
and you know how much we want people of this character. I have
been informed that there is in Hartop's[15] Walloon Regiment a
Captain called de Bauff,[16] who is of very great sufficiency in this
trade. If your Lordship could find a [*p. 33*] way of knowing this
officer's mind, you would do a piece of agreeable service to her
Majesty. The leave of his superiors must be obtained for him, his
employment which he now has must be preserved to him, the Queen
will establish him during his being abroad on her account very well,
and at his return he may depend on a very handsome reward.
    Your Lordship will please to manage this matter so as not to let
it take wind, unless you perceive that the man may be spared, and
may be made willing to go where the Queen shall think fit to send
him.
         I am with great respect, My Lord,
               your Lordship's obedient and most humble servant
                                                  H. St. John

9. [*p. 35*]   Whitehall. 9 March 1710/11
My Lord,
    I was extreamly glad to find by the honour of your letter of the
6th N.S. that your Lordship was safely arrived at the Hague, and
had begun to enter upon business with the Pensioner [Heinsius]. I
do not doubt but in a little time we shall see the good effect of your
Lordship's negociations, particularly in contributing towards a
proper regulation of the government of the Spanish Low Countries;
which, as your Lordship observes, is in a very distracted condition at
present; and therefore no time should be lost in putting it upon a
better foot.

[14] The proposed expedition against Quebec.
[15] Hartrop was colonel of a Walloon regiment of infantry. He had served
for 30 years with considerable distinction and Marlborough pressed to have
him promoted by 'Charles III', the Austrian claimant to the Netherlands.
[16] Recently promoted brevet Lieutenant Colonel by Marlborough for his
services in Flanders.

Your Lordship will find in the newspaper from my office a short account of a villanous action which I think is not to be parallelled in history. Monsieur de Guiscard[17] has four wounds; [*p. 37*] but none mortal, as we hope. The chirurgeons beleive that he will recover, there being no bad symptoms as yet: and it is pity he should dye any other death, than the most ignominious which such an attempt deserves. Mr Harley is in a very good way at present, and I hope not in the least danger of his life.

I must deferr writing till next post particularly and fully to your Lordship, the hurry I am now in making it impossible to do it by this post.

> I am ever, my Lord,
>> your Lordship's ever faithful and most humble servant
>>> H. St. John

10. [*p. 39*]   Whitehall. 13 March 1710[/11]
My Lord,
               I yesterday received your Lordship's letters of the 10th, 13th and 17th of this month N.S., but the Queen's indisposition, as well as the extraordinary hurry of this day's business, hinders me from giving so particular an answer to them as I will do by the next post. I cannot however omitt desiring your Lordship to make a bargaine, if you can do it upon any reasonable terms, with de Bauff the Ingineer, concerning whom I wrote to you some time since. I can hardly beleive his circumstances to be so good as to incline him to refuse going, for this summer's campagne, upon a service, where the Queen will employ him, and where he will be sure of much more advantage than he has hitherto had, according to my information, in Flanders.

Our friend Mr Harley is quite out of danger, [*p. 41*] his feavour having this day entirely left him.

> I am ever, my Lord, with much respect and truth
>> your Lordship's most faithfull and most obedient servant
>>> H. St. John

11.   [*pp. 41–7.*] [*This letter, dated 20 March 1710/11 O.S. is printed exactly in* Letters and Correspondence of Bolingbroke, *ed. Gilbert Parke (London, 1798), i, pp. 120–2.*]

---

[17] Antoine de Guiscard, abbé de la Bourlie (1658–1711), a French adventurer in the British service, who, when discovered in traitorous correspondence with France, stabbed Robert Harley. He died shortly afterwards of the wounds which he received in the ensuing struggle. Harley was ill for some weeks, but made a good recovery. See H. T. Dickinson, 'The Attempt to Assassinate Robert Harley, 1711', *History Today*, xv (1965), pp. 788–95.

12. [*p. 47*]   Whitehall. 20 March 1710/11
  My Lord,
              The mail, which came in yesterday, brought me the
favour of your Lordship's letter of the 26th N.S., and I have the
satisfaction to tell your Lordship upon it, that Mr Harley will in all
probability be well in a week's time, and fit to enter again upon
business. But I am sorry to let you know at the same time, that
Monsieur de Guiscard is dead, and has thereby escaped being made
that publick example, which his villanys deserved.

   Your Lordship will see by my letter to my Lord Marlborough, of
which you have herewith a copy, under how great concern her
Majesty is on account of the advices we have received concerning
the stopping the march of the King [*p. 49*] of Prussia's troops,[18] and
the difficulty in settling the funds for subsisting the Imperial and
Palatine troops in Flanders. I shall not trouble your Lordship on
the first head, it being a matter out of your province; but on the
second, besides the orders given to my Lord Marlborough, which you
will please to take, as if they were particularly addressed to yourself,
I cannot help repeating, and adding, that one way or other this
matter must be terminated without delay; that the common cause is
at stake; and that you cannot go too far in exerting the Queen's
authority, nor in speaking plainly and resolutely in her name. It
were to be wished that the Dutch might be induced to depart from
their objections against the dutys on corn, brandy, and white salt,
and nothing ought to be neglected to bring them to it; since then this
whole work would be done at once. On the other hand your Lordship
must not be wanting to speak in very strong and urgent terms to the
States of the Spanish Low-Countrys; and lay before them how ill a
return they are going to make by [*p. 51*] this obstinate proceeding
to the Queen, who has entered with so much compassion into all
their sufferings, and has thought fit to make it a particular article of
her instructions to your Lordship, that you should contribute all
you can to the ease of their people, and settle a better regulation of
government than has been hitherto observed amongst them.

   Her Majesty approves very well of your Lordship's writing to the
States General with earnestness upon this subject. You cannot use
too much of it either to them, or to any other persons concerned in en-
forcing her Majesty's sense upon so critical and important a matter.

_____

   [18] Frederick I of Prussia (1659–1719) threatened to withdraw his troops
from the allied army, if the British and Dutch did not support his claims to
inherit the Orange-Nassau territories of the late William III. The issue was
resolved when the young Prince of Orange, the other claimant, was accidentally
drowned.

I shall be glad to receive the copy you mention of the Regulation of Power for the Spanish Low-Countries, signed at the Hague, as soon as your Lordship can send it.

Your Lordship knows so very well the need of good intelligence from France, that I shall not take upon me to recommend to you the improving it as far as possible. It is certain that we have hitherto been not a little deficient in that point: [*p. 53*] which has been so much to our detriment, as the enemy has drawn great advantage from their care in managing it. Your Lordship is acquainted with the several reports lately spread concerning the Pretender, and his designs. It is true, we lay no great stress upon them. However, it is a satisfaction to know the ground of the rumours which are given out, and whether he makes the campaine, or comes to Dunkirk, or what his real intentions are.

I send your Lordship inclosed extracts of letters from my Lord Townshend[19] concerning one Seaton[20] a Scotchman who was seized by his Excellency's order in his way to France. You will please to examine further into that matter, and endeavour to give a full and exact account of it: upon which I may send your Lordship more particular directions from her Majesty relating to the whole affair.

I am, my Lord,
your Lordship's most faithful and most humble servant

H. St. John

[*p. 55*]   Here follow copies of Mr St. John's letter to the Duke of Marlborough, and of the extracts from Lord Townshend concerning Seaton, both referred to in the foregoing letter.

i.   Whitehall. 20 March 1710/11
My Lord,
            I received yesterday the honour of your Grace's letter of the 27th inst. N.S., and have laid it before the Queen, who was under the greatest concern imaginable to hear of the strange and unexpected step, which the King of Prussia has taken in regard to the march of his troops.

Her Majesty was particularly surprized to observe herself joyned with the States in his Prussian Majesty's letter to your Grace, as if she had given equal occasion to that Prince of raising complaints against her conduct in relation to his pretensions. Her Majesty knows of nothing that she has been wanting in towards [*p. 57*] procuring

---

[19] Charles, 2nd Viscount Townshend (1674–1738), was ambassador and plenipotentiary at The Hague from 1709 to 1711.

[20] Several Scottish families with the surname Seaton or Seton supported the Jacobite cause.

him due satisfaction on all the representations that have been made to her. Nothing has been omitted by the Queen in doing all she could at Berlin, in Holland, and here, for complying with every article of his demands, even the most unreasonable, as particularly that of the additional charge of her Majesty's share of 10000 crowns on account of the 8000 Prussians in Italy. I do not enter into the nature of the dispute with the Dutch, nor how little ground there may be in justice and equity to show so much violence against their proceedings in relation to the succession. The King himself chose to follow the methods of law in that country: and it can't be reasonably expected that the States should carry their complyance so far as to break through the constitution of their republick to gratify him. However, the Queen has all along, as your Grace knows, repeated her most pressing instances that some expedients might be found to give his Prussian Majesty the utmost satisfaction possible. This being the state of the case, your Grace will easily imagine how extraordinary a surprize [*p. 59*] it was to her Majesty to hear that the King of Prussia had taken so suddain and violent a resolution, especially since she understood that he was in very good temper and well satisfyed; and did not think of meeting with the least difficulty in any part of the service towards which his Majesty's troops were to have concurred.

I am, my Lord, to acquaint you that the Queen and the Lords of the Councill heard with great approbation the letter which your Grace wrote to the King of Prussia on this occasion:[21] and her Majesty desires you to continue to talk and to write to that court and its ministers in the same style.

Monsieur Bonet[22] was with me last night very late after the Committee was up. He began to talk to me of the affairs of Hildesheim, Loo and Deeien, Quedlinburg,[23] and several other things as trifling and inconsiderable as those are; at last he came to the arrears of subsidys, and to the Queen's part of the extraordinary sum of 10000 crowns. I took that occasion of interrupting him, and telling him, that the Queen was extreamly surprized at the accounts which she had received from Holland [*p. 61*] of the orders given by his master to stop the march of his troops: and at the manner in which he has joyned the Queen and the States together in complaining that

21 Marlborough's letter to the King of Prussia, dated 27 March 1711 N.S., can be seen in *The Letters and Dispatches of Marlborough*, ed. Sir George Murray (London, 1845), v, pp. 284–5.

22 André Louis Frédéric Bonet de Saint Germain, a Frenchman who acted as the Prussian resident in London from 1697 to 1720.

23 Hildesheim, Loos, Dieren and Quedlinburg were small towns in Germany Holland and Flanders, where the King of Prussia had pretensions.

he has had no satisfaction upon the representations he has made; since there is so little ground for these complaints with respect to the latter; and since there is absolutely none at all with respect to the former. I endeavoured afterwards to shew him what reasonable objections there lay against the King of Prussia's pretensions in the several points above mentioned, if we had any inclination to make them: and at the same time, notwithstanding this, what steps the Queen as well as the States have taken out of their great regard for his Prussian Majesty to comply with, and even to humour him. I told him further, that since the King his master had for considerations of such little moment thought fit to stop his troops to expose the common cause in such a conjuncture as this, and to run the risque of breaking through all the measures of the campaine, and giving the enemy an advantage which without his assistance they could not have had: [*p. 63*] he was not to expect that the Queen would pay one farthing of his arrears, or interest herselfe in promoting his pretensions, and much less give him those extraordinarys he demands, until his orders of halting were revoked, and the troops were actually in march. I think, I have not exceeded the Queen's intentions upon this occasion; and I hope that this manner of treating him here will have its due effect, whilst, perhaps, it may be proper for the Ministers in Holland to speak in somewhat a smoother style.

The next point contained in your Grace's letter relates to the funds to be provided for the subsistance of the Imperial and Palatine troops in Flanders. This is likewise a very great addition to our other misfortune. I find by my Lord Orrery's letters that this matter turns upon the same difficulties it did several months ago, and that some complyance on the one side, or the other, would make it much more easie. Monsieur Vryberge[24] was with me this morning, and endeavoured to justify his masters for insisting on the objections they make to the funds proposed by the States of Brabant; [*p. 65*] and desired that the Queen's ministers might joyn with the Dutch in over-ruling those gentlemen in the points they contest. I find that her Majesty hopes, if the necessity of affairs should require that this business should be forced upon the States of the Spanish Low-Countrys; yet there should be more than ordinary care taken to let them see that it is intended to put their government upon a better and more regular foot for the future: and that they shall be releived from the oppressions which they suffer at present. That the consolation of a more advantageous prospect hereafter may make them

---

[24] Marinus Dibbout van Vryberge or Vrijbergen (1657–1711), the Dutch envoy in London.

bear this constraint with less reluctance. For it is certain that the hardships they have undergone have sowered their minds, and made them more obstinate and more tenacious in this article of the funds. Monsieur Vryberge informed me, that the States consented to all the methods proposed for raising the 450 m. guilders which remaine to be provided for the Imperial and Palatin troops, except the dutys on corn, brandy, and white salt. I found the objection made in Holland to these impositions was, that, in case they were laid, the people of the [*p. 67*] Spanish Netherlands could make those commoditys themselves at a cheaper rate than they were at present imported by the Dutch. This, indeed, according to her Majesty's opinion, may be a very popular argument in Holland, but cannot be of equal weight in the provinces under the Spanish government. And therefore the Queen is very sorry to observe, whatever the true reason may be at the bottom, that those people have such a plausible pretence given them for refusing to comply. All I have to say upon the whole matter, is, that one way or other this point must be immediately determined. For neither the obstinacy of the Council of State in Flanders, nor the little views of gain in the Dutch, are so much to be considered as to suffer the common cause to receive such a terrible blow, as so great a diminution of our army on that side would certainly prove. And therefore I am to tell your Grace, and I am to write the same to my Lord Orrery, that the Queen depends upon it that you should insist, and not fail to lay this whole weight of her Majesty's authority upon it, that this [*p. 69*] important point should be forthwith decided, if we are not so happy as to have it ended before this comes to your hands. But I am directed to give your Grace this caution, that in all cases due care should be taken that England may not be loaded with any further expence, nor come into any share of the burthen on this account.

After this long letter I have still one point more to trouble your Grace about, which Monsieur Vryberge mentioned in his discourse to me this morning. The treaty with Denmark for their troops expires in July next, and, as I understand, the States have given orders to their Minister at Copenhagen to take care to renew, and prolong that treaty. I beleive, that no such orders have been as yet given from hence. But I take the Queen's sense to be, that if this treaty is to be renewed, and that the Danes insist to have new articles and conditions added to it, her Majesty would rather have the project formed, and considered in Holland, than at Copenhagen. But if there be no further intention than to have a bare renewal of it as it now stands, it is not much matter in what place that be done. [*p. 71*] However, I should be glad to hear from your Grace by the first opportunity what the sentiments are in Holland upon that subject. In the mean time I shall avoid entring into discourse with Monsieur Rosenkrantz[25] concerning it, who has already attempted once or twice to debate that point with me.

I am, my Lord,
    your Grace's obedient faithful humble servant
        H. St. John

ii. Extract of a letter from my Lord Townshend to Mr Secretary St. John, dated at the Hague, the 30th January 1711.

Having been some time since informed, that one Seaton a Scotchman being a person disaffected to her Majesty's government was to go from Rotterdam to Bruges to conferr there with my Lord Drummond,[26] and afterwards to continue his journey to France upon some bad design; and [*p. 73*] Mr Walpole[27] having received orders formerly from Mr Boyle[28] to inform himself of the behaviour and motions of my Lord Drummond; I thought it for her Majesty's service to acquaint Mr Cadogan with this affair, and to desire him to have enquiry made at Bruges after the said Seaton, and to cause him to be arrested after he had left that place, and should be upon the road to France, as being the best means to discover by the papers that might be found about him the design of his journey, and the truth of my intelligence. Mr Cadogan having accordingly given the necessary directions, the said Seaton was arrested the 22d instant on his way to France having a false passeport: which being a sufficient reason for seizing him, is the only one which has been yet alledged to him for doing it. You have inclosed copies of the most material papers found about him, which prove no more than that he was going to France. I keep the originals, because the paper, which concerns the route and direction for Seaton's journey, seems to be writ by the same hand that gave me the advice, and gives just reason to think that he, from whom I had [*p. 75*] the information, is a rogue that intended to play a double game, to get money on both sides, and rather to amuse me for his own advantage, than to make any material discovery, which I will take the first opportunity of examining into. Seaton is kept prisoner by the

---

[25] Ivar Eriksen Rosenkrantz, the Danish envoy to London, 1702–3 and 1709–14.

[26] James, Lord Drummond (1673–1720), was heir to the Earl of Perth. He was imprisoned for his Jacobite sympathies in 1696 and 1708. In 1715 he fought at Sheriffmuir, but was forced to follow the Pretender into permanent exile.

[27] Robert Walpole, Secretary at War 1708–10.

[28] Henry Boyle, Secretary of State for the Northern Department 1708–10.

Commandant at Bruges, and I shall write to have him continued in arrest until her Majesty's pleasure be known in this matter.

iii. Copy of a letter from Monsieur du Guay,[29] Intendant of Marine at Dunkirk, to Marsaull, found about Seaton; enclosed in Lord Townshend's letter of 30 January 1711.

Le 4 Decembre 1710

J'ay receu, Monsieur, votre lettre du 24 du passé, et ay mis sur le champ à la poste celle qui l'accompagnoit, très fâché de la lethargie de nos amis, mais il ne faut pas perdre courage, à la fin ils s'evoilleront.

Ne pouvies vous pas faire donner à notre ami Seaton de ces passeports, qui se vendent [p. 77] chez vous, sans attendre celuy que vous demandes. Je crois que ce seroit le plus court, et je luy en ferois donner icy un autre pour passer nos rivieres.

Tout à vous, Monsieur
R.G.

Le Sieur Marsaul

iv. Copy of the paper found about Seaton, enclosed in Lord Townshend's letter of 30 January 1711.

Il vous faut aller à Anvers, loger aux trois jambons au marché des herbes, l'hôte vous donnera le passeport.

D'Anvers vous irez à Gand.

De Gand à Bruges; logés à la Maison des Tailleurs.

De Bruges prenés la barque (logez à l'ange de Nieuport) pour Nieuport. Prenez le chariot pour Dunkerque.

Logez à la Chasse Royale, demandés à parler à Monsieur du Guay, Intendant de Marine, où [p. 79] vous trouverés un passeport pour plus avant.

Ecrivés moy de Bruges ce que vous aurés faire et de Dunkerque.

Mon addresse à Monsieur Roberdeau Marchand, et sous son couvert pour Marsaull à Rotterdam.

Vous trouverés de mes lettres à Dunkerque avec plus d'instructions.

Vous irés loger à V—— à la ville de Verdun.

Allés loger à P. chez Madame Morel au petit St. Jean, Rue des vieux Augustins.

v. Extract of a letter from Lord Townshend to Mr Secretary St. John [no date].

---

[29] Du Guay was believed to be planning a Jacobite expedition. In fact he attacked the Portuguese settlement of St. Sebastian in Brazil.

Since mine of the 30th past Monsieur Marsaull, the person that gave me the information about Seaton, has been here; and I have examined him more particularly on that affair: and he told me, that having got acquainted with the said Seaton at Rotterdam, he professed to him several times his desire of going to France to promote the [*p. 81*] interest of the Pretender, and to see if that court could not be prevailed upon to attempt something in his favour in Scotland; and that being a relation to the Earl of Perth,[30] he hoped by his means to have some credit at the French court; but that he designed first to conferr with my Lord Drummond at Bruges, and from thence continue his journey to Paris: upon my asking him whether he was not instrumental in getting Seaton a passeport, he owned he was; and that it was in a false name; and that he gave him the route and instructions for his journey; and the letter from a person whom he says is Monsieur du Guay, Intendant at Dunkirk, for his assistance there; and he said, he did all this in order to gain a confidence with Seaton, and by that means to find out his whole design and intrigues, and to discover them to me: and that he accordingly had given me advice of Seaton's departure for France. I asked him, whether he ever discoursed with Seaton on matters of this nature in the presence of any other person; he said that Seaton never would venture to speak to him on this subject, but when they two [*p. 83*] were alone together. This is the substance of all that he told me of this affair; neither did I let him know that Seaton was seized, who is still continued in arrest until I have her Majesty's pleasure about it, Marsaull is one of a very indifferent character and consideration; and therefore I can't see how far he is to be depended upon as to Seaton's designs; except that he was certainly going to France, of which I sent you a sufficient proof.

13.   Whitehall. 27 March 1711
    My Lord,
            The Baron de Waleff,[31] who brings your Lordship this letter, has represented to the Queen his case in relation to his advancement in the army: and her Majesty upon consideration thereof has thought it reasonable, that he should be promoted to the rank of Major General. And [*p. 85*] I am commanded to acquaint

[30] James Drummond, 4th Earl of Perth (1648–1716), was Governor to the Pretender.

[31] Blaise-Henri de Corte, Baron de Walef (1661–1734), commanded the dragoons of Liége which were in the Queen's pay. He was the only mercenary commander to follow the Duke of Ormonde on the separation of the army in 1712. The Queen had been anxious for some time to promote his career and she awarded him a pension on the Irish establishment.

your Lordship with her Majesty's pleasure herein, that he may have your Lordship's interest and recommendation in the Queen's name to obtaine from the government of the Spanish Low-Countries a commission of Major General in the service of King Charles: and that his commission may bear date from the first of January last. I have wrote to the Duke of Marlborough upon the same subject: and I hope Monsieur de Walef will not fail of succeeding in his pretensions.

> I am, my Lord,
> your Lordship's most humble and obedient servant
> H. St. John

14. [*p. 87*]   Whitehall. 27 March 1711
    My Lord,
         The Duke of Marlborough in his letter of the 31st saying nothing to me of the report mentioned in your Lordship's of the 30th of March, that the States General have agreed to the augmentation of the duty upon salt, I fear there is no ground for it; but that the old difficulty still subsists. What way you will be able to remove it, I cannot tell; but I find the Queen very averse to an expedient touched upon in the Duke of Marlborough's last dispatches; which is, that her Majesty and the States should advance two hundred thousand Gilders to enable the Imperial and Palatin troops to march: which summ is to be repaid as soon as the funds are found for it. The Queen thinks, that no hopes of this kind ought to be given; since our allyes have been but too much used to persist in the [*p. 89*] wrong, upon a confidence of our yielding; and to refuse that burden which properly belonged to them, on an assurance that it would be taken up by us to whom it did not belong at all.

I need say nothing to your Lordship concerning the Regulation of Gouvernment for the country where you are; your Lordship is sufficiently apprised of her Majesty's inclinations in general; the particular means of pursuing these you, who are on the spot, can best judge of: and where any difficulty arises, I shall, in the clearest manner I am able, convey her Majesty's pleasure to your Lordship.

I am very sorry to find that it is so hard to prevail on the ingineer de Bauff to accept of an offer so much to his advantage. I wish, your Lordship did not frighten him by naming the West Indies to him; but although the troops now embarquing should not be designed for that part of the world, yet, I think, no capitulation of that kind must be made with him. He does no where but whither her Majesty sends both officers [*p. 91*] and troops which she has the greatest regard for. He may have twenty shillings p. diem established, be assured of a considerable gratification at the end of the year, keep his employments in the service where he now is, and merit the protection and favour of the Queen. If, upon a second proposal, he should think fit to accept these terms, he must come immediately post to London, since we hope in a fortnight that Mr Hill[32] will sail.

> I am ever, my Lord,
> your Lordship's obedient and most humble servant
> H. St. John

P.S.   I forgot in the body of my letter to acquaint your Lordship, that I have writ by the Queen's order to the Duke of Marlborough, that he should insinuate to Prince Eugene, how agreeable it would be to her Majesty, if by his good offices the Marquis Paleotti[33] might be reestablished in the Emperour's service. The Queens [sic] commands me to mention the same thing to your Lordship, and would have you do all that lies in your power to promote it.

15. [p. 93]   Whitehall. 30 March 1711
    My Lord,
            I am very glad to find by your Lordship's letter of the 2d of April [N.S.], which I received on Wensday last, that the difficultys about the fund for furnishing bread and forage are likely to be removed; and that the Dutch will consent to the augmentation of the duty upon salt. But I must own, that one cannot forbear having some contempt for the mean policy your Lordship mentions of their delaying the publication of their agreement, and sinking the fund; since the common cause must thereby run so great a risk in so essential a point, as the maintaining such a number of troops, for the view of so inconsiderable a gain to some Dutch merchants.

As to the miseries which those countries are represented to labour under, I readily enter into a lively notion of them; and at the same time I must let your Lordship know, that we flatter ourselves here, [p. 95] that your endeavours will be successfull in that point, and that you will be able by degrees in some measure to redress the hardships, those poor people suffer. It is a thing very necessary for the common good, and very proper to support the honour of her Majesty's service, that the Queen, who delights to be every whelse [sic] else the refuge of the oppressed, may not seem to countenance

---

[32] John Hill, the brother of the Queen's favourite, Abigail Masham, was promoted Brigadier General in 1711 against the wishes of Marlborough. St. John promoted his claims to command the expedition against Quebec.

[33] Ferdinando, Marquis de Paleotti, was the brother-in-law of the Duke of Shrewsbury. He had been ordered to leave Italy because he had fought a duel with his superior officer. Shrewsbury and others now pressed Charles III to give him a commission as a Colonel of Horse in the Netherlands.

the misfortunes of that country, and give way to the utter ruin and destruction of it.

Her Majesty having made an Order in Councill tending to the improvement of trade, I send your Lordship a copy of it herewith inclosed [missing]. The Queen's pleasure is so fully explained in that paper, that I need add nothing to it, but to desire your Lordship to be particularly carefull in having it executed in those proper places in Flanders, which are under your direction. I have sent the same to my Lord Raby,[34] who, I question not, will give directions for what is to be done in Holland.

I am, my Lord,
your most obedient humble servant
H. S. John

16. [*p. 97*]   Whitehall. 30 March 1711
My Lord,
        My publick letter is but short, and this shall not be long; so that you will come off cheap by this post.

The method taken of setting negociations of peace on foot by the channel of the Duke of Lorraine,[35] we are informed of; and I have seen the Duke's letter to Monsieur de Begue[36] on this subject, as well as the answer concerted at the Hague; which, though it be dry, yet gives sufficient room for making of overtures. A peace must be had; and all mankind sees plainly now, in how vile a manner former opportunities were neglected of making a better than at this hour we have reason to expect.

I think, the resolution which your Lordship takes with respect to the Arenberg family[37] is extremely right. Your predecessor, I doubt, made himself a party in all those disputes.

If De Bauff the ingineer is to be had, I must [*p. 99*] desire your Lordship to send him over without loss of a moment.

I am ever, my Lord,
your faithful and most humble servant
H. St. John

[34] Thomas Wentworth, Lord Raby and, from 1711, 3rd Earl of Strafford. A former envoy-extraordinary to Berlin, he was appointed ambassador to The Hague in 1711 to succeed Townshend.

[35] Leopold Joseph Charles, Duke of Lorraine (1679–1729), had lost his territories to France in the course of the war. He hoped to act as mediator between the principal combatants.

[36] Joseph, Baron de Begue, was the Duke of Lorraine's envoy at The Hague from 1707 to 1714.

[37] Alexander van der Capellan, Duke of Arenberg or Arendsbergen in Guelderland. He was a member of the Council of State of the Netherlands, governor of Mons, and claimed to be grand bailiff of the county of Hainault.

17.   Whitehall. 6 April 1711
   My Lord,
                At the same time that I acknowledge the receipt of your
Lordship's letters of the 6th and 9th, I must beg your excuse for not
writing by last post. I was so much out of order then, that I could
not go through my dispatches; besides that there was nothing in the
letter of the 6th, which was the only one I then had of yours, that
required an immediate answer.

   I have since laid before the Queen your Lordship's letter of the 9th.
Her Majesty is very glad to observe [*p. 101*] that there is so fair a
prospect of settling funds for the Imperial and Palatin troops; and
makes no doubt but that your Lordship has taken all the pains
possible, and laid all the stress proper both with the Dutch and the
Councill of State in order to bring that matter to bear.

   The Queen is very sensible of the miserable condition of that
country: and is [*sic*] it is her intention that your Lordship should
on one hand endeavour to make them do every thing that is practicable and reasonable for the service of the common cause; so she is
desirous on the other hand that you should be a screen to them
against all tyranny, and oppression, from whatever quarter it may
come. We are not ignorant here of the views which the Dutch have
in respect to those provinces, and how by barrier, by mortgage, or
by enclosure they contrive to reduce them absolutely to their
obedience.

   As to the case, which your Lordship mentions concerning the
money lent and to be lent upon the revenues of the posts, it is a
pretty shocking observation that the Queen is to be the guarantee
for a loan [*p. 103*] of this extraordinary nature made by the Dutch,
and especially at a time, when under pretence of disability they
directly refuse to furnish their quotas for the sea service, in spight of
the obligations of all sorts, which lye upon them to do otherwise.
Her Majesty therefore approves very much of your Lordship's backwardness to engage in this matter, and desires that before you do,
you should be better assured of the indispensable necessity, which is
the plea used for it, than your Lordship seems to be at present: to
which end your Lordship will be pleased to talk with the members of
the Councill of State, and such others as are most proper and able
to give you the best and most authentick informations: and to
write again upon this subject, before you go any further in it.

   The Queen is very well satisfied with the care your Lordship takes
to improve our intelligence abroad, and particularly to get into
the secret of the correspondence with St. Germains. We are on our
part not idle, and I make no doubt but that one way or other we

shall get more lights than usual of the pernicious designs, which may be carrying on; and consequently be better prepared to defend ourselves against them. [*p. 105*] As to the Scotch Lord[38] you mention, there seems to be no doubt but that he has fixed his residence at Bruges for the convenience of corresponding with France: and I don't very well understand upon what foot he was let go, and suffered to continue there: but I will be better informed of it, in order to take measures to spoil his trade. In the mean time, I hope your Lordship will have him as narrowly observed as can be.

We expect from your Lordship a more particular account of Seaton, of whom I know nothing further than what I communicated to your Lordship before. It is certain, he must by one means or other be put out of the way of carrying on those projects, which we have so much reason to suspect that he is engaged in.

Mr Harley's cure has proved much more difficult, and tedious, than was at first expected: however, I hope, that by next week he will be able to come abroad.

> I am, my Lord,
> your Lordship's obedient and most humble servant
> H. St. John

18. [*p. 107*]   Whitehall. 10 April 1711
My Lord,
          I am extream glad to hear by your Lordship's letter of the 13th, that the very difficult affair of the augmentation of duty on the quatre especes is likely to be determined.

As to the loans on the Post Office I have already sufficiently explained her Majesty's sentiments to your Lordship in a former letter.

I thank your Lordship for the account you sent of the intelligence which you had received. We flatter ourselves that by the care which your Lordship takes, we shall be better informed than we used to be. As to the news of the Pretender's embarquing at Brest, it is true we have heard it by more ways than one: but still their armaments by sea don't seem equal to such an enterprize; neither have we any account of troops drawing together for that purpose.

I must acquaint your Lordship, that my Lord Shaftesbury[39] has the Queen's leave to go to [*p. 109*] France for his health.

> I am, my Lord,
> your Lordship's most humble and most obedient servant
> H. St. John

[38] Lord Drummond.
[39] Anthony Ashley Cooper, 3rd Earl of Shaftesbury (1671–1713), the author of the *Characteristicks*, was in ill health. He planned to go to Naples, passing through France. He died in Naples.

19.   Whitehall. 17 April 1711
   My Lord,
            I received this afternoon a duplicate of your Lordship's
letter of the 16th (which was lost with the mail) together with those
of the 20th and 23d; but it is now so late, and I have so much
business upon my hands, that I shall not say any thing to your
Lordship upon them this night. Tomorrow I shall dispatch a messenger to Holland express, and I will not fail to write by him particularly upon all the points of business contained in your Lordship's
letters.
            I am, my Lord,
                your Lordship's obedient and most humble servant
                                                    H. St. John.

20. [*p. 111*]   Whitehall. 20 April 1711
   My Lord,
            Since my last, wherein I only acknowledged several of
your Lordship's letters to me, I have received that of the 27th,
which came to hand this morning: though I intended to have writ
amply to your Lordship by the messenger, yet the great multitude
of business, and the haste we were in to dispatch him with the
resolutions taken by her Majesty upon the Emperour's death,[40]
hindered me from doing it.
   I am sorry that Monsieur de Bauff could not be had; I think, he has
refused a very good offer. The troops, with which he was to have gone,
are now ready to proceed; and I hope we shall not want him.
   We are very sensible here of the difficultys and uneasieness which
your Lordship has from the miserable condition which those
countries are in; and from the necessity and consequence of those
charges which must be laid upon them.
[*p. 113*]   A resolution of the States of the 14th of April has been
sent over and communicated to me to be laid before the Queen;
desiring that orders may be sent to her Majesty's ministers to concurr with the Dutch in all manner of means for raising the necessary
summs; and refusing to consent to the raising the customes on corn,
brandy, and salt, as extreamly prejudicial to their subjects; since
the government of the Spanish Netherlands declines continuing the
prohibition of making brandy of corn in that country, or laying a
proportionable duty upon it. I have her Majesty's orders in answer
to this resolution to acquaint Monsieur Vryberge, that the Queen's

---

   [40] Joseph I (1678–1711) had just died on 6/17 April 1711. He was succeeded
by his brother Charles, the Austrian claimant to the Spanish Empire.

directions have been already given to your Lordship to joyn in all proper measures for obliging those provinces to raise the sums requisite for supporting the troops which it belongs to them to pay: but to take care at the same time, that this be done with the greatest regard possible to the ease of that people. Her Majesty makes no doubt but that your Lordship will apply this general rule in every particular instance very properly; and she leaves it to your Lordship's prudence to make the due use of it.

[*p 115*] As to the latter part of your last letter, though I have not yet been able to lay it before the Queen, and to have her directions upon it; yet I know so much of her Majesty's mind upon that subject, that I may venture to tell you that the Queen will expect that the Imperial and Palatine troops should one way or other be maintained. And her Majesty thinks, that this is the least they can do in return to that concern she expresses for the oppression they suffer, and the inclination she shews to redress the grievances, and releive the calamities of that people. I think it ought on all occasions to be inculcated, that the way to encourage the Queen in these good sentiments, and indeed to pursue their own interest, would be to do every thing that falls to their share for the support of the warr. And at the same time your Lordship, who is sent to be a patron to them, should endeavour to obtain a better regulation of their government, which would soon make amends for the charges which they are obliged to bear. And the present nice conjuncture of affaires is to be enforced as an argument why the burthen of them is more than ordinary at this time.

[*p. 117*]   I am, my Lord, with true respect,
        your Lordship's obedient and most humble servant
                    H. St. John

21.   Whitehall. 23 April 1711
  My Lord,
        I have been hindered by the tide of business, which has pourred in upon me every day, hitherto from acknowledging your Lordship's private letter of the 20th of this month N. St.

It is not possible to bestow your time and pains better than in endeavouring to settle a good correspondence in France; for though I flatter myself, we are already got into methods of knowing more of the enemy's affairs, than those able ministers, who went before us, ever did: yet I am far from thinking that we have so full, so quick intelligence; and that through so many different channels as is necessary and practicable.

[*p. 119*] The allowances, craved by the man your Lordship speaks of, are very great; and unless you have very great reason to beleive that he can arrive at better accounts of the enemy's designs and preparations than generally our spyes are able to do, I think, one would hardly employ him. If you are of opinion he may deserve the reward he asks, I think your Lordship should make the best bargain you can with him, and send him to Paris. If he continues there, the expence will be so great that neither your extraordinarys, nor my secret service money will suffice to maintain him; and in such case, her Majesty will make it up to us.

I have not had an opportunity yet of speaking to the Chancellor [of the Exchequer],[41] who has hitherto been but little abroad, and entred but little into business, of the proposition which your Lordship makes of a commission to take up for the publick service what money you please. I will not fail to talk to him about this matter, as soon as I possibly can; but, I fear, the rules of the Treasury, and the consequence of the president [*sic*], will be difficultys in the way; especially since in case of any charge beyond what the [*p. 121*] extraordinarys are given, or will suffice for, it always may, and always will be allowed for upon representation made to her Majesty.

I must entreat your Lordship, if any opportunity offers, to say something civil in my name to the Counts d'Ursel[42] and Milan;[43] to whom I must very speedily write, and would have done so sooner, had I not been for some weeks past ill in my health, and at the same time overloaded with business.

I beleive your Lordship's countenance to those two gentlemen may be very properly given; after the trust which the Queen put in them this spring.

I am, my dear Lord, with the greatest truth,
your must faithfull friend, and most obedient servant
H. St. J.

22. [*p. 123*]   Whitehall. 24 April 1711
My Lord,
My letter by this post will be very short; but I inclose in it the papers which I received from Monsieur Vryberge, relating to

[41] Robert Harley, still recovering from his wound.

[42] Conrad Albert Charles, 1st duc d'Ursel (1665–1738), was a member of the Council of State of the Netherlands. Formerly a supporter of Philip V, he had changed sides and had been rewarded with the governorship of Namur. He was reputed to be the most influential man in Brussels and on good terms with Orrery.

[43] The Count van Milaenen or de Milan Visconti, who had also changed allegiance from Philip V to Charles III.

the Spanish Netherlands; and the answer, which by her Majesty's order I have returned to that Minister.

I am, my Lord, with all possible respect,
your Lordship's obedient and most faithfull humble servant
H. St. John

Here follow Monsieur Vryberg's letter to the Queen, and Secretary St. John's answer; mentioned to be inclosed in the preceding letter.

i. Madame,
Les troupes Imperiales et Palatines estants venues dans les Pais Bas de commun concert de vôtre Majesté, et de leurs Hautes Puissances [*p. 125*]. Il est tres juste que votre Majesté et l'Etât prenne soin en commun pour leur entretien, et que touts les contracts et engagements à cette fin soient faits et signez tant de la part de vôtre Majesté, que de la part de leurs Hautes Puissances; n'estant pas raisonable de mettre à la charge de l'Etât d'estre seul guarant pour les negotiations, qu'il faut faire à la charge des Pais Bas Espagnols pour la subsistance des dites troupes: leurs Hautes Puissances ont deja pour le bien de la cause commune interposez si souvent leur credit dans des telles negotiations que leur credit en a extrement souffert; et qu'il n'est pas possible pour elles d'y continuer: c'est pourquoi, Madame, les Seigneurs Etats Generaux des Provinces Unies ont ordonné per une nouvelle resolution du 28 d'avril nouveau style, le soubsigné leur envoyé extraordinaire de prier votre Majesté comme il a l'honneur de faire par ce present memoire, pourqu'il plaise à votre Majesté d'ordonner et authoriser les ministres pour concourir avec les dits Seigneurs Etâts ou leurs Deputées en tout ce qui regarde les dittes troupes, et qui sera trouvé bon de commun concert. Fait à Londres le 21 Avril/2 May 1711.
M. Van Vryberge

ii. [*p. 127*]   Whitehall. ce 24 Avril 1711
Monsieur,
J'ay receu la lettre de votre secretaire du 9/20 de ce mois, avec l'etrait des resolutions des Seigneurs Etats Generaux du 14 N.S.touchant l'affaire des fondes pour la subsistance de troupes Imperiales et Palatines aux Pais Bas Espagnols: aussi bien que votre memoire du 21e sur le même sujet. Et ayant eu l'honneur d'en faire rapport à la Regne, sa Majesté m'a commandé de vous faire sçavoir là dessus, que les ordres qu'Elle a toujours donnés à ses Ministres à l'egard de cette affaire ont été de concourir avec les Deputées de l[eurs] H[autes] P[uissances] pour obliger le gouvernement des Pais

Bas Espagnols à lever les sommes necessaires pour le payement des troupes, dont ils sont chargés, et à contribuer à toutes les depenses de la guerre auxquelles ils doivent fournir. Mais en même tems sa Majesté leur a recommandé d'avoir tous les egards possibles au soulagement de ces pauvres provinces, qui ont souffert extrémément, étant reduites par les [*p. 129*] grandes oppressions à un etat tout à fait pitoyable. J'ay renouvellé depuis peu cette instruction generale à my Lord Orrery; avec order [*sic*] de s'en servir comme d'une regle dans tous les cas qui tomberont en dispute. Sa Majesté ne doute point que Messieurs les Etats Generaux n'approuveront fort une regle si juste et si équitable: et on peut etre assuré que le comte d'Orrery, aussi bien que le duc de Marlborough ne manqueront pas de concourrir avec les Deputés de l[eurs] P[uissances] pour faire lever les deux sommes de 450000 et de 850000 francs de la maniere proposée dans la susdite resolution: s'il se trouve qu'il n'a nul autre moyen de le faire egalement seur et practicable, et plus accommodé aux necessités de ces provinces equisées. Car quoi que l'intention de sa Majesté soit de soulager ce peuple autant que faire se pourra, Elle entend pourtant toujours en premier lieu que les interets de la cause commune n'y souffrent pas.

Je suis, &c.
H. St. John

23. [*p. 131*]   Whitehall. 27 April 1711
My Lord,
          I acknowledge the receipt of your Lordship's letter of the 30th of April, and your note of May 2d together with the enclosed advices.

The Queen is very well pleased with the care which your Lordship takes in regulating the affaires of the Netherlands. Her Majesty expects that the people of that country should furnish the necessary supplyes which are demanded of them for the service; but she would have your Lordship at the same time make them as easy as possible in all instances which may not be prejudicial to the interest of the common cause. Since it is but too certain that they have for some time laboured under the weight of a very severe treatment.

It is confirmed from all hands that the Dutch are at present just in the temper which [*p. 133*] your Lordship apprehended. But we hope, when they come to consider cooly of the matter, they will be of opinion that as long as the summs are raised which we expect from them, it is much more eligible to have them with the good liking and ease of the country, than by involving it in unnecessary difficulties.

The post is just come which has brought me your Lordship's letter of May 4th with the enclosed; but it is so extreamly late, that I have not time to say anything to your Lordship upon them.

I am, my Lord, with great truth,
your Lordship's most humble and obedient servant,
H. St. John

24. [*pp. 135–41*] [*This letter, dated 1 May 1711, is printed exactly in* Letters and Correspondence of Bolingbroke, *ed. Parke, i, pp. 181–2.*]

25. [*p. 141*]　　　　　　　　　　　　　　　Whitehall. 8 May 1711
My Lord,
　　　　　I am to return your Lordship my thanks for the favour of your letters of the 7th and 11th inst. N.S.

I agree entirely with your Lordship that good management from the beginning would have prevented all the grievances and disorders, which those provinces now complain of, and consequently all the difficultys which your Lordship meets with in obtaining of them those things that are necessary for the service of the warr.

I think your Lordship's letter to the Pensionary, of which you sent a copy in yours of the 7th, was extremely well; and though it procured only a general answer, yet it had that effect, which is all we can [*p. 143*] hope for from great part of your Lordship's conduct in such distracted circumstances of affaires, that it will exonerate the Queen's administration, and shew that nothing has been omitted, which her servants could do towards making those provinces more easie; and notwithstanding all the complaints, which have been made in Holland of your behaviour in these matters, I cannot but own that I am glad you have pursued it, since I am sure that your Lordship will in all cases take care that the common cause don't suffer by your indulgence to these people. And it is good that the Dutch should find by degrees how little their absolute dominion over those countrys is liked in Brittain; and also how far the Queen is from approving that rapine and violence, which has been exercised there ever since the country was reduced to King Charles.

I don't very well comprehend how it comes to be a hardship that the Imperial and Palatine troops are put to their charge, since I am sure they have very few troops of their own to be employed. And though it be prejudicial to any country to have their revenues mortgaged for a considerable time, [*p. 145*] yet when they complain of a mortgage of 18 years, your Lordship, I am sure, will not fail to put them in mind that we in Brittaine have mortgages of 32 and of 99 years on several branches of our revenue.

I have not yet authority to say to your Lordship that Seaton should be released, though we have no more than what you mention against him. But, however, we have this advantage from having taken him up, that the Pretender has one emissary the less to employ.

I am, my Lord, with much respect and truth,
your Lordship's obedient and most humble servant
H. St. John

26. [*p. 147*]   Whitehall. 22 May 1711
My Lord,
                I received your Lordship's letters of the 14th, 18th, and 21st, all together about a week ago; and directed Mr Tilson[44] to acknowledge them; but having no new commands from her Majesty upon the heads of business they contained, I did not trouble your Lordship with an answer my self.

I have now the favour of your Lordship's letters of the 25th and 28th, which continue to represent the great difficultys you have to struggle with in finding funds for maintaining the Imperial and Palatine troops. But, I hope, your Lordship's great zeal and application will at last surmount all the opposition that is made in that matter either by the Dutch on one hand, or the Councill of State on the other. I have nothing particular at present to observe to your Lordship upon that subject, but to repeat the same orders you have already had, to take care that [*p. 149*] the service be provided for; but to have it always in your view to chuse the expedients which may be the least burthensome to that exhausted country. I was glad to hear by a private letter, which I received last post from the Hague, that the States begin to think seriously of making a better Regulation of Government in the Spanish Netherlands, and that your Lordship will be desired to come to the Hague to be present at those consultations, and assist with your opinion and advice upon that occasion.

If my Lord Drummond comes over hither, as your Lordship suspects he designs to do, we shall take the best care we can to have him narrowly watched, as your Lordship has done on your side of the water.

As to the Pretender's journey which has been so industriously given out by several ways, I take it to be rather an amusement to alarm people here, than any real design; and I have by the post which

---

[44] George Tilson was formerly secretary to Lord Raby when the latter was in Berlin and was now one of the under-secretaries of state in St. John's office.

came in this morning received so particular and authentick an account of the different destinations of the ships which have been [*p. 151*] equipped at Brest, that I think there is no room left to apprehend their being intended for a descent on any part of Great Britaine.

> I am ever, my Lord,
> > your Lordship's most humble and obedient servant
> > > H. St. John

27.   Whitehall. 1 June 1711
    My Lord,
            I have this night received the favour of your Lordship's letter of the 8th N.S.; but have only time to read it, and cannot say any thing particular to your Lordship upon the contents of it.

I make use of this opportunity to send your Lordship the inclosed memorial relating to the interests of the Marquiss de Paleotti, which her Majesty approves as a proper project for doing service to that [*p. 153*] gentleman; and I am to recommend it to your Lordship's particular care to promote it effectually with the States of the Spanish Low Countries. I have writ to my Lord Raby to procure directions to the Dutch Deputies[45] to join with you in getting the matter setled. I shall only add, that, in doing this, you will do a pleasure to the Duke of Shrewsbury,[46] and lay an obligation upon his Grace.

> I am, my Lord,
> > your Lordship's most humble and obedient servant
> > > H. St. John

Here follows the memorial, mentioned to be inclosed in the preceding letter.

Memoire au sujet de l'affaire de Monsieur le Marquis de Paleotti.
    Pour faire reüssir les pretentions de Monsieur le Marquis de Paleotti, il faudra une lettre de sa Majesté la Reine à my Lord Raby son ambassadeur extraordinaire à la Haye, pour [*p. 155*] recommander les interests du dit Marquis aux Etâts Generaux d'une maniere à les porter de prendre une resolution de concert avec sa Majesté pour luy donner les appointements entiers du colonel de cavallerie, à sçavoir en qualité du colonel et capitaine, comme s'il

---

[45] The two Dutch Deputies to the Netherlands since 1706 were Johan van den Bergh (1664–1755) and Frederick Adriaen van Reede, Baron of Renswoude (1659–1738).
[46] Charles Talbot, 1st Duke of Shrewsbury, the Lord Chamberlain, was married to Adelaide Paleotti.

avoit actuellement un regiment au service de sa Majesté Catholique
dans les Pais Bas, avec assurance du premier regiment qui viendra
à vaquer, et Messieurs les Deputés de Leurs Hautes Puissances à
Brussels doivent être chargés de l'execution de la dite resolution
conjointement avec les ministres de sa Majesté.

28.   Whitehall. 12 June 1711
    My Lord,
            Your Lordship's letters of the 11th and 15th came yester-
day by the way of Holland, and this morning the mails from Ostend
brought the favour of yours of the 20th. This makes me [*p. 157*]
wish that your Lordship would preferr the conveyance by Ostend,
which often brings the letters earlier than that of Brille.

    I wish the hasty departure of Prince Eugene with so large a
detachment, as he has taken from our army, do not prove very
prejudicial to the common cause.[47] But at the same time I readily
agree with your Lordship, that it will be a very great ease to you to
be freed from the many difficultys you were like to meet with in
providing the remaining funds for the subsistance of those troops,
as well as a particular pleasure to that oppressed countrey to part
with guests, who have been so chargeable and so unwellcome.

    The Queen has been informed that they are very apprehensive
in Brabant upon the death of the Archbishop of Mechlen,[48] least the
Dutch should hinder the putting another in his place. And as I find
her Majesty to be extremely fearfull of the ill consequences, which
may happen, if we and the States should be too meddling in ecclesi-
astical affairs in the Spanish Netherlands; I am commanded [*p. 159*]
to desire your Lordship to send a full state of that matter, and in the
mean time to proceed very cautiously in it; and not make any step
where there is the least doubt, without having fresh orders from
hence.

    I was glad to find by the same letter, which brought me an
account of your Lordship's illness, that you was in so fair a way of
recovery. I hope, before this comes to your hands, you will be
restored to your former state of health. Her Majesty thinks it
proper, if your Lordship is in a condition to take the journey, that
you should go to the Hague, now the Dutch Deputies are sent for
thither, that you may concert with them there a better plan for the

---

[47] Prince Eugene marched to the Rhine with all the Imperial troops to
guard against a threatened French incursion into the Empire.
[48] Humbert Guillaume de Précipiano, Archbishop of Mechlen or Malines
from 1690 to 1711. The vacancy created by his death was not filled until
December 1715.

government of the Spanish Low Countries; and leave them without any excuse in that matter by reason of your absence. Besides, as my Lord Ambassador Raby is ordered to come over hither for a little while, the Queen thinks your Lordship's presence at the Hague may be usefull to her affairs, if there be any thing extraordinary to communicate [*p. 161*] during his Excellency's stay here.

> I am, my Lord,
> your Lordship's most faithful humble servant,
> H. St. John

29. [*pp. 161-71*] [*This letter, also dated 12 June 1711, is printed exactly in* Letters and Correspondence of Bolingbroke, *ed. Parke, i, pp. 242-47.*]

30. [*pp. 171-75*] [*This letter, dated 26 June 1711, is printed exactly in* ibid, *i, pp. 261-63.*]

31. [*MS. Eng. Letters e. 4, p. 1*]   Whitehall. 26 June 1711
    My Lord,
          I am to acknowledge the favour of your letters of the 22d, 25th, and 29th instant with the inclosed papers.

As to the demands of the Imperialists, I agree with your Lordship in thinking they were unreasonable; but the occasion of their halting so long in the Netherlands, I suppose, was to see whether the detachments, which the French made, were really intended for Germany; or designed only as a feint to amuse us.

What service the leaving the Hussars may be [*p. 3*] of to the publick, we are not able to judge here; but the Queen commands me to say, that by the answer which the States of Brabant returned to the Duke of Marlborough's letter upon that subject, they did not shew themselves so well inclined to the common cause as they ought to be; for we might reasonably expect that they would make no difficulty of maintaining that one regiment, now they are eased of so great a load as the rest of the Imperial and Palatin troops.

The Queen is sorry to find that the Dutch continue still to lay such severe burthens upon the poor people of the Netherlands; as she is, on the other hand, to observe the backwardness which the Council of State shew towards doing any thing for the service of their prince, and for the common interest.

The Dutchess of Bisacchia's[49] memorial I will lay before the

---

[49] Probably minor Neapolitan nobility. Bisaccia is a small town *c.* 70 miles east of Naples. The Duke of Bisaccia was serving in the French army in the Low Countries at the beginning of the war.

Queen by the first opportunity, and endeavour to procure her Majesty's orders to my Lord Dartmouth[50] to write to the Duke of [*p. 5*] Argyll to obtaine of King Charles the permission which is desired: and the opportunity of obliging the Duke of Aremberg will very probably be an inducement for the Queen to comply with what is asked in the memorial. I wish the late differences about exchange of prisoners may not be an occasion of some objection to the Duke of Bisacchia's coming to Brussels.

I am sorry your Lordship has been so much indisposed, but, I hope, you are now perfectly recovered. If the States continue to talk of any inclination to settle the government of the Netherlands upon a better foot, which they express in all their letters hither, your Lordship's presence at the Hague will be of great use in that affair, as well as in many others in the absence of my Lord Raby.

I am, my Lord, with much respect,
your Lordship's obedient and most humble servant
H. St. John

32. [*p. 7*]   Whitehall. 29 June 1711
My Lord,
        Having laid Seaton's papers before the Committee of Council at the Cockpitt, I am to acquaint you that the Lords are of opinion that he should not be released immediately, but that it may be proper for your Lordship to endeavour once more to find out what his errand to France was; and, perhaps, by promising good usage on the one hand, and by threatening him with very ill on the other, you may be able to extort some confession from him. In the mean time your Lordship will be pleased to order the jaylor to subsist him, and care will be taken here for answering that expence.

I transmit to your Lordship a copy of a petition from the Corporation of Tiverton, which was put into my hands by the Attorney General,[51] in the behalfe of one Mr Gatchell. By the inclosed your Lordship [*p. 9*] will be fully apprized of the subject matter of this complaint, which I desire you will be pleased to examine into the merits of, and give Mr Gatchell such assistance therein as your Lordship shall think reasonable.

I am, my Lord,
your Lordship's most humbel and obedient servant
H. St. John

[50] William Legge, 1st Earl of Dartmouth (1672–1750), was the Secretary of State for the Southern Department.

[51] Sir Edward Northey (1652–1723) was Attorney General 1701–07 and again from 1710 to 1718.

Here follows the copy of the petition to the Attorney General, mentioned to be inclosed in the preceding letter.

Tiverton. 16 May 1711

Sir,

One Mr Ludovicus de Wulfe, merchant of Ghent in Flanders, having (when the French took possession of Flanders) given orders to one Mr Edward Gatchell, of this town merchant, for goods to the value of three or four hundred pounds; and [*p. 11*] Mr de Wulfe having received such goods into his custody, and refusing to pay for the same, Mr Gatchell did in October last was twelve months, send his son to Ghent to demand the money so due to him from the said Mr de Wulfe; and he refusing to pay it, was forced to commence a suit before the magistrates and councill of Ghent against Mr de Wulfe for the same, who has kept Mr Gatchell's son there ever since by delaying of the suite, and preventing a final sentence against him, and thereby has put Mr Gatchell to a great expence and charge. Wherefore, at his request, we desire you will be pleased to get a letter from one of her Majesty's Secretaries of State to my Lord Orrery her plenipotentiary at the Court of Brussells, in favour of his son Mr John Gatchell, desiring his Lordship to recommend the matter aforesaid to the consideration of the magistrates and councill of Ghent, for a speedy end and determination therein; in doing which you'll oblige [*p. 13*] Sir, your ready humble servants,

Wm Wood	George Thorne Mayor
Peter Barton	Robt. Burridge
Nathl: Thorne	Roger Chamberlin
Saml: Burridge	John Upcott
Geo. Davey, junr.	Will: Upcott
Daniel Deyman	John Tristram
	Richd. Spurway
	Fra: Plumpton
	Geo: Davey, Senr.
	Robt. London
	William Frost

Whitehall. 13 July 1711

33.

My Lord,

I have received the honour of your Lordship's letters of the 2d, 6th, 9th, and 13th instant, N.S.

If I had been certain of your Lordship's going to the Hague in time, you should not [*p. 15*] have failed on your arrival there to have met with the best accounts I could have given you of the Queen's sentiments on the several heads of business which are now in transaction. To supply this, in some measure, I will write to you by this post at large, and wherever you may be pressed in matters which you have no answer to give to, or wherein, perhaps, it is most expedient to be silent as long as possible, you will please to referr the ministers to the orders you shall receive from hence: or to my Lord Raby's arrival in Holland, who will be in very few days dispatched from hence.

Monsieur d'Ahlfelt,[52] the Danish Minister, will not fail to enquire what instructions you may have received from Court relating to the Treaty with his master,[53] which is now expired, and which they would renew with us upon very extraordinary terms. Your Lordship may let him know, that when our ambassador left the Hague, we were in hopes that the Pensionary [Heinsius] and he (Monsieur d'Ahfelt) would have settled that matter to common satisfaction; [p. 17] that you make no doubt, but that my Lord Raby will come back instructed to finish what the Queen so very much desires; but that you hope the King of Denmark will not insist on such termes as Britaine and Holland cannot comply with; particularly, you will put him out of hopes of obtaining the additional subsidy demanded; and represent to him how hard and unreasonable the Queen and the States must think such an article to be, when they paid so much levy money for these troopes at first, when they are engaged in so burthensome a war against France, and when they are entred into new expences at the instances of his Court, and the other Northern Confederates, to support the Act of Neutrality.

If he, the Muscovite, or Polish Ministers complain that the contingent for this service is not compleat, your Lordship will let them know that eight Palatine battalions, and one of Retinghen are provided, and that there has been no want of good will to find the remaining three, since Monsieur Seckendorff,[54] a Major General of King Augustus [of Poland], has been [p. 19] sent into Germany to negotiate for them, with very ample powers from the Duke of Marlborough.

The unreasonable proposals, that have been made to us, have hindred us from being able to conclude a treaty for them hitherto, but we hope still to find them, and no endeavours shall be neglected on the Queen's part to this purpose; but we must observe, that the

---

[52] Hans Heinrich Ahlefeldt, Danish envoy to The Hague 1710–14.
[53] Frederick IV of Denmark (1671–1730).
[54] Friedrich Heinrich von Seckendorf (1673–1763) was an experienced officer who had fought in Flanders under William III and Marlborough. He joined the forces of Augustus, Elector of Saxony and King of Poland, in 1709, but continued to serve with the Saxon troops in Flanders.

complaint to be made on our side is much better founded. The Saxon recruits for Flanders, amounting to more than 4000 men, have been raised some time, and subsisted by the money of the Queen and States; and yet they are kept from marching under pretence that three regiments are still wanting to compleat the contingent of the Neutrality.

The Minister[55] of the Elector Palatine[56] will probably be sollicitous to know what orders you may have concerning the demand of bread and forage, lately insisted on by him for the eight battalions of his troops sent to the north. I have yet no positive orders [*p. 21*] from the Queen upon this subject, but your Lordship may very properly say, that her Majesty will not fail to do whatever can in justice be expected from her; insinuating at the same time, how hard we think it to furnish forage to any troops, while it is to be had in the country where they serve, and especially when that country is the frontier chiefly exposed to the danger which those troops are employed to prevent.

The Dutch Secretary[57] was at Windsor yesterday, and put into my hands a resolution of the States of the 17th instant, N.S., founded on the extravagant demands made by Count Werthern[58] and the Baron Gersdorff.[59] Your Lordship will please to let the Pensionary and such other of the Dutch Ministers as speak to you on this subject, know, that her Majesty looks upon it to be an affair of the utmost danger, and nicety; that the Committee of Council has this morning been in debate upon it; that on Sunday the whole will be reconsidered before her Majesty at Windsor; and that the resolutions then taken will, without loss of time, [*p. 23*] be communicated to the States. Your Lordship will please to give the Dutch Deputys to understand, that the Lords of the Councill are afraid that the concessions made by them in the Conference to the Polish Ministers, may even be too large how carefully soever they may be expressed. That they think, the balance of power in the North, and the Protestant interest in Germany, deeply concerned in the measures which the Northern Confederates seem at this time

[55] Daniel Steingens.

[56] Johann Wilhelm of Bavaria-Neuberg, Elector of the Palatinate (1658–1716).

[57] Vryberge had recently died in London. Simon van Slingelandt (1664–1736) was Secretary to the Council of State in The Hague and later Pensionary of Holland.

[58] Georg, Count Werthern (1663–1721), was minister, later Chancellor, for Augustus of Saxony-Poland and commander of the Corps of Neutrality.

[59] Wolf Abraham, Baron Gersdorff, was Saxon envoy at The Hague from 1698 to 1719.

engaged in the pursuit of, and that the greatest deliberation should be used by us in resolving what to do, and the greatest firmness afterwards in executing those resolutions.

    I am, my Lord,
        your Lordship's most humble and most obedient servant
                                    H. St. John

34.   [*p. 25*]   Whitehall. 17 July **1711**
   My Lord,
             I am to acknowledge the receipt of your Lordship's letters of the 16th and 24th instant.

I hope your Lordship will be able to obtain for Mr Walef what he desires, and what he seems with so much reason to expect. The step cannot be thought very extraordinary in his case, who can be preferred no other way; since it has been made in many instances where there was not the same pretence, and where there was as little relation to the King of Spain's service.

I am sorry to find that your Lordship's health is so bad; I doubt you have but little rest at the Hague; and the uneasieness of being every day a witnesse to new difficulties brought upon us may very well encrease that indisposition.

[*p. 27*]   The Pensionary's confession to your Lordship acknowledges a very great truth; but they have the misfortune in Holland very often not to see the opportunity, till it is fleeted by them; like the fellow in the play, who never finds out the jeast till half an hour after it is made.

I have nothing more to say to your Lordship upon the affairs of the north, in which, as great as the danger is, and as pressing as the necessity of taking a resolution is, I find the Lords of the Council very doubtfull what to advise. To employ our contingent for support of the Neutrality, in an actual war with the Swedes, or to give the Saxon troops our pay, whilst they engage in the same cause, are equally contrary to our interest, and destructive of the end which we proposed to ourselves by entring into the Act of Neutrality. On the other hand, to lose the service of the Saxons and of the Danes too, (for I hear Monsieur D'Ahlfelt has received his orders,) in this critical conjuncture of affairs, and in the midst of a campagne, would be very fatal.

[*p. 29*]   By letters from Mr Whitworth[60] we find, that the Dutch Minister[61] at Vienna has pressed, as well as the Queen's, that a

---

[60] Charles Whitworth (1675–1725) was sent by the British government to Vienna, Berlin and Dresden, before returning to his position as envoy-extraordinary to the court of Peter the Great of Russia.

[61] Jacob Jan Hamel-Bruynincx (1662–1738) was the Dutch envoy to Vienna.

detachment should be made from Hungary, since the war in that country is concluded; and the old excuse for doing nothing against France at an end. But then he has desired, that this body of troops should be sent to the Rhine instead of reinforcing the Duke of Savoy's[62] army, which is the use her Majesty hoped they might be applyed to, and thought that the States concurred in. If we had not done wondring at any thing which can happen, this would have surprized us a little; since we looked upon adding 8000 men to the Duke of Savoy's army before the end of the campagne as a measure concerted and settled between the Queen and the States. Besides, tis so apparent that no number of troops whatever can act offensively, and with vigour, upon the Rhine; whereas on the side of Savoy a very considerable effort and a powerfull diversion might be expected, that we are the more at a loss to account for this order to Monsieur Bruninx. But I ask your Lordship pardon for saying so much to you [*p. 31*] upon this subject, since, I doubt, it is too certain that neither for the Rhine, nor for Savoy, nor for any other part of the service, shall we obtain of the Austrian Ministers one single regiment.

>   I am, my Lord,
>   your Lordship's most humble and obedient servant,
>   H. St. John

35.   Whitehall. 20 July 1711
>   My Lord,
>   My dispatch by this post will not be very long: by that of
Tuesday next, I am likely to give you more trouble.

Inclosed your Lordship will receive a copy of the Attorney General's opinion in the case of Seaton, which my Lords of the Committee of Council thought necessary to take: and if [*p. 33*] nothing more material can be got out of him, or be produced against him, than has yet appeared, my Lords see no reason for confining him any longer.

>   I am, my Lord,
>   your Lordship's obedient and most humble servant
>   H. St. John

Here follows the copy of the Attorney-General's opinion to Mr Secretary St. John, mentioned to be enclosed in the preceding letter.

>   Sir,
>   Having by your letter of the 17th instant signified to me,
that one Seaton having been by the Queen's order taken up, and

---

[62] Victor Amadeus II (1666–1732).

confined at Bruges, and it appearing by the papers found upon him, that he was going into France; requiring my opinion, how far a subject of her Majesty is [*p. 35*] punishable for an intention of going clandestinely into France; I do humbly certify, that by an act made in the 3d year of her Majesty's reign for preventing trayterous correspondence with her Majesty's enemies, it is enacted, that if any of her Majesty's subjects shall, during the present war with France, voluntarily go, or repair, or embark into any vessel, with intent to go into France, or the dominions of the French King, such person is guilty of high treason: and that if Seaton embarked from England with such intent, though he might go round by Holland, such embarking is high treason within the act. But if he did not go from England with such intent; but being in Flanders, did there first intend to go thence into France; such intention will not be high treason within the said act. Yet if, by the papers found about him, it shall appear, he had such intention in order to serve her Majesty's enemies, the same will amount to a misdemeanour; but such misdemeanour is not punishable by the laws of England. However, her Majesty may [*p. 37*] by Privy Seal command Seaton to return to England; and if he shall not return thereon, he will thereby forfeit his goods and chattels.

I am, Sir,
your most obedient humble servant
Edw: Northey

15 July 1711

36. [*pp. 37–43*] [*This letter, dated 20 July 1711, is printed exactly in* Letters and Correspondence of Bolingbroke, *ed. Parke, i, pp. 279–82.*]

37.   [*p. 43*]   Whitehall. 24 July 1711
My Lord,
            Her Majesty commands me to communicate to your Lordship her sentiments concerning the interests of the Duke of Savoy, and the demands of that Prince, in the present conjuncture of the affairs of Europe. The use which your Lordship is to make of this information, is, to discourse in confidence with the Pensionary on the subject, to feel the disposition of the States, and to endeavour to draw them into a concurrence with her Majesty.
[*p. 45*]   Your Lordship will therefore please to begin by acquainting this Minister, that the Marquis del Bourg[63] having been sent hither

---

[63] Ignace Francois Solaro, Marquis del Bourg or Delborgo, envoy of the Duke of Savoy at The Hague and, for a time, to London.

to desire in his master's name the Queen's support in any new turn which affairs may take by the death of the late Emperour; and particularly, the Treaty of Marriage between the Prince of Piemont and the eldest Arch-Dutchess, daughter of Joseph, which his Royal Highness designs to propose;[64] the Queen made no difficulty to promise what he desired, and her orders to her ministers are accordingly given.

The objection of carrying by this match a title to the hereditary countries of Germany into the House of Savoy, was, you may be sure, made: but the Minister of Savoy gave a ready and satisfactory answer, which his Royal Highness has since confirmed to it, by offering that the Arch-Dutchess should in this case previously to the marriage renounce all claim to those territories; and by shewing, that one renunciation or other ought to be made, whoever she marryes; [p. 47] since, as it might be thought unreasonable that any pretensions to the hereditary countryes of Germany should be brought into the House of Savoy; so, it would be a very great hardship upon his Royal Highness, if her pretensions to the succession of Spain should go along with her into any other family. On this occasion the Marquis del Bourg insisted very much on that article in the Treaty of 1703, wherein it is said that no third person shall be superinduced in the succession to the monarchy of Spain after the House of Austria in prejudice of the family of the Duke of Savoy.

Your Lordship will represent to the Pensionary that the Queen came so readily into this proposition of the marriage, because she is convinced that in justice, and in good policy, a particular regard ought to be paid to the interests of the House of Savoy in the present scituation of affaires.

Your Lordship will propose to the Pensionary to consider of this matter with two views. If [p. 49] the Empire and the Dominions of Spain are to be united in the person of King Charles, the Ministers of Savoy pretend their master will then be reduced to the very condition which he has sacrificed all to avoid; and that his dependency upon the House of Austria must in this respect be worse than his dependency on the House of Bourbon: that the former will have more pretences to chicane with him, and to exercise their power over him than the latter can possibly find: of which these Ministers think the Court of Vienna have given of late many remarkable instances.

If the Empire and the Dominions of Spain were to be separated, the immediate right in such case to the Spanish succession devolving upon the eldest Arch-Dutchess, daughter of Joseph, his Royal Highness judges that it would be thought not only his but the

[64] This proposed marriage did not take place.

publick interest, to unite by the marriage proposed, the immediate and the remote titles.

As these observations appear to the Queen to have a great deal of foundation, so they [*p. 51*] lead her Majesty to many other reflections, which your Lordship will propose and enforce to the Pensionary; letting him know at the same time that in so perplexed a case, where such different interests are to be reconciled, and where so much consideration is to be had not only of the present but of future ages, she can discern no clue so likely to extricate us out of these difficulties as that of the marriage. On that foundation the Duke of Savoy may most agreeably, and in the softest manner to the House of Austria, find that safety, which he apprehends himself in danger of losing; and without it, there is no possibility of preserving the present or future quiet of Europe, as far as it may be affected by these disputes.

The Queen, my Lord, considers that a Duke of Savoy by the very scituation of his country must of course become the first sacrifice to whichever of the two great families of Europe shall be in condition to encroach on its neighbours. His interest must therefore eternally be to prevent the exorbitant power of either; and it must [*p. 53*] be ours, by necessary consequences, to secure him in such a state as may enable him to do so.

If we suppose the whole monarchy of Spain, or even the territories belonging to it in Italy, together with the Empire vested in King Charles, it seems natural to conclude that his Royal Highness must and will from that minute become the vassal of France: as he would inevitably be of the House of Austria, should that House grow as formidable to Europe as it has anciently been. And thus the power which is so happily scituated, and which naturally should be used for supporting a ballance in Europe, will be constantly employed to help to destroy it.

Her Majesty considers further, that any accession of strength to the House of Savoy will probably be exerted with vigour, when the common interest may be in want of it. Whereas by a fatal and tedious experience we have found that all the acquisitions gained at the expence of the maritime powers for the [*p. 55*] House of Austria have been of no advantage to them in the prosecution of their war against France.

It may likewise be observed, that by the first system of this war, it was intended not only to rescue Spain out of the hands of the House of Bourbon; but also to keep that monarchy and the Empire divided: there would otherwise have been no need of the renunciations made in favour of Charles the Third. But if the Empire and the Dominions of Spain are to unite in the person of this Prince, the system of the war is essentially altered; what effect this alteration will have upon the Duke of Savoy is evident: perhaps, it may have the same on some other princes concerned in the Allyance.

By what I have writ to your Lordship, you are, I beleive, sufficiently informed of the instances which the Duke of Savoy makes here; and of the effect which these instances have in the Queen's mind. Without therefore mentioning to you any further the arguments [*p. 57*] made use of by the Count de Maffei[65] and the Marquis del Bourg, or any more general reflections on the same subject, I shall conclude this part of my letter by acquainting your Lordship, that the point which we perceive his Royal Highness really drives at, and the composition to which he would be glad to be reduced, is, the possession of Milan either as the dower of the Arch-Dutchess, or otherwise; and that he waits only to discover whether he can obtain what his security requires by the concurrence of the allyes, in order to hearken to the propositions of France, and to endeavour to succeed on that side if he fails on ours.

Your Lordship will please to debate very calmly and very fully with the Pensionary the several considerations proposed in this letter, and such others as may occurr to you; and to let him know, that the Queen would be glad to be informed of his sentiments, and by him of those of the rest of the Dutch Ministers; how far they incline to be of her Majesty's mind, and what other expedients they can offer to prevent the loss of the Duke of Savoy to the common [*p. 59*] cause.

The other point, which I am by her Majesty's orders to write to your Lordship upon, concernes the affairs of the North, and the unhappy dilemma which the demands of those princes seem to reduce us to. I enclose a copy of a letter which Monsieur D'Elorme,[66] the Saxon Resident, sent me on Sunday [*missing*]; and which is the first communication that we have had of the propositions made by King Augustus,[67] except the resolution of the States of the 17th instant delivered to me by the late Monsieur Vryberge's secretary. Your Lordship will perceive that in this letter, besides the alternative of sending back the Saxon troops, or of employing the Corps of Neutrality against the Swedes in Pomerania, it is desired that the Queen may propose some other expedients for securing his Polish Majesty and the Empire from a suddain invasion.

Your Lordship will be pleased to acquaint the Dutch Ministers,

65 Annibale, Count de Maffei (1667–1735) served the Duke of Savoy as envoy to The Hague and to London between 1699 and 1713.
66 Charles Pierre D'Elorme, Saxon resident in London from 1710 to 1714.
67 Augustus II, Elector of Saxony and King of Poland (1670–1733).

that her Majesty is under the utmost concern to find the common cause [*p. 61*] at this point of time so distressed in a matter, which she hoped the States had good assurance of being able to keep off, at least till the end of this year; and the whole conduct of which has been by her Majesty from first to last left to their direction; that the Queen hopes, the Northern Ministers have not insisted upon their first propositions, but have yielded to some middle way, which the wisdom of the States may have found out: since on the demands, as they were first made, the Queen is unable to resolve herself, or to advise them.

To enter into an actual war with Sweden either by employing the Corps of Neutrality, or by paying the Saxon troops whilst they are employed according to the desire of King Augustus, is contrary to the intention of all our engagements: on the other hand, to stand by and behold the destruction of Crassau's[68] army, and the conquest of Pomerania, has something very mean and cruel in it.

We have had some accounts which give us reason to beleive that it might be satisfactory to the Northern Princes, and particularly to the King of Denmark, if the Corps of Neutrality [*p. 63*] advanced to the frontier of Pomerania with the army of the Northern Confederates, and if a declaration was at the same time made to the Swedes, with the consent of those Princes, that no injury should be offered to them; but that the country of Pomerania should be preserved; provided the Swedish General would consent immediately to disband his troops, or to some other condition which might effectually put it out of his power to disturb the peace of the Empire. This, it is pretended, would be using the King of Sweden[69] in no other manner than we used the King of Denmark before the beginning of the present war; that it would save his army, which might otherwise be cut to pieces; and his province, which might otherwise be lost, and, perhaps, not so easily regained.

I am directed to mention this to your Lordship that nothing may be omitted, which can be thought of, on a subject of so much consequence: but it is easie to see, that if the Swedes continue refractory, we are then under an obligation of attacking them; and that there is little room to expect, the Swedish [*p. 65*] Ministers or Generals will consent to any terms of this sort without an express

---

[68] Ernst Detlof von Krassow (1660–1714) was in command of the Swedish troops after the defeat of Charles XII at Pultova in 1709. His forces in Swedish Pomerania continued to threaten both Saxony and Poland.

[69] Charles XII of Sweden (1682–1718) had abandoned his forces after the battle of Pultova and sought refuge in Turkey. He did not rejoin his Swedish troops until 1714.

order from their King; which it is impossible, considering the distance he is at, should be procured in any reasonable time. Besides which, the common character of that Prince, and the short and peremptory answer which he has lately given to Mr Jeffereys,[70] afford little room to hope that he would yield to necessity, or take such measures as any other Prince or State upon earth would take in his circumstances.

Upon the whole matter your Lordship knows very well how little share the Queen has had in all the steps that have conduced to bring these difficulties upon us. You will therefore lay it, as much as you can, on the Dutch to extricate us out of them; and testify the Queen's disposition to back and to support the best measures which they shall be able to take in so great an emergency.

I beleive, I need not tell your Lordship how much more necessary it is to observe the secret as to the former part of my letter, than as to the latter. The former should, indeed, [*p. 67*] be only communicated to the Pensionary himself, and that in confidence; and by the answer which we shall have from him, it will be plain what we are to depend upon from the Dutch.

Your Lordship will do well to let Count Sinzendorff[71] know, that we want no arguments to convince us of the necessity of keeping firm in the present exigency of affairs: and you may insinuate very properly to him, that the Queen's character, as well as the part she has taken in supporting the interests of the House of Austria, leave no room to doubt of her good intentions to the common cause, or to entertain any jealousies of her conduct. Upon this occasion your Lordship may say, that her Majesty thinks she gave a very great instance of her zeal for the prosecution of the war, in sending Mr Whitworth to Vienna to solicite that a detachment might be made from Hungary, now that all pretence of diversion from the malecontents is at an end, and when she empowered him to have made such offers of assistance to that Court, as would effectually [*p. 69*] have enabled them to march the 8000 men desired for the reinforcement of the Duke of Savoy's army, if there had appeared the least inclination to do it.

> I am, my Lord, with much respect,
>> your Lordship's most humble and obedient servant
>>> H. St. John

---

[70] Captain James Jefferyes had served as a volunteer in the Swedish army from 1707 to 1709. Between 1711 and 1715 he was the British resident in Sweden.

[71] Philipp Ludwig, Count Sinzendorff (1671–1742), was the Imperial ambassador to The Hague.

38.   Whitehall. 27 July 1711
    My Lord,
    I have very little to trouble your Lordship with by this post,
which you have reason to be glad of, since my last dispatches were
of so unreasonable a length.
    The share, which we have in the affairs of the North, being
chiefly managed at the Hague, [*p. 71*] all I shall say to your Lordship
upon them is, to desire that you will be pleased yourself, or else that
you will order Mr Harrison[72] to transmit full and frequent accounts of
what passes in relation to the Act of Neutrality to the Queen's
Ministers residing at the Northern Courts, that they may be rightly
informed of the sentiments of the maritime powers, and be thereby
enabled more effectually to promote her Majesty's service.
                I am, my Lord, with much truth,
                    your Lordship's most obedient humble servant
                                                        H. St. John

39.   Windsor Castle. 31 July 1711
    My Lord,
                I have laid your Lordship's letters of the 31st of July and
4th of August, which were received [*p. 73*] on Sunday last, before the
Queen; and am commanded to let your Lordship know, that the
Dutch Secretary had put into my hands the resolution of the States
concerning French prisoners some days ago, so that we expected to
hear from your Lordship on that subject.
    We have at this time no prisoner of any consequence, that I know
of, except the Mareschal de Tallard,[73] and the Comte de Ligondé[74]
who married my Lady Huntington. These gentlemen have always
been both as to their exchange, and as to their license of absence,
under the Duke of Marlborough's care: to whom I have writ to be
informed on what foot they now are, and how many of them may be
at this time on parole in France. You may assure the Dutch Ministers,
that her Majesty will very willingly contribute her endeavours to
procure satisfaction of the debts owing by the French prisoners in
Holland; but, I beleive, the States themselves will think that there
would be something inhuman in our conduct if we should closely

[72] William Harrison (1685–1713) was recommended by St. John for the post
of secretary to Lord Raby (Strafford), the British ambassador at The Hague.
[73] Camille d'Hostun, Comte de Tallard, Marshal of France (1652–1728),
had been taken prisoner at the battle of Blenheim in 1704. In October 1711
he was allowed to go home on parole.
[74] Michael de Ligondez, a French Colonel of Horse, had also been captured
at Blenheim. In 1706 he married Frances Hastings, the widow of Theophilus
Hastings, 24th Earl of Huntingdon.

confine the [*p. 75*] Mareschall de Tallard who has been already so distinguished in hardship.

Upon which occasion I must acquaint your Lordship, and your Lordship may insinuate the same to the Pensionary, that the Queen is so sensible of the ruin which has been brought on the private affairs of this unfortunate man by his long confinement at Nottingham, and his being denyed the liberty of going home on his parole, which has been granted to all the rest, that she would certainly before now have indulged him in this request, had it not been for the alarm which the very rumour of such a favour to the Mareschall once occasioned in Holland.

Might your Lordship not further insinuate how great a regard the Queen has shewn to them, that she has had consideration even of their suspicions. It would not be proper for your Lordship to propose to them, but might not they think that giving the Mareschall leave to go into France for six months would procure some satisfaction to [*p. 77*] their subjects, who have money due to them from the French prisoners, and might not they intimate such a proposition to us?

As to the affairs of the North, your Lordship will want little instruction from hence. My former dispatches shew you the Queen's sentiments on every side of this affair; and you see that her Majesty chuses rather to concurr with and to second the Dutch, than to take the lead at this time of day, and go about to mend a game which other people have spoiled.

As to any conversation, which I may have had here, I can only say, it is impossible I should ever suggest that we are not obliged to cover Poland; since I have read the Act of Neutrality too often to be ignorant of the import of it. I may, perhaps, have said, in reasoning with the Danish and Saxon Ministers, that the Swedes object to us as an instance of our partiality to the cause of their enemies, that we went out of the Empire to take Poland and Jutland into that Neutrality. But I ask your pardon for troubling you upon this [*p. 79*] subject. When princes act such a part as the Northern powers at this time do, their Ministers must very often cavil de lanâ Caprinâ.

My Lord Strafford will be hastened back to the Hague; and your Lordship will be pleased to assure the Pensionary, that he only stays the longer to go over the better informed, and the more fully instructed.

Brigadier Sutton[75] arrived here on Saturday night express from

[75] Richard Sutton was an experienced soldier who had served under William III and Marlborough. He came to London with Marlborough's plans for breaching the defensive fortifications of the French, the *ne plus ultra* lines, and capturing Bouchain. Sutton was later commander of the garrison at Bruges.

the Duke of Marlborough, with news of very great importance, and which we received with very great satisfaction.

Her Majesty is desirous that nothing should be neglected, which may enable his Grace to improve his first success, and to push with some vigour on that side, since the Court of Vienna will suffer us to do so upon no other. Your Lordship is therefore to acquaint the Dutch Ministers, that you have orders to insist with the Council of State, that directions may immediately be given to such parts of the ten provinces from which the Duke of Marlborough shall have occasion to demand forage, waggons, pioneers, or any other assistance for the operations [*p. 81*] of the army, that they do furnish him with the same whenever they shall be required by him to it, without staying for the consent of the Council of State or any other order.

Her Majesty makes no doubt but the Dutch Deputies will receive these directions; and they and your Lordship insisting peremptorily on the same proposition, she takes it for granted this step will be made.

We suppose that these orders, or such as may be equivalent to them, are given already to those parts of the country which are under the government of Holland.

If this letter finds you gone from the Hague, you will please to write to the Pensionary, and to lose no time in promoting that which the Queen apprehends can admit of no delay.

I am, my Lord,

your Lordship's most obedient humble servant

H. St. John

40. [*p. 83*]   Windsor Castle. 6 August 1711

My Lord,

Her Majesty commands me to enclose to your Lordship the petition of Mr David Whyte [missing]. The case appeares extreamly hard, and the contravention to the Treaty very gross. The Queen therefore is pleased to direct that your Lordship do take this affair up with warmth, and oblige the magistrates of Bruges to do justice to the petitioner; unless you find the facts to have been mistaken, in which case your Lordship will please to let me hear from you, and to attend her Majesty's further pleasure.

I am, my Lord,

your Lordship's most obedient humble servant

H. St. John

41. [*p. 85*]   Whitehall. 7 August 1711
My Lord,
                I received on Sunday last the favour of your Lordship's
letter of the 7th instant from the Hague, and of the 11th from
Roterdam.

The proposal, which was made by Monsieur Palmquist[76] concerning the body of Swedes in Pomerania, might indeed have been very
advantagious to the common cause to have it accepted, and is no
other than what the allyes offered to the Senate of Sweden last year.
But I must be of opinion, that the Danish and Polish Ministers were
not in the wrong, when they suspected that he wanted sufficient
authority from his master, who might have done, in this case, as he
has done in others; gained time in his distress, and given up his
Minister, when he thought his affaires mended.

I hear from the Hague, by letters of the 14th, that there is at last
another expedient agreed [*p. 87*] upon to satisfy the Northern
Confederates, which will not be so agreeable to the interests of
Sweden, but which we cannot be very justly reproached for, since
our present circumstances laid us under very great difficulties; and
the conduct of the King of Sweden increased them, by leaving us
almost nothing to say in answer to the instances of the Muscovite,
Polish, and Danish Ministers.

What has been done in relation to the affair of the Bishop of
Antwerp[77] being agreeable to her Majesty's former instructions, I
have nothing more to say to your Lordship upon that subject.

As to the Queen's sentiments concerning the affair of the Duke of
Savoy, which your Lordship was directed to communicate in confidence to the Pensionary in order to prepare his mind for what
will be every day more and more pressed upon him, I could wish that
you had not left any thing in writing with him, but had only argued
the matter thoroughly in conversation.

Count Werthern's complaint against Mr Jeffereys [*p. 89*] for
having in a memorial to the King of Sweden called his master only
King Augustus, is not well grounded: since Mr Jefferyes had given
him the title of King of Poland in his first memorial, which for that
very reason the King of Sweden would not receive; and he must
either have come back from Bender without so much as entring upon
business, or he must have changed his style, as he did.

As to the business of forage for the Palatine troops employed in

76 Johann Palmquist was Swedish envoy to The Hague between 1703 and
1715.
77 Peter Joseph von Franken-Siersdorf, Bishop of Antwerp from 1710 to
1727.

the Neutrality, which that Elector's Minister[78] mentioned to you, it will be very soon adjusted upon a reasonable foot, and to their satisfaction. I beleive there is little danger of the Elector's recalling those battalions, though his Minister, according to the present laudable custom among our allyes, could not forbear threatning it.

Monsieur Walef's case the Queen thought a very just and a very compassionate one: and what your Lordship said upon the backwardness which the Dutch shewed to comply with her Majesty [*p. 91*] in it, however it was taken, is no more than what there was occasion given for.

I am, my Lord, with respect and truth,
your Lordship's most obedient humble servant
H. St. John

[PS]   Her Majesty has commanded me to send your Lordship the inclosed petition [missing] of Mr Migliorucci, that you may endeavour to procure him just satisfaction.

42.   Whitehall. 17 August 1711
   My Lord,
               I have received the favour of your Lordship's letters from Brussells of the 17th and 20th instant N.S. for which I now return you my thanks.

I agree with your Lordship in the judgment which you make of the conduct of the people of the [*p. 93*] Provinces where you are: on which occasion I can offer no other rule to your Lordship than that, which was at first given you, of using all endeavours to oblige them to do what is reasonable and necessary for the prosecution of the war, and screening and protecting them where ever any oppression is attempted upon them.

The Dutch indeed are to be at the expence of all the extraordinaries for sieges; and they may well be so, not only on account of the immediate advantage which redounds to them; but also on account of that great accession of wealth and power, which those conquests are likely in time to produce to their State. But, I beleive, the number of waggons and pioneers necessary for that undertaking which our army is now engaged in, can at no time be furnished any way but by the neighbouring countries. The war languishes in every other part; and it would be [a] pity to have the operations on any account retarded on that side where [*p. 95*] it is pushed.

I am, my Lord,
your Lordship's most humble and obedient servant
H. St. John.

[78] Daniel Steingesn.

43. [*pp. 95–9*] [*This letter, dated 24 August 1711, is printed exactly in* Letters *and* Correspondence of Bolingbroke, *ed. Parke, i, pp. 337–39.*]

44. [*p. 99*]   Whitehall. 28 August 1711
     My Lord,
                I am to acknowledge the favour of your Lordship's letter of the 31st August N.S.
     I have received one of the same date from the Duke of Marlborough, and in it the consultations and reports of the Council of the Finances at Brussells, with a letter from Mr Laws[79] [*p. 101*] to Mr Cardonnel[80] concerning the refusal which is made to provide for the regiment of the Hussars according to your Lordship's requisition. Her Majesty was extreamly surprized to find so ill a return made to her kindness; and her good offices towards the redress of their grievances so ungratefully acknowledged, in matters that are necessary for the publick service. She expects a more ready complyance on the part of the Councills of State and Finances; and I am commanded to acquaint your Lordship, that the Queen thinks fit you should represent her concern at this their proceeding in very strong terms; and let them know, that she does insist upon their providing bread and subsistance for the regiment of Hussars which serves in the Duke of Marlborough's army. And if they appear obstinate in their refusal, your Lordship will please to take all proper means to compell them to make provision for so necessary a service: the delay of which has already put the Duke of Marlborough to some difficulties to procure advances to preserve the regiment, and keep the men from starving. I [*p. 103*] hope, before this comes to your hands, your Lordship will have the Dutch Deputy with you; and by your joint representations and united authority you will carry this point, which has been refused with a very ill grace, and is an unhandsome requital of her Majesty's indulgence to those Provinces.
     The other matters I am to speak to your Lordship upon shall make the subject of another dispatch.
                I am, my Lord,
                     your Lordship's most humble and obedient servant
                                                    H. St. John

     [79] John Laws acted as secretary to Cadogan and then to Orrery in Brussels, and took control of British diplomacy during their absence.
     [80] Adam Cardonnel was secretary to the Duke of Marlborough. He was dismissed from his offices and expelled from the House of Commons in 1712 after being charged with the misappropriation of government funds.

45.   Windsor. 4th September 1711
     My Lord,
               I am to return your Lordship my thanks for the favour
of your letter of the 7th, which I received here on Sunday last.
     I am glad Mr Pesters[81] is gone to the Hague [*p. 105*] upon the
errand mentioned by your Lordship, since upon the present foot of
government the people of those Provinces will have no great reason
to be satisfyed with us; and we, perhaps, shall have much reason to
complain of them. The sketch of the plan, which your Lordship
draws, is calculated to prevent both these mischiefs; and will therefore, I hope, have the approbation and concurrence of the States
General without any material alterations.
     We shall expect to hear at the return of Mr Pesters what their
resolution is: and whether the project be agreed to, or not. I beleive
your Lordship will do very well to transmit it hither.
               I am, my Lord,
                    your Lordship's most humble and obedient servant
                                             H. St. John

46. [*p. 107*]   Whitehall. 14 September 1711
     My Lord,
               I acknowledge the receipt of your Lordship's letter of
the 17th instant.
     It is very surprizing, that, after what the Queen has done for the
people of the Netherlands, and the endeavours which her Ministers
have used to free them from oppression, and restore tranquillity
among them, they should make the ungratefull return of refusing to
maintain one regiment of Hussars, notwithstanding the load of so
many Imperial battalions and squadrons is taken from them.
     If this is their affection to the common cause, and this the treat-
ment we are to expect, it is high time to establish some new Regulation of Government. Her Majesty therefore commands me to let
you know, that she would have you join your best endeavours with
the States Deputies in order to effect it; and that she would [*p. 109*]
have been glad to have received from your Lordship the plan proposed for that purpose, at the same time as it was sent to the Hague.
     As to Seaton, I can only say to your Lordship, that the fond from
whence the expences of his journey into France were to be supplyed,
ought to be his support in gaol, and pay the fees at his coming out.
               I am, my Lord,
                    your most obedient humble servant
                                             H. St. John

---

[81] Ernest de Pesters (1665–1728) was Pensioner of Maestricht and Dutch
receiver of war contributions in the Netherlands.

47. [*pp. 109–13*] [*This letter dated, 25 September 1711, is printed exactly in* Letters and Correspondence of Bolingbroke, *ed. Parke, i, pp. 365–7.*]

48. [*p. 115*]   Whitehall. 25 September 1711
    My Lord,
           I have your Lordship's letter of the 28th instant [N. S.] to acknowledge: and I am very glad to find by it, that the new Regulation of Government for the Netherlands is so near being finished; and that the States approved the plan your Lordship formed with so little alteration. I hope, the Council of State and Finances will make as little difficulty in submitting to it.
    I am sorry to find the Province of Flanders, and some others, so strenuously oppose the interest of the common cause, by refusing supplies of forage for the subsistance of the army: but as I have acquainted your Lordship formerly, the Queen's intentions are, that you should upon all occasions endeavour to make them comply with what is necessary for the prosecution of the war: and however burthensome the present demands may prove, her Majesty would have your Lordship [*p. 117*] join your good offices with the Duke of Marlborough for the performance of them: since the armies being obliged to continue near Bouchain, till it is put in a posture of defence, and the destruction which the French have made of the neighbouring country make these measures not only excusable, but absolutely necessary.
    I thank your Lordship for the copy of the intercepted letter: if it was wrote by a spy of France, I wish all they have may be as little informed.
           I am, my Lord,
               your Lordship's most humble and obedient servant

                                                      H. St. John

49. [*pp. 117–19*] [*This letter, dated Windsor Castle, 30 Sept. 1711, is printed exactly in* Letters and Correspondence of Bolingbroke, *ed. Parke, i, p. 385.*]

50. [*p. 121*]   Whitehall. 9 October 1711
    My Lord,
           The inclosed petition and affidavit [*missing*] of Joseph Jackson of London merchant will inform your Lordship of his case; which, as it appears to be just and reasonable, I am to recommend it

to your Lordship to afford the petitioner such assistance, as you shall think necessary, for the recovery of his goods.

I am, my Lord,

your Lordship's most obedient humble servant

H. St. John

51. [*pp. 123-31*] [*This letter, dated Whitehall, 9 October 1711, is printed exactly in* Letters and Correspondence of Bolingbroke, *ed. Parke, i, pp. 392-5.*]

52. [*pp. 133-7*] [*This letter, dated Whitehall, 15 October 1711, is printed exactly in* ibid, *i, pp. 408-9.*]

53. [*p. 137*]   Whitehall. 26 October 1711
My Lord,

The mails, which arrived lately from Holland, brought me the honour of several letters from your Lordship, of which the last is of the 26th instant N.S. I return your [*p. 139*] Lordship many thanks for them, and the accounts you give of your endeavours to introduce and settle the new Regulation. I hope you will be able happily to finish that affair, which is so essential to the good government of those Provinces for the future.

Her Majesty has been pleased to give your Lordship leave to come over to Great Britaine; and I am commanded to signify the same to you; and that your Lordship upon the receipt of this letter may immediately come away, if you shall think fit. This part of my orders is the more agreeable, because it gives me hopes of embracing your Lordship here in a short time.

I am faithfully, my Lord,

your Lordship's obedient and most humble servant

H. St. John

Appendix
[*To the Earl of Orrery*]

[*p. 141*]   Whitehall. 13 March 1710/11
My Lord,

The inclosed is a copy of a letter which Mr Secretary St. John received yesterday, which by his order I transmit to your Lordship, and am with the greatest respect,

My Lord,

your Lordship's most humble and obedient servant

T. Hare[82]

[82] Thomas Hare was one of the two under-secretaries of state in St. John's office.

Here follows the memorial to Mr Secretary St. John, mentioned to be inclosed to the Earl of Orrery in the preceding letter.

Gand. Le 19 Mars 1711

Monsieur,

Nous avons eté fort consolés, lors que nous avons entendu le changement que [*p. 143*] sa Majesté Britannique a fait dans son gouvernement, car nous avons fondé la dessus nos esperances d'être delivrés de tant d'extortions, piliages, et autres mauvaises directions, dans nos pauvres païs, faites par le General Cadogan, et ses adherans, tant de nôtre pais comme d'ailleurs.

Et nous ne sommes pas veritablement trompés, car peu de tems apres nous avons veu le dit Cadogan dignement depouillé de la charge que Sa Majesté luy avoit conferé dans nos provinces, pour le bien du public, et de la quelle il ne s'etoit jamais servi que pour le sien particulier, avec des moiens indignes, et avec de plus cruelles extortions faites a nos miserables provinces.

Cet illustre apotiquaire (de ravagieuse memoire) n'a jamais donné ses emplâtres, ni concourru à donner aucune charge, qu'a ceux qui luy ont mis devant les jeux, [*p. 145*] et mis en main des bourses pleines d'or, sans considerer le bien de la cause commune, et sans avoir aucun egard à nos bien intentionnés compatriotes. Je parle de ceux qui sont portez pour l'auguste maison d'Autriche, et pour ses Hauts Alliés.

Cette verité n'a été que trop confirmée, et tres pernicieuse à nos pauvres compatriotes par la surprise de Gand, et particulierement par l'amnestie procurée contre toute justice, (dans un crime si enorme de felonnie,) par le dit General Cadogan, et par son chef, sous pretexte de supposés privilèges, dont ils en tire des sommes immenses.

Cette amnestie, dis je, non seulement a laissé impunis les traitres convaincus, mais les a rendu si orgeuilleux contre les bien [*p. 147*] intentionnés, que les fidels serviteurs du Roy Charles et de ses Hauts Alliés, sont par eux foulés au pied, et persecutés par ces malins esprits qui ont toujours trouvé leur asyle et protection par des voyes indignes, aupres le dit Cadogan et son chef.

Dont la rapacité est connuë à tout le mond, ils n'en ont neantmoins aucune honte, ils sont hardis meme de mettre leurs mains rapinantes dans le Chateau Royal de Teruure [*sic*], aiant fait enlever quelque tems passé, et transporter en Angleterre, les plus varies tableaux qui s'y trouvoient, disant etre par ordre du Duc de Marlborough, et ceux qui les gardoient en ont meme receu quittance.

Nous sçavons fort bien que le Roy notre maître en est tres touché, et que à son tems il en fera des justes plaintes à sa Majesté la Reine d'Angleterre.

[*p. 149*] Nous avons bien lieu, avec touts nos compatriotes bien intentionnés, d'etre infiniment obligés à la Reine de la Grande Britagne de nous avoir delivrés des mains de ces Barrabbas, et de nous avois envoyés en sa place un tres digne et tres zelé Ministre, comme est Monsieur le Comte d'Orrery, duquel nous esperons, comme des Deputés de Hollande, du soulagement à nos peuples affligés, et un promt redressement du gouvernement à nos languissans païs.

Nous [*sic*] espérances commencent neantmoins à se perdre, aiant veû le depart de Bruxelles du Secretaire Lawes vers la Haye (que nous croions à toujours) envoié avec des grandes promesses par certains malins esprit de nôtre gouvernement, pour donner tous les faux pretextes, des sinistres impressions, au dit Comte d'Orrery, à fin qu'il laisse couvrir les choses, et qu'il continue [*p. 151*] le gouvernement sur le malheureux pied qu'il a eté jusques à present, et particulierement à fin que mettant dans les magistratures, ou dans le management des affaires, des gens de probité, et bien portés pour la cause commune, et utilité publique, l'on ne decouvra pas les belles conduites autant du dit Cadogan que celles du dit Lawes et ses adherants, qui a eté toujours un indigne instrument des rapines, et un malin fomentateur de desunion.

Nous plaignons fort notre sort malheureux, et en meme tems le zelé et brave cavalier du Comte de Orrery, qui nous croions peut etre deja sinistrement informé à la Haye par l'interessée malice du dit Lawes, pour se conserver en charge avec quelques uns des nos compatriotes, adherants à luy et à ses indignes maximes. C'est dont nous pouvons aisement nous persuader, puisque [*p. 153*] le dit Cadogan et son chef ont fait, et font, leur possible pour maintenir le dit Lawes dans l'emploi de secretaire, non seulement pour avoir la main, et diriger par son moyen à leur mode les affaires, et favoriser ses adherants (ennemis du bien public) mais pour rendre, s'il leur sera possible, le dit Comte de Orrery la victime de leur passion, en luy attribuant tous les sinistres accidents qui pourroient arriver à notre desuni et deplorable païs par les intrigues de ces gens là.

Nous avions cru, Monsieur, etre de notre devoir, et du zele et attachement que nous avons pour l'auguste maison d'Autriche, et pour ses Hauts Alliés, de vous en donner part; quoique vous en sçavez, peut etre, plus que nous, à fin qu'avec votre prudence ordinaire vous ôtres, Monsieur, tous les obstacles qui pourroient empecher la bonne direction et union [*p. 155*] dans notre gouvernement; et causer la derniere et irreparable ruine de notre pauvre païs, et miserables sujêts, et qui pourroient rendre infructueux le zele et bonnes intentions, envers notre patrie, que le dit Comte de Orrery a pour le service du Roy notre maître, de sa Majesté Britannique, et de ces Hauts Alliés.

[*Unsigned*]

INDEX

Abbott, Richard, receiver, 121
accountants to the crown, 112, 126, 131
accounting, 8, 12, 14, 16–17, 21, 23, 26–9; officers, 14, 18–19, 29
Act of Neutrality, 178, 180, 188, 189
Ady, John, deputy chamberlain, 113
Ahlefeldt, Hans Heinrich, 178, 180
aids, 101, 108, 119
Aldworth, Richard, receiver, 124; William: auditor, 122; receiver, 124
alienations without licence, 105, 109, 111
amerciaments, 103, 108, 110, 111, 116
Amsterdam, 138
Anderson, Samuel, sworn clerk, 112
Anne, Queen, 141, 149–57, 160–99
answers in equity, 99
Antwerp, bishop of, 191
apposals of sheriffs, 111, 115, 116
apposers, foreign, 108, 110, 111, 115, 116
appraisement, writs of, 127
appraisers, 127
Arden, Thomas, sworn clerk, 112
Arenberg, Alexander, duke of, 163, 176
Argyll, see Campbell
Arkesden, great court, 16, 20, 24
Armiger, Gabriel, sworn clerk, 99
armoury, see masters
arms, prohibited, 5n, 28
army paymasters, 100, 106, 110
Ashburnham, Bertram, 91
assarts, 109
assessments, 101, 108, 119, 125; rolls of, 100
assize, clerks of, 109
Astle, Thomas, 91
attachment, writs of, 99
attorney general, 102, 176, 177, 181; (duchy of Lancaster), 9n, 12, 14–15
attorney(s); duchy of Lancaster, 14–15; king's (Wales), 39, 44. See also clerks; Common Pleas; Exchequer; King's Bench

audit of accounts, 6–7, 12, 16–17, 21, 23, 25–8
auditors, 40, 111, 117, 126; (duchy of Lancaster), 4, 7, 9n, 12, 20–1, 25–8; of exchequer, 106, 118–24; of imprests, 115, 117, 118, 124; of land revenues, 118; of receipt, see writers of the tallies; of revenue from Lancaster and Cornwall, 125; of revenue of recusants, 124
Augmentations, court of, 40, 118; records, 107
Augustus II, 142, 178, 185, 186, 191
Austria (Austrians), 137, 138, 139, 183, 184, 187, 197, 198; minutes, 181
Ayloffe (Ayliffe), Benjamin, deputy keeper of duchy of Lancaster records, 1n, 6n; Henry, king's remembrancer, 98, 100; William, 98
Aymys, Richard, messenger, 135

Badby, Edward, sworn clerk, 104
bailiffs, 17–18, 22, 28, 101, 104, 108, 115, 117, 119, 120, 127; county, 20, 23–4; of franchise, 19–20, 23–4; of hundred, 40, 41
bailiwicks, grants of, 109
Baker, Michael, marshal, 125, Richard, marshal, 125; Thomas, sworn clerk, 114
Ball, William, sworn clerk, 112
Ballow, Henry, deputy chamberlain, 113; William, usher, 126
Bank of England, 146
Bankes, Richard, messenger, 126; usher, 126
Barcelona, 146
Barlow, Richard, sworn clerk, 104
Barnet (Barret), William, messenger, 135
barons of exchequer, 98, 99, 102, 103, 107, 110, 113, 114, 115, 116, 117, 119, 125, 126; cursitor barons, 103
barrier fortresses, 137, 138, 164
barrier treaty, 138, 140, 146